Transforming Culture

A Model for Faith and Film in Hollywood

C<small>HRISTINE</small> G<small>UNN</small>-D<small>ANFORTH</small>

WIPF & STOCK · Eugene, Oregon

TRANSFORMING CULTURE
A Model for Faith and Film in Hollywood

Wipf & Stock
A Division of Wipf and Stock Publishers
199 W. 8th Ave., Suite 3
Eugene, OR 97401

www.wipfandstock.com

ISBN 13: 978-1-55635-996-5

Manufactured in the U.S.A.

Transforming Culture

"*Transforming Culture* introduces a unique Christian moving-image communication model based on solid theological and communication theories. This is a very timely source of information for the film industry, which aims at relating moving image communication to faith. Implementing the model of *Transforming Culture* can be influential to the American Christian film industry and can help spearhead cultural transformation in a country such as South Africa, a young democracy diverse in culture and religion. The model is based on, and is an expansion of, the notion of prophetic imagination initially introduced by the renowned American theologian, Walter Brueggemann. It is a necessity on the bookshelf of the film producer, the communication academic and student, and the theologian."

—Johan Coetzee, Professor of Biblical and Religious Studies,
   University of Johannesburg

"In the rough and tumble of modern media and film, Danforth formulates a dynamic model to guide makers of Christian film and TV video in creating an alternative consciousness to that of the dominant culture. The wide reach of her model evokes excitement for rebuilding Christian culture at the same time that it exhibits the conflicts and disagreements that gnaw at the divided Christianity of our time. This merger of Walter Brueggemann's understanding of the prophetic imagination with socio-rhetorical strategies of interpretation leaves no doubt for readers that they are encountering an energetic young scholar with a strong desire to make the twenty-first century a better place for humankind."

—Vernon K. Robbins, Professor of New Testament and Comparative Texts,
   Emory University

"I find strong reason to believe that we need imagineers—like the prophets of old—to cultivate an alternative consciousness to that of the predominant secular culture. Spirit-filled narratives and stories are the best bet for criticizing and energizing persons and communities to re-imagine life in a transforming way. Christian communicators in both the Church and the moving-image media industry can use this model to bring about a transformation of our culture."

—Joseph Palakeel, Founder of IMPACT, India

"Christine describes effective Hollywood storytelling for faith film in a profoundly biblical sense that, if utilized, can impact our culture for God. He will take the ordinary everyday stories and let them take flight in the hearts of people so that they may relate His complete work in Jesus. Our hearts yearn to hear about the new creation in stories that we can relate to in our milieu."

—Regardt van den Bergh, director, *The Visual Bible: The Gospel According to Matthew, Faith Like Potatoes, The Hansie Story*, and *The Lamb*

To our children, Grace and Michael John

Many are willing that Christ should be something,
but few will consent that Christ should be everything.

—Alexander Stuart Moody

Contents

Contents

Foreword

IT IS CLEAR TO any vigilant observer that late capitalism is now headed toward a catastrophe. There are many facets to this coming trouble and many signs of the approaching disaster, notably the environmental crisis. At bottom, however, the coming crisis is rooted in the fact that propagators of late capitalism have signed on to a false account of reality, one that focuses on wealth, power, and control, that relies upon military power, and that issues in an entitled sense of insatiable pursuit of commodities. That false account, moreover, is so comprehensive as to be totalizing for persons across the ideological spectrum, so totalizing as to be totalitarian, impatient with any dissent and intolerant of any alternative. Indeed it is nearly impossible to think or imagine or act outside the grip of that narrative construal of reality.

There is hope, however, in the recognition that this narrative construal of reality through the lens of wealth, power, and control is just that, a narrative construal. That is, it is a shrewd, sustained "social construction of reality" that is effective because the mechanisms of its construction are kept invisible. The recognition that it is a construal, however, leads to an awareness that this story we tell about ourselves is not a "given." It is, rather, a chosen narrative that can be unchosen for the sake of a more adequate account of reality.

There is a long line of interpreters who were able to stand outside the hegemonic ideology of their day and urge an alternative perspective on reality. Most spectacularly, the prophets of ancient Israel given us in the Hebrew Bible stood, for the most part, firmly against the hegemonic ideology of the day that served the interests of the Davidic dynasty, the Jerusalem temple, and the entourage of urban elites who clustered around king and temple. These prophets, in their daring poetic cadences, urged a strong critique of that dominant ideology and appealed to the ancient covenant of Sinai as an available, adequate alternative.

Foreword

In this book, Christine Gunn-Danforth makes powerful and suggestive connections between that ancient prophetic practice and the current possibility of the use of film as a mode of symbolization that could echo and replicate the prophets. The happy burden of this book is that the connection is largely persuasive and lays down an urgent summons for those who would engage in powerful communication that contest for the governing symbols of society. It is Gunn-Danforth's proposal that film may now provide a medium for dissenting alternative imagination that follows in the train of those ancient voices. While attending to the subversive models of the Hebrew Bible, this book pays close attention to the possibilities of narrative in a society that relies upon and is propelled by icon management. The capacity of Gunn-Danforth to move back and forth between ancient models and contemporary possibilities is rich with suggestion. We may hope her book will evoke further thought and effort from folk who are able to mobilize film for transformative purposes. The daring thought that this medium can be put to such possible use is not unlike the readiness of the old prophets to use images and metaphors that were essentially alien to them for the sake of the message. Good communicators in every context know that any available material can be turned to critical thought and empowering summons, that is, to transform the medium for the sake of the message. Gunn-Danforth's challenge is precisely that the most powerful medium among us can be employed for health and life, and not be necessarily in the service of death and destruction. This welcome book summons its readers to think afresh in the midst of an enormous crisis. I am pleased to have been present with the author in the inception of the argument, and glad to add my voice to this hope-filled possibility.

Walter Brueggemann
Columbia Theological Seminary
July 21, 2008

Acknowledgments

Thanks be to my precious Savior, Jesus Christ, who has been my rock and fortress, remaining faithful to complete the good work that He had started.

I would like to express my deepest gratitude to the following:

Professor Walter Brueggemann, whose wise counsel, writings, and conversations have shined a guiding light on the path of this endeavor since our initial meeting in Chicago in 1994—in glad solidarity.

Professor Johan H. Coetzee, who has continued to guide me in this interdisciplinary effort with wisdom, encouraging me to achieve my utmost for his highest.

Professor Quentin J. Schultze, for having continued to support this endeavor with enthusiasm and generosity. I am most grateful.

Regardt van den Bergh, for allowing your God-given vision and God's grace to be so evident in your support and encouragement of the genre *Jonahre,* and to *Rudolf Markgraaff* for graciously making all documentation and information regarding the making of *The Lamb* available to incorporate in this book.

John A. Gunn and *Helena Gunn* (my parents), for your long hours of discussion through this composition and loving, prayerful encouragement that made this endeavor possible. *Ralph Gunn,* for your brotherly support, love, and prayers and for holding me accountable not to lean on my own understanding but in all my ways to acknowledge Him.

Michael A. Danforth and our children, *Michael John* and *Grace,* for your faith, hope, and love that you give to me unconditionally; you are each God's grace manifest to me.

University of Johannesburg, for the copyright of the material contained in this book that was completed as part of the Ph.D. dissertation in 2004.

Wipf & Stock, thanks to K. C. Hanson, Jim Tedrick, James Stock, Kristen Bareman, and all of your gracious team that have gone the extra mile to get this out in record time. I am indebted to you one and all. Thank you also *Amanda Bird*, the copyeditor, for your meticulous work.

To all those *friends and family* that have been on this journey with me, thank you for your encouragement and prayerful support through the many peaks and valleys stretching over the past 14 years.

Abbreviations

JBL   Journal of Biblical Literature
ZAW   Zeitschrift für die alttestamentliche Wissenschaft
JSOT   Journal for the study of the Old Testament
HTS   Hervormde teologiese studies

CHAPTER 1

Theology of Communication

Is There a Model for Faith and Film in Hollywood?

BACKGROUND

IT HAS BEEN AN astounding turnaround to see a laughing stock and object of great scorn become one of the greatest stories ever seen. This ironically describes not Jesus but the 2004-screened version of the story of Jesus as produced by Mel Gibson. Breaking all kinds of viewing and box office records, *The Passion of the Christ* is now seen as a Hollywood success story, and the question is, *How can we repeat this?*

Is there a model that can be followed? Was it a matter of faith-hungry audiences, or was it merely media hype that got people out to see a Hollywood icon, Mel Gibson, gone "astray"?

These were the questions baffling Hollywood producers, film critics, and television and radio talk show hosts in 2004. However, it must be noted that before and after Mel Gibson's success with *The Passion*, many films and television shows have experimented with explicit and implicit portrayals of faith. Still, the question that is capturing the attention and imagination of theologians and communication scholars from Cambridge to Hollywood is, how can these two disciplines be integrated and yet be practically viable for successful Hollywood-style productions?

The moving pictures have become the present generation's form of entertainment, education, and companionship. They have facilitated communication of the gospel to millions, crossing cultural and language barriers. This interaction between media and humankind has subsequently become a major influence and function of narrative, determining dominant ideologies and confirming them to the masses.

1

Societies have been stifled by belief systems perpetuated by the popular media and promoted as truth. Ideologies motivated by profit margins and that which sells to mass audiences have led to a humanist, postmodern morality. The purpose of both the *narrative* literature of the Bible and modern Christian moving-image communication in narrative format is to effectively establish a *consciousness alternative* to that of the popular culture. Walter Brueggemann calls this process Prophetic Imagination. This forms the basis for understanding the paradigm that describes the theological purpose which reveals to modern day storytellers how to communicate biblical truth in the moving-image media in an oral/aural culture. The world today, 2,000 years later, is closer to first-century biblical oral/aural culture than any time before. Hearing and not reading is back again, as it was in ancient Israel, as the main source of learning—thus consistent with the worldview of the inspired authors of the Bible, who shaped the biblical narrative forms to elicit faith in a sovereign God (a Prophetic Imagination). This book explores the task of the Christian moving-image media producers to similarly elicit a transformation of culture in their audiences.

PROPHETIC UTTERANCES

We live in a hegemonic environment encultured by dominant ideologies. Through the dominant media messages we struggle to hear the voices of truth. These popular media narratives co-opt our imagination and convince us that mimicking the styles and trends of those in control will lead to power, affluence, and success. Hegemony drives the consumer culture of the West and drove the apartheid era of Africa and instituted the Nazi quest for superiority into a monstrous Holocaust. These outcomes of hegemonic power are just some of the extreme examples of evil resulting from the power, affluence, and religion of the empire that allows no rivals.

The role of those in such a situation can be metaphorically likened to the Jews in exile.[1] Generating new modes of speech, giving fresh expression to new possibilities, is the hard, faith-filled work of those with a prophetic voice. It is in the utterances of the Old Testament prophetic literature that the power of revolutionary utterances is identified. Revolution in this sense is defined in terms of Jacques Ellul's[2] description of a dialectic, with

1. Brueggemann, *Cadences of Home.*
2. Ellul, *Presence,* xxxiv.

the world and its life on one side and the text of the Word of God on the other, establishing a style of life through the speech of hopeful subversion. Brueggemann describes the cadences of speech that ushers the hearers in exilic circumstance back home as subversive hope. However, the intent and message of the speech is just as important as the mode of articulation, which must be a playful, artistic rendering that will be able to re-describe and thus subvert the dominant consciousness of the hegemony to fresh alternatives. Wars of terrorism, famines, moral disintegration of social life and institutions, the abundance of wealth, and the depersonalization of humanity have become overwhelmingly familiar, and any array of human solutions has proved inadequate.

It is through film and television—the popular narratives of our time—that we are constantly confronted either with confirmatory messages, otherwise named priestly communication, that substantiate the claims of the popular culture or with prophetic messages that criticize the culture, implicating a biblically based lifestyle and wisdom. Prophetic communication, or theologically termed Prophetic Imagination, can thus be understood as the criticizing of the dominant order or status quo and energizing the imagination to an alternative consciousness.

In the book "Christianity in the Mass Media," Quentin Schultze introduces the idea of prophetic communication reflecting on religious communicators, using the wisdom of the ages to discern the present. However, in Schultze's work this prophetic terminology is understood as speaking from a particular "tribal" Christian context into the world, and it is important to note that a broader definition of prophetic is being discussed here. Rather, the ancient Hebrew prophets are considered as models of a medium of rhetoric/communication that identified social domination and injustices and spoke creatively to bring about a confrontation with the dominant reality. In this manner they established an alternative consciousness; a re-imagining of the present reality leading to a future filled with hope. The term hopeful subversion is used by Cambridge Professor Jeremy Begbie to refer to the act of bringing a language to bear upon a social context, allowing hearers to see the need for exchanging the existing paradigms of meaning for a just and righteous alternative. The imagination plays a central role in this work of criticizing and energizing to newness, arriving at new possibilities for social and cultural contexts.

Thus, the prophet is not an isolated future teller that is uninterested in history and tradition but one who uses the imagination and community's symbols to bring to expression a transforming vision of society. The Prophetic Imagination paradigm can be used to express a purpose for faith and film that would transform culture to establish an alternative biblical reality. This paradigm also provides a fresh new approach to expressing transformative messages through technological mediums, taking the Hebrew biblical prophetic texts as impetus and developing popular cultural messages that encapsulate an alternative reality.

Examples of such recent films in 2008 are *Expelled*, *Prince Caspian*, and *Take*. These films all appeared in theatres within a month of each other and criticized popular notions and practices in society to allow for new understandings of reality. *Expelled* addresses in a docudrama (or *edutainment* style) the expulsion of those who would research the credibility of intelligent design theory, in essence implying that Darwinism provides inadequate answers. Even though the evolution theorists themselves admit the theory's inability to describe what caused the start of all life, certain paths of discovery are forbidden. *Expelled* draws links between annihilation of research evidence pointing to a higher being or intelligent design and the amorality that caused the Holocaust. Viewers discover that Darwinism undergirds Nazi idealism and resulted in the idea of designing a perfect race; since no higher being had to be respected and no morality had to guide the process, the Nazi rulers used what they thought the most expedient methods. Through the movie, the audience participates with interviewer Ben Stein in a process of rational discovery. The surprising course it takes comes as a shock and thus provides the impetus for provocative discussions on freedom, the American education system, dominant ideologies, and agendas. The movie speaks prophetically to American audiences, suggesting that they do not really possess the freedom they believe is theirs. It challenges and potentially transforms their accepted social framework by considering the parallels between it and societies that have denied God in their research and subjugated areas of study to purely humanist explanations.

I will interject here and note that in the study of communication we are not immune to these trends. There is an ever increasing gap in our current research, as Quentin Schultze pointed out in his speech, "The God-problem in Communication Studies." Pertinent to the discussion in this book is the study of biblical prophetic rhetoric as a paradigm that is largely ignored in the study of rhetorical theory. The study of modern Western rhetoric is situated exclusively in classical Aristotelian and

Athenian roots. Prophetic rhetorical theory and praxis as exhibited in the ancient Hebrew texts predates these texts yet are marginalized in rhetorical study. Prophetic rhetoric constitutes consummate rhetorical practice and recognizable forms of invention, arrangement, and style. Lipson expressed this, saying, "It is ludicrous to think that Hebrew prophetic orators, (and other cultures that pre-date the western world's paradigm of rhetorical theory) could have sustained their longevity and power without a well-honed understanding of how to communicate for significant social functions . . . to convince and persuade, or without conceptions and practices of language that supported their purposes."[3]

SOCIAL CONTEXTS

According to the Lausanne Committee for World Evangelization, "Two thirds of all people in the world are oral communicators—who can't, don't, or won't learn through literate means."[4] We are closer to ancient Israel's context than at any time before. The Hebrew prophets lived in an oral culture, and their messages contributed to its oral tradition. These prophetic voices did not desire to persuade but rather to inform the culture in ways that would criticize the dominant consciousness and at the same time energize to a new, alternative style of living. They were always aware of the particular culture and circumstances surrounding the lifestyle they addressed.

Today communicators are realizing the power of a voice not just to persuade but as vehicle for social transformation. In South Africa's post-apartheid era, old modes of thinking and doing have necessitated social transformation. The work of reconciliation and acceptance has posed many seemingly insurmountable problems. Social problems abound in the country, as in the rest of Africa, with the ever increasing AIDS epidemic and escalating crime rates; humanist methods have provided no effective resolutions.

However, efforts to bring about social change by communicating values through the media resulted in a series of films broadcast on South African national television stations. These do not overtly address the Bible but are culturally situated stories that have begun to do the work of prophetic rhetoric by promoting key biblical values such as acceptance,

3. Lipson, "Egyptian Rhetoric," 3.
4. The Lausanne Movement, "Global Issue."

perseverance, and forgiveness. These films, produced by Curious Pictures, are titled collectively as *Heartlines* and *edutain* the audience through stories. This culturally situated *edutainment* is not happening around camp-fires but around television screens, to deliver a message for a new reality that, if adopted, is able to sustain a better future for South Africa. It is exciting to see theologically grounded messages of acceptance, love, and forgiveness being expressed in culturally relevant storylines and effecting cultural transformation.

Take, a U.S. film released a month after *Prince Caspian* and *Expelled*, similarly addresses a social issue—restorative justice. If adopted by all U.S. states, this practice would make a large positive impact on death row inmates and their victims. This movie is startling yet poignantly energizing, with a storyline that is both informative and entertaining. It expresses a view that has been silent and, if heard, could bring transformation. Societal, culture-specific change as the purpose of communication is a major factor that the field of communication/rhetorical study must consider; the purpose needs to transform the practice of communication. Rather than to persuade, the goal is to stimulate new patterns of thinking and, in so doing, change society to reflect the justice, freedom, and peace resulting from a biblical style of life.

BIBLICAL STORYTELLING IN HOLLYWOOD

Chronicles of Narnia

It is recently that the Narnia series of films have brought the theological imagination of one of the Inklings, C. S. Lewis, onto the screen. The second film after *The Lion, the Witch, and the Wardrobe* is *Prince Caspian*, released in theaters May 16, 2008. This film brings biblically based myth-making to centre stage, with content that is filled with biblical imagery and themes. The success of the series has been cemented with the alliance of Walt Disney Pictures and Walden media. The first of the films based on C. S. Lewis' seven Narnia books tells the metaphorical story of *Narnia*, a fallen world of mythic creatures ruled by evil, the White Witch. It is the four children with unfettered imaginations who enter Narnia as transforming agents to convert the lost world into a harmonious, peace-ful one. One of the children, however, betrays his siblings; then appears the lion, Aslan, who must sacrifice his life to redeem the loss and restore Narnia. Although written as an imaginary tale, this story is interwoven with core biblical themes of salvation, betrayal, and redemption through the sacrifice of innocent life. These myths serve as prophetic imagery that brings some key biblical truth to expression in every strand of plot and subplot portrayed.

In *Prince Caspian* the story begins with a civilization that has become obsessed with self-preservation and progress in a city on a hill. The inhabitants have declared war on the misfits of Narnia, mythic lowly creatures that can not fend for themselves. However, the wise counsel and teaching Prince Caspian receives from his tutor inspires this prince from the evil empire to defect for the good of the Narnians. He needs help and calls on the already "baptized" princes and princesses of the first movie: Lucy, Edward, Susan, and Peter. They come at the sounding of the horn to take up their gifts of power, given to them in Narnia by Aslan, to assist Prince Caspian to set the enslaved Narnians free. We see in this imagery the plot and picture of Moses setting the captives free yet being part of the structure of the dominant empire and its mentality. Prince Caspian, like Moses, receives power to lead the captives to freedom in a battle in which earth and waters are moved by God (Aslan) to save the oppressed minorities. The water rising to overthrow the army of the kingdom that reminds us of the paradigmatic prophet Moses, who in exile could imagine a life of freedom beyond this oppressive social reality and lead a people to freedom through the power of a living just, God.

These prophets of old established new paradigms of meaning that was communicated rhetorically to transform their culture to embody new realities. Our films in the twenty-first century are reflecting the patterns of the prophetic voice in imagery derived from biblical passages. It is time for us to sit up and have ears to hear and eyes to see. The prophetic rhetoric has possibilities for revealing modes of practice rich and meaningful in a postmodern, relativist culture looking for new ways of communication within an information-dominated society.

It is the work of the prophet par excellence to use the imagination to inspire meaning through narrative. Embedded in symbolic imagery, the stories of our time are not at first recognizable as prophetic, but with similar purpose, do serve as parables to shake the dominant ideologies of our aural/oral culture. This was the work of literary geniuses like Isaiah, Jonah, and Moses, prophets who used their information from God to change culture by well chosen imagery and purposeful communication rather than mere cognitive strategies of persuasive speech. C. S. Lewis provides an example of how to incorporate biblical truth in storytelling for society today.

THEOLOGY OF COMMUNICATION
(See Chapter 7)

What this leads us to is the need for a theology of communication, not only to create stories that artistically render biblical truth, but to give us the tools to analyze and critique films by evaluating whether they contain biblical truth.

This requires understanding communication according to its Latin root *communicare*, "to share," or literally, "to make common," and establishes the role for biblical moving-image media: *to create and share a biblical culture on earth.* In this book this is called creating and sharing the *Lifestyle of the Believer* component. The process of communicating via moving-image media enables God's image bearers, as agents of God's "common grace" in the media, to share the images and message of truth to establish an alternative consciousness. "*Common grace*—that is, carrying out God's work of maintaining creation by promoting righteousness and restraining evil"[5] is therefore fulfilling the cultural commission.

To communicate truth through the moving-image media employing the prophetic theology comprises the *Bible* component as well. This redeems culture by displaying a dynamic spiritual order of an alternative consciousness. Producers and directors managing moving-image media messages, according to this paradigm, are required to become a "...culture-creating cult, men and women of another type arrayed for the great battle of principal against principal."[6]

As Rossouw explains, "Culture is the interpretative and coping mechanism of society, it is the way in which people understand themselves, their world and the appropriate interaction with one another and with the world they live in."[7] This "sharing" and "making common" of the communication process could be instrumental in affecting culture in terms of biblically based truth. It is necessary, when formulating the content of messages for biblical filmmaking, to understand the decay of the material order of the culture. As part of the *Life* component of the model,

5. Colson and Pearcey, *How Now Shall We Live?*, 33–34.
6. Ibid., 37.
7. Rossouw, "Theology," 804.

it is necessary to take into account the cultural shift from a modern to a post-modern culture (or late-modern, as some prefer to call it).

THE IMPORTANCE OF NARRATIVE FORM

Incorporation of biblical truth in productions poses two problems. One is that many theologians cannot understand how communication can be termed biblical if it is not explicitly Christian. I want to suggest with this model based in a theological paradigm of Prophetic Imagination that biblical communication happens in our culture when moving-image media narratives create an alternative consciousness. This in turn creates a style of life reflecting truth and exercises God's common grace to fulfill the cultural commission, establishing communities of *Shalom*.

The other practical problem is that Christian producers with little theological/biblical training attempt to communicate biblical truth using the moving-image media. Without a certain communication-savvy, theological grid to work with and monitor the message that is the medium, their attempts can easily result in distortion of the biblical truth. This brings us to why a *theology of communication* is necessary, versus merely understanding a Christian worldview. Producers are looking for an appropriate theology that applies the biblical truth of God's Word in terms of life, so that it can be practically implemented in moving-image narrative storytelling. Within the narratives of the Bible we find the essence of an alternative consciousness. It is in this story, entertaining and educating us in terms of biblical truth, that a viable theology of communication for the moving-image media in the new millennium is discovered.

No *explicit narrative format suitable for use as a model* currently exists to accomplish effectively this task of communicating a biblically based message through film and television.

The function of storytelling as moving-image narrative has not progressed to a theoretical study, and most scholarship is epistemologically thin. Since the 1940s and 1950s, media scholars have turned to the humanities for research and methodology. This is problematic because media scholars have "discarded an important historical and philosophical link to the great traditions of rhetorical analysis and critical inquiry. . . . Consequently, although there is some marvelous work on narrative by these scholars, it is virtually unknown by media researchers."[8] Schultze

8. Schultze, *American Evangelicals*, 8.

identifies three reasons for the lack of stated theory and structured critique:

> First, much television criticism is frequently done by people who like to watch a lot of television rather than study television. Second, art criticism in general today is under the shadow of modern subjectivism, which holds that there really are no standards for criticism; one critic's views are as "accurate" as any other critic's views. Third, the field of communication produces many researchers who are methodologically sophisticated, but theoretically uneducated.[9]

In the film arena, however, some competing theories exist from which valuable perspectives can be gleaned for the transcendental moving-image media. (See chapters 7 and 12).

The research developed in this book establishes a practically viable theoretical and theological basis for a biblically based moving-image narrative genre. It draws from cultural studies, theology, socio-rhetorical criticism, narrative and imagination theory, and European structuralists to examine the role of popular moving-image narrative in culture and society. The book proposes a new purpose and genre for the mass media.

A NEW MODEL FOR HOLLYWOOD PICTURES

The biblical genre proposed here as model for faith and film in Hollywood presents the elements of narrative as a means for bringing to the audiences of the twenty-first century a message of redemption through, and hope in, the power of a living God. The church has been culturally resituated from a position of socioeconomic hegemony in the past to its current place in a radically secularized Western culture. As a result, the church and its message are poorly situated to respond to the new cultural, intellectual situation. That the church and Christian programming are no longer the dominant intellectual forces in society and can no longer count on cultural reinforcement is being increasingly evidenced. The television series "Touched by an Angel" was pulled off the networks in the U.S. for containing the name of God in every program. The research solution proposes a preaching that is recast in an entirely different mode and genre using the technology of moving-image communication to affect the present cultural context. This book likens the crisis of transcendental

9. Ibid., 118.

communication through film and television and preaching today, meta-phorically, to the situation of the ancient Hebrews in Babylonian exile. Therefore, the solution lies in the study of biblical texts that deal with the theological and communication issues of a faith crisis in exilic circum-stances. The book of Jonah is such a text, and as it is analyzed from a socio-rhetorical perspective, the answers to our own dilemma crystallize in many helpful layers from the rich textures of the text.

We will use scholar Vernon Robbins' work on socio-rhetorical criti-cism, *Exploring the Texture of Texts*, in conjunction with the three para-digmatic models developed in this book that incorporate theology and communication theory, to compare authorial intent in biblical literature and a producer's purpose in moving-image technologies. Brueggemann writes, "(R)hetoric among the decentered not only has a different inten-tion, that is, to propose a countertruth that subverts, but *also a different style or mode of articulation*."[10] The key to communicating transcenden-tally via a new genre to a culture in which Christian faith is in exile, as Brueggemann[11] explains, is to cast the message as a "testimony" to a new reality. The purpose of the transcendental communication is to "state and reinforce the exilic community in a particular identity, in a plot that has a specific Yahweh as its key character."

> It is the plot that resists despair and that allows Israel to refuse
> assimilation . . . *the subversive utterance of countertestimony* (i.e.,
> about a God who will not "fit" and about a world governed by this
> God who will not accommodate or compromise) and *the playful,
> hyperbolic, ironic utterance* that keeps the uttered future elusively
> beyond the control of the rulers of this age, who would like to tame
> the elusiveness into a large, domesticated generalization that can
> be administered.[12]

It is to this end that the canonical book of Jonah speaks forth new-ness in a format probably not recognized by scholars as the very essence of what Brueggemann calls for in homiletics today. The book of Jonah, although placed among the prophetic books of the Old Testament, is the only biblical book without a defined genre. It is discovering the mode of storytelling in this biblical text that reveals some startling insights into the form's relevance to the message. Marshall McLuhan's mantra, "The

10. Brueggemann, *Cadences*, 57.

11. Ibid., 53.

12. Ibid., 53, 57–58.

medium is the message," is the essence of effective communication.[13] If this is true for biblical authors, then discovering a theological purpose for biblical messages would also lead to an understanding of what the modern mediums that encapsulate this theological message should look like. Thus this book delves into prophetic communication dealing with the imagination and working that into a film format.

This discourse is then described as a genre that communicates a Prophetic Imagination result as authorial intent. This can be readily accommodated in modern storytelling in film and television, presenting producers and audiences with a useful theologically based model for directing as well as understanding programming with a transcendental message. It is the medium complemented by the form, style, and theological composition of biblical narratives—particularly well-exemplified in the canonical book of Jonah—that points to an effective technique for communicating in the current faith context. The comparison of authorial intent and worldview is made possible by the similarities the Bible shares with other great literary works. Robert Alter has emphasized this aspect in his work, stating, "The interpreter may assume artistic deliberateness on the part of the Biblical authors and use the artfulness of the narrative as a conduit to the author's worldview, just as he would any great work of literature."[14]

Applying socio-rhetorical criticism (see Chapter 3) as methodology, the narrative book of Jonah is analyzed to extrapolate biblically based elements of a rhetoric that subverts the dominant consciousness and communicates the transcendental in narrative format. These insights, developed from theology and communication disciplines, will show how film and television media can employ transcendent truth in storytelling for the contemporary cultural situation of faith. The ultimate goal is to elicit faith and hope in God, establishing a Prophetic Imagination perspective with the audience in "exile."

As with the book of Jonah, other canonical texts and non-canonical narrative texts contain some of the critical elements to establish a Prophetic Imagination. The book of Jonah is chosen as it presents a biblically poignant and concise example of the elements necessary to capture the essence of a prophetic, narrative rhetoric appropriate for moving-image media to subvert the secularized, dominant culture. These elements will be identified,

---

13. McLuhan, *Understanding Media.*
14. Quoted in Patrick & Scult, *Rhetoric*, 18.

defined, and compared to other canonical texts, as well as to moving-image media, to show the critical relevance of implementing them as a means of communicating a Prophetic Imagination through film and television.

UNDERSTANDING THE CONTEXT OF FAITH AND FILM

Contemporary Culture as Mission Field

This book is designed to identify the role of the moving-image media—film and television—in society today and to research the elements of a narrative genre that will effectively communicate the purpose and message of a biblical theology through these channels.

First, the role of the moving-image media is described in this book in terms of its function and purpose in the "modern western culture," as termed by Newbigin in "Foolishness to the Greeks." The First World is considered as the mission field for the gospel. Newbigin describes the "modern western culture" as taking

> as fact that the individual's area of making his own decisions has increased enormously. With the aid of modern technology, modern man chooses when he will live, to whom he will talk, how he will behave. . . . The old patterns of belief and behavior that ruled because they were not questioned have largely dissolved. . . . It is natural in a culture controlled by this kind of experience, for religion also to be a matter of personal choice, unconditioned by any superhuman or supernatural authority.[15]

It is to this culture, where truth in the Word of God and faith in a God of the impossible has largely disappeared, that the work of Old Testament scholar Walter Brueggemann brings a perspective that is biblically based. Based on his thesis, termed Prophetic Imagination, a biblical paradigm inspires the theology of communication for redeeming culture outlined in this book.

The task of prophetic ministry into such a mission field is to nurture, nourish, and evoke an alternative consciousness and perception that contrasts with the consciousness and perception of the dominant culture in society. Therefore, every act of a ministry that would be prophetic should be geared toward evoking, forming, and reforming encultured society so that an alternative community is constructed. It is a measure of our enculturation that various acts of ministry—for example counseling, ad-

---

15. Newbigin, *Foolishness*, 13.

ministration, television, film, and even liturgy—have taken on lives and functions of their own. As Brueggemann writes, "There has come a dryness, a legalism in ministries which bore people because they are something in their own right and not as elements of the prophetic ministry of formation and reformation of an alternative community."[16]

Clifford Christians recognizes this limitation in terms of evangelical mass communication: "Devoid of a theory of culture, evangelicals attach communication technologies exclusively to the Great Commission and celebrate their alleged cost effectiveness in winning souls."[17] Inarticulate about symbolism and the power of a theologically defined purpose to affect culture, Christian moving-image communicators have merely adopted techniques of the secular marketing mentality and scientific stimulus-response theories of the mass media.

Only as the prophetic injunction to convert cultural forms through language and narrative is heard can the Christian communicator's purpose for moving-image media messages be effective in establishing God's kingdom on Earth.

CONCLUSION

How these elements are used to accomplish the Prophetic Imagination purpose of the Jonah narrative is a critical question for developing a multi-layered biblical communication genre that will achieve the same purpose through moving-image narratives today. These communication elements are identified within the biblical narrative of Jonah through socio-rhetorical criticism and are then built into the interdisciplinary models to form a theology of communication. This presents an exemplum to develop and analyze film and television narratives according to biblical elements. The basis of such a genre accomplishes a Prophetic Imagination purpose through form, style, content, and intent. Substantive communication theory and theology corroborate in the following chapters, proving this fusion a timely and useful foundation for answering the many questions about the value of biblical storytelling in film in a postmodern and post-Christian culture.

---

16. Brueggemann, *Prophetic Imagination*, 13.
17. Christians, "Redemptive Media," 331.

CHAPTER 2

A Prophetic Imagination Purpose

INTRODUCTION

WALTER BRUEGGEMANN HAS COINED the phrase "Prophetic Imagination." It refers to the mission of the Old Testament prophets, who used evocative language to establish an alternative voice in contrast to that of the popular culture of their day. In this chapter, I will examine this concept and its theological variables, demonstrating how biblical narratives share a common purpose with film and television narratives of faith today.

What has mostly been focused on when communicating faith through the moving-image media are the aspects of religion considered to be safe and neutral that are often used because of their immediate visual qualities. These aspects comprise a specific set of signifiers for producers and audiences that represent received and confirmed components of religious life. For example, in the words of Ferre, "the Roman collar as an acceptable signifier of religion, church, piety; the southern evangelical, Protestant in some nonspecific way, sometimes black; the Hindu guru, almost always pathetically distracted and comic; the generalized religious 'psychotic,' zealous, often violent, sexually confused and repressed."[1] God and religion as portrayed on television and in film have become a popular theology, part of the generalized cultural fabric of a society's story system. A God of history that is capable of jettisoning these stereotypes for the rich variety of religious experience and for a deeper sense of religious life is missing.

---

1. Ferre, *Channels*, 33.

The first condition that needs to be secured is the clearly defined purpose for Biblical moving-image media; and from that point deductions and conclusions on how that translates into unique elements of content, format and style can be made. In order to achieve this purpose, various perspectives have been considered—both those based on audience-related statistics and those rooted in the Great Commission. Few producers, however, have understood these media as powerful communication tools for shaping values, icons, and behavioral patterns of the popular culture.

This book proposes Walter Brueggemann's concept of Prophetic Imagination to serve as a purpose for biblical film and television productions. This concept forms the basis for a theology of communication that enables a biblically based purpose to be implemented in storytelling. Prophetic Imagination provides a most important theological lens through which all phases of messaging for a moving-image production can be directed and examined. Since the dominant culture in the West today is now post-Christian—no longer relying on Judeo-Christian truths as the basis of public philosophy or moral consciousness. This places the *Lifestyle of the Believer* in what Brueggemann has likened to an exilic circumstance.

> I believe that this sense of (1) *loss of a structured reliable "world"* where (2) *treasured symbols of meaning are mocked and dismissed* is a pertinent point of contact between those ancient texts and our situation. . . . The most remarkable observation one can make about this interface of *exilic circumstance* and *scriptural resources* is this: Exile did not lead Jews in the Old Testament to abandon faith or to settle for abdicating despair, nor to retreat to privatistic religion. On the contrary, exile evoked the most brilliant literature and the most daring theological articulation in the Old Testament.[2]

This was the task of the prophets of old, and today the producers and directors of moving-image media need to find ways to present symbols through narrative to breathe life-giving interpretations of an alternative reality into the dulled dominant culture. The cultural context is rapidly becoming postmodern, meaning that it is resistant not only to biblical truth but to any truth claims whatsoever. It is for this reason that the book of Jonah as an exilic/post-exilic narrative will be examined in later chapters to discern the creative interplay of Prophetic Imagination through content, context, and message in a uniquely crafted format and style.

2. Brueggemann, *Cadences*, 2–3.

This is an example of the message and medium fulfilling together the intent of the communication aptly described by communication scholar Marshal McLuhan in his statement that "the medium is the message."[3] It is the medium that in its form resonates with the artistic playful, invitational, prophetic message that will address with charismatic power this crisis of a cultural conflict between two worldviews—secular naturalism as dominant consciousness and a Biblical *lifestyle of the believer* as the alternative.

Concentrating mainly on Brueggemann's model of Prophetic Imagination (see Appendix A), this chapter orients the book to consider both secular and religious forms of moving-image communication as well as its elements of alternative consciousness that reveal the world of Yahweh as a kingdom reality.

PROPHETIC IMAGINATION

In personal interviews with the renowned Old Testament scholar Professor Walter Brueggemann conducted at the November 1994 Society of Biblical Literature Conference in Chicago and again at Columbia Seminary in 1999 as well as in continuing discussions, the applicability of Prophetic Imagination to the moving-image media has been discussed. The following represents Brueggemann's ideas from which a purpose for effective, transcendental, biblical television and film can be developed.

The understanding of Prophetic Imagination begins by being freed from the stereotypical association with *prophetism*, which regards prophets as social protesters or future-tellers. *Prophets*, as defined in terms of Prophetic Imagination, were "concerned with most elemental changes in human society and . . . understood a great deal about how change is effected. . . . Most of all, they understood the distinctive power of language to speak in ways that evoke newness 'fresh from the word.'"[4]

The church today is a dynamic community of people influenced by various communication strategies. A certain culture has arisen from the presentation of the Gospel, Old and New Testament, through these communication technologies. The enculturation has become institutionalized, and a gradual loss of identity and abandonment of faith, hope, and sincere "agape" love is evident in society. Religion has become stereotyped and

3. Williams, *New Communication*, 13.
4. Brueggemann *Prophetic Imagination*, 9.

17

has lost its impact, meaning, and purpose, as seen in the moving-image media today.

An analysis of the media and the contemporary church, from the perspective of Prophetic Imagination, provides a platform for drawing parallels between historical biblical references and the popular culture. "What we understand about the Old Testament must be somehow connected with the realities of the church today."[5]

The task of Prophetic Ministry is to bring this enculturation and traditionalism into an effective interface with contemporary society by achieving a consciousness that is alternative to that of the popular culture.

The first two concepts to define are *alternative consciousness* and *dominant consciousness*. The alternative consciousness *criticizes* the dominant consciousness. It does what *liberal* tendencies have done by rejecting and delegitimizing the dominant culture. However, this is a dichotomous process, in that as it *criticizes* it also *energizes* with a promise of newness, of another time and situation, which a community of faith moves toward.[6] (Therefore, it also does what *conservatives* have done by living in anticipation of the newness promised by God.) In prophetic communication, the elements of criticizing and energizing are held in a delicate equilibrium; the prophet is thus concerned with the future as it impinges on the present.

The difficulty is to define the concept *alternative* for and in a community that on the whole does not even understand that an alternative exists. The term "alternative" means hope other than or different from a particular constant—i.e., the consciousness or intrinsic framework of an individual. Crossan notes, "If they are to be religiously successful, television must as surely as parables, act to 'shatter the deep structure of our accepted world . . . remove our defenses and make us vulnerable to God.'"[7] The "dominant consciousness" is therefore defined as the most prominent and generally accepted belief framework of a group of people, i.e., the popular culture. The culture of a community is reflected in, as well as established by, the *power* held by communication technology (see Chapter 7). As seen in the context of the utterance of Jesus's parables 2000 years ago, Christ formulated his message for the contextual culture of his time,

5. Ibid.

6. Brueggemann, *Prophetic Imagination*, 44, 62.

7. Crossan, *Dark Interval*, 122, in Arthur, "Reflections," 125.

to persuade his audience of a referential context that would otherwise be beyond their knowledge or understanding. These simple stories (narratives) reflected the "accepted world" of the listener but included truths that shattered its deep structures.[8]

Theologically, the perspective follows that God created people as co-creators of culture who now shape their "ways of life" (see Chapter 7). The prophetic communicator steps out of the commonplace culture to "reshape" that culture according to the world of God. This creational perspective would argue that humans as storytellers are mini-creators who use symbols in narration as agents of cultural change on behalf of the Creator. "Prophetic" means, in this view, to let one's communication be shaped by God and not just by the existing culture.

The moving-image media has the power to support one mythological reality over another. C. J. Arthur notes, "The question is, how can that *power* be used in a way that is theologically acceptable, such that the reformed perceptions of the world which are fostered (*as an alternative*) are in line with a vision that is not transcendence blind?"[9] (italics and insertions mine). One differentiation based on Jacques Ellul's description of this power is whether the media uses messages to confirm through propaganda popular cultural beliefs, or acts as is proposed—prophetically criticizing while at the same time energizing a culture to believe in new realities.

PROPHETIC THEOLOGY

The prophetic media is committed to applying the biblical truth of God's word to the real world of sin and human fallenness. Theologically, Moses is the paradigmatic prophet used by Brueggemann to identify the criteria inherent to an understanding of prophetism as part of the Prophetic Imagination. Brueggemann writes that the non-Israelite antecedents to prophetism, namely "the Canaanite phenomenon of ecstasy (1 Samuel 10 and 19) and evidence from Mari concerning institutional offices of prophecy in the cult and court" are not discarded.[10] However, this book takes prophecy to mean the work of the Hebrew prophets whose literary records are found within the pages of the Old Testament, men of Israel,

---

8. Ibid., 121–22, in Arthur, "Reflections," 125.

9. Arthur, "Reflections," 126.

10. Brueggemann, *Prophetic Imagination*, 15.

and spokesmen of Israel's God to the nation of which they were members. Robert Scott wrote, "Their message was addressed to men of their day, in the conditions and circumstances under which they lived and in language which only men of their own nation and time could fully understand."[11] The dynamic of prophetism is born out of a social-political reality that is so radical and inexplicable that its cause can be nothing less than a theological hope for the awaiting newness. Prophetic *criticism* and *energizing* to newness is a result of an experience from within a culture, not merely an appropriation of external sources.

ROYAL CONSCIOUSNESS

Israel as a new socio-political community emerged out of Egypt as a result of an internal yearning for freedom directed towards a God who is able to loosen the chains of the *royal consciousness*, exposing gods with no power.

The royal consciousness is that belief framework that imposes rules and standards by those in control to gain power for selfish gain. Moses' faith in God's sovereignty over the mythical legitimacy of Pharaoh's world broke out of this dominant passive reality.

This dialectic between *religion* and a *political-social reality* is the first aspect evidenced by the paradigmatic model of Moses. The political and economic arrangements of the Egyptian Empire provided no alternative than to serve the interests of those in charge. It was the productive functioning of this order that warranted its existence. Moreover, the religion of static triumphalism propagated by Pharaoh seemed unquestionable. The lords of the Egyptian regime were static gods of the people who remained gods as long as the people believed in their power. This led to the politics of oppression and exploitation.

To define the royal consciousness, Brueggemann explores three general characteristics (as identifiable in the Solomonic period) that reflect the Egyptian empire and are comparable to the dominant culture today. Moses brought forth a revolution, both religious and political, which sustained itself until the year 1000 B.C. It was a work that resulted from the engagement of the religion of God's freedom with the politics of justice and compassion. It was not just a religious idea, but a new social community and culture—in the words of Brueggemann, "A community that

11. Scott, *Relevance*, 1.

has historical body, that had to devise laws, patterns of governance and order, norms of right and wrong, and sanctions of accountability."[12] In 962 BC, following 40 years of David's leadership, Solomon's achievements returned to the religious and political presuppositions of the pre-Mosaic imperial situation. According to George Mendenhall, this shift in the social vision of Solomon, which he describes as the "paganization of Israel" was contradictory to that of Moses.[13] In other contexts, scholars like Gerhard von Rad and Brueggemann term this return to pre-prophetic reality "enlightenment."[14]

Based on the Solomonic achievements as a paradigm, in stark contrast to the Mosaic vision, the three elements that summarize a royal consciousness against which the prophetic ministry must speak are the following: "economics of affluence," "the politics of oppression," and "a religion of immanence." Our sociology is predictably derived from, legitimated by, and reflective of our theology.[15]

WELL-BEING AND AFFLUENCE

Well-being and affluence were evident in the Solomonic achievements. Archaeological findings of artifacts and building remains support the description in 1 Kings 4:20–23 of a well-ordered and secure social situation. According to Brueggemann, "Judah and Israel were as many as the sand by the sea; they ate and drank and were happy. Solomon ruled over all the kingdoms from the Euphrates to the land of the Philistines and to the border of Egypt; they brought tribute and served Solomon all the days of their life. Solomon's provision for one day was thirty cans of fine flour and sixty cans of meal, ten fat oxen, and twenty pasture-fed cattle, a hundred sheep . . ."[16]

However, this satiation and the abundance of a consumer society eradicated all anxiety about survival and subsequent dependence on God, establishing a culture with a *royal consciousness*. This consciousness is characterized by a grudging acceptance of *life* that is not fulfilling. The words of wisdom of the "philosopher" in Ecclesiastes 2:10–11 describe

12. Brueggemann, *Prophetic Imagination*, 16.

13. In Brueggemann, *Prophetic Imagination*, 31.

14. Brueggemann, *Hope*, 31.

15. Brueggemann, *Prophetic Imagination*, 17–18.

16. Ibid., 32.

this futility: "Anything I wanted, I got. I did not deny myself any pleasure. I was proud of everything I had worked for, and all this was my reward. Then I thought about all that I had done and how hard I had worked doing it, and I realized that it didn't mean a thing" (GNB).

The counter-culture of Moses was characterized by an economy of equality and by life in a world of scarcity. The vision of the Mosaic experience was: "He that gathered much had nothing over and he that gathered little had no lack; each gathered according to what he could eat" (Exod 16:18), and God provided the rest. "This was the food that the Lord was giving you to eat . . . manna" (Exod 16:31). Brueggemann notes that in the royal community, however, love for your neighbor, "(c)ovenanting which takes brothers and sisters seriously, had been replaced by consuming, which regards brothers and sisters as products to be used."[17] This community, inured to suffering, believed it could live as self-made men and women. In an economics of affluence in the dominant culture of media messages it is the same satiation which makes the people numb to pain. This kind of "happiness" that satiated security breeds with disregard for neighbor is without passion or joy of freedom. This surely leads to the politics of social oppression, the second element characteristic of the empire.

OPPRESSIVE SOCIAL POLICY

Oppressive social policy was the foundation of the Solomonic achievements. Citizens working for the benefit of the state were mobilized for the sake of those in charge and to support their extravagant lifestyles. In 1 Kings 11:28 it is written that Jeroboam was an able young man, and when Solomon noticed how hard he worked he put him in charge of all the "forced labor" (GNB).

The nature of government and the role of people and leaders are disputed in 1 Kings 12, showing the struggle the Israelites had with this new self-understanding.

The Mosaic experience had the following vision:

> And if your brother becomes poor and cannot maintain himself with you, you shall maintain him, as a stranger and sojourner he shall live with you. Take no interest from him or increase, but fear your God; that your brother may live beside you. . . . For they are

17. Ibid., 33.

my servants, whom I brought forth out of the land of Egypt; they shall not be sold as slaves. (Lev 25:35–42)

Brueggemann writes, "This is all over by the time Solomon gets around to forced labor to enforce his rule."[18]

The royal consciousness management mentality governs by cost-accounting principals and has no time for the politics of justice and the mystery of God's provision. The philosopher of Ecclesiastes writes, "Then I looked again at all the injustice that goes on in the world, the oppressed were weeping and no one would help them. No one would help them because the oppressors had power on their side" (Eccl 4:1 GNB). Although a conventional Hellenistic dating can be ascribed to Ecclesiastes, the book likely speaks to a situation like that of Solomon where weariness, boredom, and satiation had become the spirit of the dominant culture. In the culture today, these same attributes and cynicism can be readily observed, replacing a vision of God's freedom with apparent security and covenanting with consumption communities that dismiss the cries of the marginal. As Brueggemann writes, the empire has "created a subjective consciousness concerned only with self–satisfaction," resulting in self-made men and women.[19]

A RELIGION OF IMMANENCE

A religion of immanence is the third Solomonic achievement. A controlled static empire now also required a radical revision of the character of God. The revelation of the liberating God in the Exodus narrative had been forgotten in the managed social reality of Solomon's empire. The land was satiated, without revolution or change or past or future. Everything was held in the now. There was no promise or hope for the future. The present was propagated as perfect, and all criticism was silenced. According to Brueggemann, there are two ways criticism is silenced, "One is the way of heavy-handed prohibition that is backed by forceful sanction." The other is suggested by the treatment of Jeroboam in 1 Kings 11:40, when the criticism of Ahijah the prophet is curiously ignored. "That is the second way of handling criticism, developing a natural immunity and remaining totally impervious to criticism."[20]

18. Ibid., 37.
19. Ibid., 42.
20. Ibid., 38.

The royal consciousness is contained in and centered around the king's taking on increasing significance and power over God. The primary vision becomes the well-being and enhancement of the visible sovereign. He is no longer a means to establishing a new community. The religion of this empire substitutes the promises and creative provision of the Holy One for the security and certainty of the imperial gods who promise the individual access to a transcendent being.

The joy of freedom and faith in Yahweh is a response to his uncompromising love: "I will be gracious to whom I will be gracious, and will show mercy. But . . . you cannot see my face; for man shall not see me and live" (Exod 33:19–20).

The royal consciousness has traded the vision of God's freedom for what seems to be a reality of imperial security. It has denied the legitimacy of tradition that requires us to remember, of authority that expects us to answer, and of community that calls us to care. It has enthroned the *present* so that, in the words of Brueggemann, "the sovereignty of God is fully subordinated to the purpose of the king."[21]

We may learn from the prophets that their God was not bound within the tradition of the past ages of Moses and David; so, too, our God is not bound within the tradition of their age or that of the first century AD. He is the living God, at work not only in the souls of individuals today but present as the final arbiter in the struggles and confusion of social life.

CRITICIZING AND ENERGIZING

It is the role of the prophet, as with Moses, to exhibit an alternative imagination and way of thinking, beyond the confines of his present reality and culture. Moses engaged in the experiences of suffering of the marginal people. The Solomonic establishment, on the other hand, embodies the dominant culture's numbness, which is the loss of passion. The imperial gods' inability to care or suffer has only to be compared with the grief, anguish, and joy of David (2 Sam 1:19–27, 3:33–34, 12:15–23, 18:33) or, conversely, with the one-dimensional narrative of Solomon. Apathy, the absence of pathos, can be defined in the connection R. D. Laing makes between behavior and experience: "If our experience is destroyed, our behavior will be destructive."[22] It is necessary to practice the proper be-

21. Ibid., 34.
22. Laing, *Politics*, 12.

havior rather than an imagined alternative, because the imperial gods are no longer able to experience their own experiences. The royal consciousness is interested in a community of behaviors—not in the expression of experiences—and can therefore be managed. This is why testimony of God's intervention in the lives of believers is such a powerful witness against the dominant culture's imperialism (see Chapter 9).

In Martin Marty's *A Nation of Behaviors*, this inability to experience rests on the supposition that nothing is truly new but that everything consists of merely a rearrangement of old behaviors, as well as the notion that things are forever.[23] There exists a denial of endings because it would be too costly to suggest that those in power are not in charge and that things will not ultimately work out. Death is one of those aspects of life that the royal consciousness chooses to deny. Brueggemann describes this, saying, "Lifton has concluded that we have no adequate way to relate to death's reality and potential, so it is dealt with by a numbness that denies."[24]

God created out of nothing, but humans must always create out of that which exists. In an Old Testament context, faithfulness to God turns humans into conduits of prophetic rhetoric, thereby transforming existing culture.

The prophet who would criticize the apathy of the royal consciousness would need to energize the thoughts of this numbed society so that its members would begin to imagine. To imagine prophetic newness as a promise at work in our history is to engage in prophetic imagination.

The prophet does not engage in futuring fantasy by asking if the vision can be implemented, because that is of no consequence until it can be *imagined*. The royal consciousness that makes it possible to implement anything and everything is the one that is *frightened of the artist*. The prophet keeps alive the ministry of imagination by conjuring and proposing alternative futures to the single one the king portrays as the only thinkable option or possibility.

The prophet *energizes* people by first making them realize that there are no real endings and by offering *symbols* adequate to the horror and massiveness of the experience that evokes numbness and therefore requires denial (see tragedy in Chapter 9). Symbols that will release experience and permit it to be redemptive bring to expression those dimensions

23. Brueggemann, *Prophetic Imagination*, 120.
24. Ibid., 48.

of reality that the royal consciousness fears and tries to subvert. Through symbols, the prophet is able to bring to public expression the fears and terrors that have been denied. The prophet Jeremiah embodies the way to an alternative consciousness such as Moses experienced in the face of the denying dominant culture. Jeremiah articulates grief in the two dimensions necessary for a language of grief.

First, his grief was for the end of his people—he really cried for them—and secondly, no one would listen and see what was so transparent to him. Jeremiah's grief is expressed as a visible, public event—as Brueggemann writes, "A play-by-play of the disaster in poetry that matches an internal wrenching in his heart and in which his very bowels are gripped by terror."[25]

Jeremiah also demonstrates the metaphoric use of language as he engages in a battle for linguistics in an effort to create a different epistemology out of which a new community might emerge. Here the aspect of *time* is also relevant. The eternal now of the royal consciousness does not know what "time" it is. Unchanging continuation of power seems safe and secure, but God knows the time and when the end will come. It is out of real tears and repentance that real newness can come, based on the unconditional love and mercy of a free God.

This is the miracle of newness that Jeremiah knew. From pain, hurt, and loneliness his tears broke barriers; without it there is no newness. Brueggemann writes that after Jeremiah, it was ultimately Jesus of Nazareth who demonstrated that "weeping must be real because endings are real and that weeping permits newness. His weeping and suffering permitted the kingdom to come," "And Jesus wept."[26]

THEOLOGICAL IMAGINATION

It is the imagination of the prophet to think and believe beyond knowledge and understanding to a genuine alternative—which is what Yahweh allows, and which can be effectively used through the media as a witness of hope and faith to the nations.

We live today like the Israelites in a kind of "exile"—the cultural exile of the popular culture. Moses reached to God (or, first, God reached to him) beyond the confines of contemporary culture and its existing bondage.

25. Ibid., 53.
26. Ibid., 61.

So, too, the Christian communicator today should strive to reach beyond the present cultural bondage. The threat being faced is the bondage of the commercial principalities and powers of moving-image media. People often attempt to fill the resulting technological emptiness with the liturgies of consumerism and commoditization. In the context of the contemporary exile, it is a recovery of the Holy Presence in communication that must first be imagined—and then practiced in ways that will counteract the debilitating powerful ideology of the dominant culture.

The practice of poetic imagination through narrative is such an act of Prophetic Imagination, carried out in a communicative *style*. Poetic imagination is the term Brueggemann uses to denote a *style* of language that is lyrical and expressive, constructing an alternative and thereby energizing people to real newness. He explains, "I am concerned not with the formal aspects of poetry but with the substantive issues of alternative prospects that the managed prose around us cannot invent and does not want to permit."[27]

The use of "mythos" as part of "logos" is what poetic imagination describes. This is a pre-Socratic understanding of discourse that parallels the development of orality and literacy, as Walter Ong has examined.

The issue in the story of the interrelations of logos and mythos is which form of discourse—philosophy (technical discourse), rhetoric, or poetic—ensures the discovery and validation of truth, knowledge, and reality and thereby deserves to be the legislator of human decision making and action. The two stories inform one another and both are necessary to a full realization of the relationship between communication and what humans are and can become.[28]

This poetic narration entailing both mythos and logos evoked images and invited perceptions in Israel that were not available apart from such poetic imagination. Earl Mac Cormac has identified that meaning in such metaphors of poetic imagination in the Old Testament results from a matrix of four interrelated elements:

> *Semantics* (the association of the semantic features of the referents), *metaphor as a speech act* (its illocutionary intent and perlocutionary performance of stimulating emotion), *context* (which offers a pragmatic interpretation of which possible meaning to accept),

27. Ibid., 45.
28. Fisher, *Human Communication*, 6.

and *culture* (the broader context in which the trope is embedded and to which it stands in a mutually influential relationship).[29]

The use of figurative language in a given context demands a certain religious historical context in which it can function. This also holds true of the marriage image in Hosea. The metaphor in Hosea 2:4–17 does not display the kind of realism that permits it to be used as a proper documentation of marriage laws. Rather, it serves as an analogy, as a communicative device in prophetic utterances similar to the parables Jesus used.

Perelman suggests, "Very often analogy is at the center of an original vision of the relationship between humans and the divine."[30] Meaning derived from such comparisons is therefore crucial to understanding the function of poetic imagery.

Similarly, the media can make available perceptions to begin to transform the self-image, communal image, and image of historical possibility, by using a narrative model with a Prophetic Imagination perspective (see Chapter 10).

Jesus, as the fulfillment of the prophets of the Old Testament, used parables as mode of teaching and educating as an act of poetic imagination that can guide our prophetic use of the moving-image medium. He invited his community of listeners out beyond the visible realities of Roman law and the growing restrictions of Jewish law. Like Second Isaiah's poetic imagination, Jesus does this precisely out of tradition itself. It is clear that he tells parables consistent with the rabbinical tradition, but his parables also serve to conjure an alternative social reality. Although specific, they are open-ended. The parable, a particular story or genre, does not leave the listener instructed to act in a certain way—i.e., it is not didactic, but intends to characterize an alternative society, which Christ calls the "kingdom of God."

PROPHETIC IMAGINATION PURPOSE IN JONAH

This reveals two aspects of effective biblical communication: to define the Prophetic Imagination perspective as the purpose of biblical moving-image media messages and to choose a suitable genre (*format* with a *style*) that includes the perspective of a poetic imagination by which to present the message. The narrative of Jonah brings these elements into

29. Quoted in Botham, "Communicative Function," 58.

30. Ibid., 57.

a congruent, inclusive whole. It allows for the communication of an alternative consciousness as authorial intent, with a dramatic and revelatory function that captures the imagination of the audience, such that a prophetic criticism is presented and the dominant consciousness of the cultural context is energized. This vivid, artistic, playful, and surprising narrative communication does nothing less than theologically shatter the deep structures of the dominant context's Jewish culture. The call to a different understanding of God as present with and interested in having a personal relationship with his created beings is revealed. The character of God and that of humans are juxtaposed to, ironically, reveal the fallen condition of humankind's heart and intentions and the merciful, forgiving love that God wants to communicate to all he has created, both Jew and Gentile. This orientation to the world—to Yahweh's world—communicated prophetically through the characterization of Jonah and the content of the narrative, reveals the skewed theology of the dominant consciousness into which this story speaks. Through a tapestry of rich metaphoric and ironical style, this narrative reflects categorizations of form such as the novella, parable, allegory, comedy, and satire, to name but a few. All these are indications of a literary jewel, a narrative that uses in extreme fashion revelatory mechanisms of storytelling to capture and shake to new revelation the theology of the Jews to hope. This is *par excellence* the task of Prophetic Imagination and ministry. This revelation of hope in the message of Jonah would uncouple Israel's witness to her God from political power, allowing her to become the suffering servant at the mercy of her enemies, the Ninevites. This newness, arising out of the suffering of Israel, enables the whole Gentile world to learn of God's merciful forgiving love. This message of God's compassion, freedom, and justice offers symbols that communicate God's plan to transform enemies such as Nineveh into brothers and his desire for the salvation not only of Israel but of all people. Israel would become the witness of God's deliverance, in the midst of the most degrading circumstances.

This school of thought resulted in the powerful songs of the suffering servant that are ascribed to an unknown prophet, namely Deutero-Isaiah, in, among others, Isaiah 53. These songs were originally written with the intent to energize Israel to fresh faith, similar to that seen in the book of Jonah. This is an act of hope-filled language that speaks metaphorically to engage the community in new discernment, just when it had given up. This language of amazement,[31] also termed poetic imagination by Brueggemann,[32] reinterprets the history and role and understanding of Yahweh's will for his people, as the work of a Prophetic Imagination. For both Jonah and Deutero-Isaiah, "The task of prophetic imagination and ministry, especially as we see it in sixth-century Judah, is to cut through the despair and to penetrate the dissatisfied coping that seems to have no end or resolution."[33] The Messiah is the fulfillment of the Old Testament quest for *Shalom*, made available through the theological shift that Israel was called to embrace through the prophetic writings in exilic and post-exilic circumstances. Brueggemann writes that Prophetic Imagination, through the hard work of recognizing the true situation of the dominant consciousness, "moves by subversive, evangelical lips uttering hopes and possibilities; it may end in new people, new community, new creation. The departure from the empire was the great point of risk for the sixth century Jews, but out of that departure came the birth of Judaism, the enactment of God's faithful capacity for newness."[34] This newness is the result of God's working in the lives of people and in history to establish *shalom*, a community of believers living transformed lives in terms of the miracle-working power of the Creator.

The *royal community* and *royal consciousness* serve the people in charge; a community of faith puts God in charge and establishes a new social community with hope, faith, and a future of promise.

An understanding of Prophetic Imagination can be grasped in the connection Zimmerli brings to fresh expression in *prophetic proclamation* and *reinterpretation*. Brueggemann writes, "Prophetic proclamation shatters and transforms tradition in order to announce the approach of the Living One."[35] "Moses discloses Yahweh the Sovereign One, . . . (who) is extrapolated from no social reality and is captive to no social perception, but acts from his own person toward his own purposes."[36] He is a God free from the bounds of social reality. For example, the community that emerges out of Egypt has not only a new religion based on the freedom

---

31. Brueggemann, *Prophetic Imagination*, 69.

32. Brueggemann, *Hopeful Imagination*.

33. Brueggemann *Prophetic Imagination*, 65–66.

34. Brueggemann, *Cadences*, 133.

35. Brueggemann, *Prophetic Imagination*, 115.

36. Ibid., 16.

of God but is also expected to adhere to certain norms and sanctions established by God. Moses receives these directly from the living God on Mount Zion. This sociological connection between theology and politics was identified by Karl Marx when he observed that, "The criticism of religion is the ultimate criticism and must lead to the criticism of law, economics, and politics."[37]

Prophecy is the discernment of how genuinely alternative God is. The awesome call to maintain the dialectic of criticizing the dominant consciousness while at the same energizing it to adopt an alternative consciousness is the task of prophetic ministry. The mass media has, however, taken on a "priestly" type of voice for the entire community of popular culture. Schultze observes that, "As priest-like institutions, the media do not try to challenge the tribe's values and beliefs. Instead, they confirm people's existing beliefs and values."[38] This media voice confirming the status quo of the empire infiltrates the minds of its audience, socializing the society/persons to be passive receivers with dim imaginations who are all too eager to submit to the dominant royal consciousness.

CONCLUSION

Although the moving-image media can never identify with any one culture or socio-economic order, neither can it reside outside culture or socio-economic orders of different kinds. Cultures and orders present both opportunities and dangers for the church, Christian media, and theology. A transition from the modern to the postmodern culture in society has brought the narrative (analogical) theology (i.e. incorporating the imagination via metaphor, symbols, and semantics) and ecumenical dialogue (keeping in touch with fellow believers and communities of believers of all different Christian traditions) into an interface that must be creatively directed to communicate biblical truth in a reality-forming way (see Chapter 7).

Prophetic Imagination as discussed in this chapter and developed by theologian Walter Brueggemann is an important theological perspective through which all phases of a moving-image media production can be examined. In a post-Christian culture the Christian in popular culture is likened theologically to being in the situation of exilic circumstance simi-

37. Ibid., 17.
38. Schultze, *Communication*, 124.

lar to that of ancient Israel. As the sacred symbols of Christians are being mocked and removed from public places, the biblically based moving-image media must, like the prophets of the Old Testament, artistically portray playful, invitational messages. These must, with charismatic power, confront the cultural and spiritual conflict between two worldviews, with secular naturalism as dominant consciousness and faith-filled *lifestyle of the believer* as the alternative.

The narrative approach has been recognized and applied in Christian film and television in America and South Africa with the film series *Narnia* and Heartlines, respectively. However, there is no coherent theological background or purpose that guides the filmmaking process. With a Prophetic Imagination purpose behind such messages, this chapter begins to show the theological aspect that undergirds a theology for communication that this book develops, to give the necessary support for the implementation of biblical narratives for the screen. The concepts of intent and dominant and alternative consciousness, integrated with *form* and *style* of the narrative, bring to the table semantics and metaphor to future fantasy that keeps alive the imagination.

Understanding messages in terms of a Prophetic Imagination gives a perspective to biblical moving-image communication that incorporates culture but also adds the pragmatic theological orientation to it. This lays a sound theological foundation for the purpose of the message before introducing the interdisciplinary models (see Chapter 4), by which to practically implement or critique theology and communication of biblically based messages via the moving-image media.

CHAPTER 3

Socio-Rhetorical Criticism as Methodology and Its Relation to the Interdisciplinary Models

INTRODUCTION

THIS CHAPTER WILL DISCUSS Vernon K. Robbins' approach to socio-rhetorical criticism as well as outline and discuss its principles. Certain aspects of the approach are linked more closely to the development of the specific interdisciplinary models put forth in this book. This congenial methodology encompasses both communication principles and socio-rhetorical critique of sacred (biblical) texts, enabling one to also draw theological conclusions for analyzing "texts" (literary, oral/aural, or visual). Detailed attention to the biblical text is given, with interaction between the world of the text's author and the present world and how to translate this into moving-image media for the twenty-first century.

Socio-rhetorical criticism is used in this book as a methodology for analyzing the biblical text of Jonah and will serve in developing a communication paradigm from which media messages can be structured to communicate with biblical authority and power. Normally, scholars work either synchronically, analyzing the text itself, or diachronically, analyzing the socio-historical background, and the two processes are separate. However, the approach used in this book is an encompassing approach dealing with all the textures of a text simultaneously—the text itself, as well as its socio-cultural setting. Most discourse is analyzed in a literary manner with characters, events, and episodes reflecting on each other and creating a world inside the biblical text. This "internal mind" of the text is essentially the *Bible* component of the three paradigmatic models (see Appendices A, B, and C) that this book proposes. This component relates to the biblical text, which must be consulted to derive motivation and educational elements relating to a biblical worldview, which the producer of the message wants to communicate. Then there is the historical approach, which deduces the world surrounding a text by looking through the text, either inwardly or outwardly, and so reconstructing the historical world surrounding the text. This "external body" component of the text is the *Life* component, which the paradigmatic models will explore, and encompasses the life that is lived surrounding the text in ancient times as well as the present time. The social and cultural texture in which the reading takes place affects the meaning external to the text, and that which is extrapolated from the text often is available for entertaining the reader precisely because of points of contact between the text and the reader's world.

The socio-rhetorical methodology recognizes that these two approaches separate the internal literary mind of the text from the external historicity of the text. This dualism imposes restrictions on the interpretation of the language, how it is used and its effects. In the development of the models by means of socio-rhetorical criticism, it is the continual interweaving of the *Bible* and *Life* components as textures of the text (in the process of finding meaning) that understands language as a social product with meaning networks and meaning effects in which the text, as well as the interpreter or reader, lives. Socio-rhetorical criticism is a postmodern reading, and this book's proposed analysis thus considers the text metaphorically as a rich tapestry of textures. As the text is viewed from different angles, different webs of meaning become evident.

This leads to the third component of the paradigmatic models, *Lifestyle of the Believer,* which emphasizes that a text must not be seen as a meaning unto itself, but as a message that is read within a world, thereby communicating with purpose and meaning relative to a particular world. The proposed communication strategy of Christian moving-image media is to incorporate elements of the biblical text (the *Bible* component) to educate, perhaps only in terms of morals and absolute truth, and to use the contemporary setting's point of contact with the message (the *Life* component) to achieve an element of entertainment. Finally, this process of communication, with elements that inhabitants of the world in which the text is interpreted can relate to, will translate the *Lifestyle of the Believer,* with meaning and purpose exemplified in story elements such as character and plot. Similar to the biblical author of Jonah, then, the producer needs to *"edutain"* (see Chapter 9) the audience with a clearly defined purpose, that of a Prophetic Imagination (see Chapter 2).

INNER TEXTURE AND THE INTERDISCIPLINARY MODELS
(Elaborated in Chapters 5 and 6)

The Prophetic Theology Model is the point from which a Christian message must start, as it refers to the producer of the message, posits God as the author of all messages, and establishes the Bible as the basis and purpose for the communication. In the process, the exploration of the various textures of the text, with particular focus on Inner Texture and Intertexture, leads to the extrapolation of the Prophetic Imagination purpose of the biblical text. This can make the message translatable for *"edutaining"* audiences of moving-image media. Exploring the inner texture provides a flat reading of the rhetorical axis of the communication (see model in Appendix D)[1] but highlights the meaning of the message as it travels intrinsically from implied author to implied reader via the narrator and characters in the story. As Robbins points out, "Various literary critics have displayed a horizontal diagram to exhibit this communication process, 'the whole narrative communication situation,'[2] and this is the beginning point for building a socio-rhetorical model for interpretation."[3] Socio-rhetorical criticism adds two aspects to the text-immanent approach of analysis developed by, among others, Anglo-American New Criticism, Russian Formalism, and French Structuralism. First, it sets these results in dialogue with results from other disciplines. In this book, this interactive quality will be used to link the Theology Model (Appendix A) with the Contemporary Communication Model (Appendix B) and develop the Edutainment Model (Appendix C). Each model employs the different textures to help understand the text and extrapolate from the Bible text biblically based messages for the contemporary media and culture. Secondly, it brings the implied author and implied reader into an interactive relationship. Unless the text is read, it lies dormant of meaning and meaning effects. Eventually the Theological Model (Appendix A), using socio-rhetorical criticism, interactively explores the world of the

---

1. Figure 2.1 is taken from Robbins, *Tapestry*, 21; Figure 2.2 is taken from Robbins, *Tapestry*, 29.

2. Chatman, *Story*, 151; Rimmon-Kenan, *Narrative Fiction*, 86.

3. Robbins, *Tapestry*, 28.

author—the *Bible* component—and the world of the text—the *Life* component—and the world of the interpreter—the *Lifestyle of the Believer*—to interpret the inner texture of the biblical text.

INTERTEXTURE AND THE INTERDISCIPLINARY MODELS
(Elaborated in Chapters 6 and 8)

It is in the process of exploring the inner texture on a rhetorical axis that the presence of "intertextuality" lends to the interpretive process another dimension, namely the vertical axis. This axis represents language and information that results from a communication transaction taking place. This communication interaction takes place between the author and reader of the biblical text, the *Bible* and *Life* component of the Theology Model (Appendix A), respectively. Other texts being read outside of the biblical text are manifestations of language that play a special role in the author's representation of the world and therefore the interpreter. In the case of the moving-image media, this refers to the producers' interpretation and application of the text for use in portraying the *Lifestyle of the Believer*. The process of exploring the intertexture, then, as defined by socio-rhetorical criticism, has as its goal "to analyze the manner in which signs and codes evoke a textual form of cultural, social, and historical reality."[4] This textual application of the cultural and social textures are delineated and defined by socio-rhetorical criticism as separate from social, cultural, and ideological textures. The latter are also differentiated and applied in different models respectively in this book. However, they all contribute interactively to the overall analysis and understanding as well as application of the text, for use in the Christian moving-image media messaging.

SOCIAL AND CULTURAL TEXTURE AND THE INTERDISCIPLINARY MODELS
(Elaborated in chapters 7 and 8)

The social and cultural textures of texts are referred to in this book as the "voice" of the text. In the words of Frow, "Socio-rhetorical criticism views voice in text as the medium for the 'consciousness' or 'vision' of the characters and the narrator, who are 'concretizations drawn from a

4. Ibid., 33.

represented world."[5] This area is dominated by the theories of anthropology and sociology, by which the cultural and social nature of the voices can be analyzed. The Final Cultural Categories proposed by Robbins are the "final topics" as Aristotle named them, which represent the cultural location of the discourse. The cultural location of the discourse is the manner in which the propositions and arguments are presented and by which people are separated in terms of dominant culture, subculture, and counterculture. For this book and the integration of theology with communication, these topics are the structure in which the model for a Theology of Communication is developed in Chapter 6.

Prophetic Imagination can be identified in the discourse of a text using the following definitions of rhetoric from Robbins's socio-rhetorical criticism model. The dominant culture rhetoric, relating to Brueggemann's concept of a dominant consciousness,[6] and for the purposes of the critical communication model, is defined by Robbins as, "A system of attitudes, values, dispositions, and norms that the speaker either presupposes or asserts are supported by social structures vested with power to impose its goals on people in a significantly broad territorial region."[7] This is, then, the working definition for understanding and extracting the *Life* component (see Appendix A) in the discourse of the "text" when explicating Prophetic Imagination elements in the Theology of Communication model, (see Appendix A) whether in a literary, oral/aural, or moving-image text. "Subculture rhetoric imitates the attitudes, values, dispositions, norms of dominant culture rhetoric. . . . This rhetoric implies that a network of groups and institutions exists for supporting persons. . . . Both sexes, all ages and complete family groups are perceived to have a stake in this rhetoric."[8] The *Bible* component or biblical worldview, in this book, refers to alternative culture rhetoric. According to Roberts "*Counterculture* or *alternative culture rhetoric* rejects *explicit* and *mutable* characteristics of the dominant, or subculture rhetoric to which it responds. . . . The term is best reserved for intracultural phenomena; countercultural rhetoric is a culturally heretical rhetoric that evokes 'a new future,' not an alien rhetoric

---

5. Frow, *Marxism,* quoted in Robbins, *Tapestry,* 34.

6. Brueggemann, *Prophetic Imagination,* 28.

7. Robbins, *Texture,* 86.

8. Roberts, "Counter-Culture," 112, and Gordon, "Subsociety," 155, quoted in Robbins, *Textures,* 86.

that evokes the preservation of an old culture (real or imagined)."[9] The alternative consciousness of Prophetic Imagination's Prophetic Theology is thus established through this countercultural rhetoric, which evokes the theme of "hope of voluntary reform by the dominant society in accord with a different model of 'the good life.'"[10] This definition of the *Lifestyle of the Believer* component in the Theology of Communication Model (see Appendix B) is delineated as ". . . a fully developed counterculture rhetoric to express a constructive image of an alternative, better way of life. It provides a relatively self-sufficient system of action by grounding its views in a well-developed, supporting ideology."[11]

The producers of programming with a biblical life worldview establish an alternative consciousness (as defined by Brueggemann) through moving-image narratives that, through the mimetic environment of the action and speech of the narrator and characters, evoke the represented world of the counterculture. It is, however, the fine balance of knowledge as well as the integration of the current social and cultural setting with the biblical worldview that must engage the audience. As this rhetoric in moving images normally entertains the dominant consciousness, the hope is to see an alternative consciousness presented to educate in terms of the biblical truth, thereby opening the door to acceptance of the *Lifestyle of the Believer.*

IDEOLOGICAL TEXTURE AND THE INTERDISCIPLINARY MODELS

(Elaborated in Chapter 9)

The ideological texture of the discourse is the point of view that each individual, as part of a group with certain presuppositions, values, and dispositions, brings to the interpretation of the text. Robbins identifies three ways to analyze the ideological texture of a text: "Analyzing the social and cultural location of the implied author of the text; analyzing the ideology of power in the discourse of the text; and analyzing the ideology in the mode of intellectual discourse both in the text and in the interpretation of the text."[12] In the Prophetic Imagination paradigm, it is the ideology of the

9. Roberts, "Counter-Culture," 114, quoted in Robbins, *Texture,* 87.

10. Robbins, *Texture,* 87.

11. Roberts, "Counter-Culture," 121, quoted in Robbins, *Texture,* 87.

12. Robbins, *Tapestry,* 111.

dominant consciousness of the society to which the alternative consciousness of the biblical worldview of the author must speak. It is, however, the
interaction of these two worldviews in the Bible that forms the discourse
that must be interpreted in terms of what represents the counterculture
group and how that influences the purpose of the communication. Thus,
the ideologies of a life "system" justify the biblical writers' place in the
world and give him or her perspective on the world. This is the point of
view from which the study of ideological texture can provide insight for
the producer of moving–image messages. It is interpreting the varying
ideologies as covertly portrayed by the characters in the biblical narrative
that overtly points to the ideologies that this book has analyzed in terms
of a Prophetic Imagination. According to Eagleton, "The term 'ideology'
'represents the points where power impacts upon certain utterances and
inscribes itself tacitly within them.'"[13] Discerning these ideologies in the
text, displayed in the narrative by the characters, the author, and implied
readers, gives an understanding of the perspective and worldview of the
biblical writers. The power of the ideology of the biblical authors affects
the communities they lived in as well as our communities today to live
a *Lifestyle of the Believer.*[14] The producer of narratives for the moving-
image media must consider the social and cultural data that can be built
into the language of a text. The ideology of power in the discourse must
be analyzed, and Robbins suggests using Foucault's guidelines for such
analysis.[15] These require a definition of the system of differentiations that
allows the dominant consciousness, as the *Life* component, to rationalize
certain objectives in institutionalized form to exert power over others.
In biblical terms, they thus indicate the ideologies of power contained
in the narrative of the *Bible.* A biblical alternative is presented as the way
of truth, the *Lifestyle of the Believer,* which can be applied to the institutions of power that hinder a Prophetic Imagination in our contemporary
contexts.

13. Eagleton, *Ideology,* 223, quoted in Robbins, *Texture,* 110.

14. Robbins, *Texture,* 111–12.

15. Ibid., 113.

SACRED TEXTURE AND THE INTERDISCIPLINARY MODELS

(Elaborated in Chapter 9)

Human relationship with the divine (God or gods) and the way sacred texts speak about realms of religious life are the issues involved in the sacred texture of a text. The presence of *God (or gods)* in a text and his relation to humans in the text is the starting point for an analysis of the sacred. However, throughout the analysis of biblical texts, the textures in and of themselves are thick with layers of meaning about God. God can act overtly as a character in the text or passively as merely a presence in the narrative. There are also characters that act as holy people; as Robbins describes, "Frequently there are holy persons of higher and lower status in a text. The interaction of these people with one another creates an environment in which subtle distinctions can be made between truly authentic religious thought and behavior and beliefs and practices that are inferior."[16] Texts may contain explicit or implicit references to the *Spirit and the spiritual realm*. "The sacred texture of a text often emerges in the context of conflict between good and evil spiritual forces."[17] *Divine history* entails the realm of eschatology, apocalyptic, and salvation history, as well as the prophetic. God's actions in and through the world can provide a glimpse of the last things (eschatology); the events of the end times or future time (apocalyptic/prophetic); and God's plan to bring salvation to humans through his continuing history with mankind. These themes reveal *human redemption* and *human commitment* to the divine in the portrayal of faithful followers and supporters of people who reveal God's ways in the text. This human commitment is not only an individual matter but takes place within a specific *religious community*. Robbins writes that it is a matter "of participating with other people in activities that nurture and fulfill commitment to divine ways. In Christian terminology, this is the realm of ecclesiology, . . . to worship God and enact obedience to God . . . with the nature of community (*Lifestyle of the Believer*) into which people are called by God"[18] *(my insertion)*.

Finally, *ethics* includes study of the responsibility that individuals have to act in terms of the spiritual interests of others and how that responsibility is treated in both ordinary and extraordinary circumstances.

16. Ibid., 121.

17. Ibid., 123.

18. Ibid., *Texture*, 127.

Aspects of the divine revealed in the text are thus the clues to begin to discern the multi-layered textures of the sacred in texts and its part in Spirit-filled productions that will be empowered by the divine to create a new Christian culture.

CONCLUSION

The socio-rhetorical criticism methodology applied to the text of Jonah provides a multifaceted postmodern approach to look at the particularity of the text, to discern its purpose, message, and uniquely rendered artistic form. In a new cultural and epistemological context it is necessary for the moving-image media to converge medium and message. Brueggemann writes that socio-rhetorical criticism provides a methodology for analyzing the various textures of a biblical text as layers of "dense text, dense people and dense God."[19] The proposition of this book for analyzing the polyvalence of the biblical text is illustrated by using the text of Jonah and applying socio-rhetorical criticism. The communication through the particularity and density of the text provides a purpose and form for human transformation that "does not happen through didacticism or through excessive certitude, but through the playful entertainment of another scripting of reality that may subvert the old given text and its interpretation and lead to the embrace of an alternative text and its redescription of reality."[20] It is to this aim that this book applies socio-rhetorical criticism as a method to discern a new model from the canonical text of Jonah that communicates through a new form "a practice of density."[21]

19. Brueggemann, *Cadences*, 76.

20. Ibid., 29.

21. Ibid., 74.

CHAPTER 4

Introduction to Interdisciplinary Models

(Refer to Appendices A, B, and C)

IN ORDER TO BE prophetic ministers in the technological age of the twenty-first century, we must regard the symbolic world of the media as both the tool and the obstacle to transforming a culture to believe. Walter Brueggemann has provided a paradigmatic theological worldview, in which believers are termed the prophets of an alternative consciousness that speaks out against the dominant culture of their time (see Chapter 2). No longer is prophetic ministry restricted to that of prophets called by God in the Old Testament, but all believers, through their lifestyle, proclaim an alternative to the world's standards, values, and dominant culture.

As the Christian moving-image media must become the voice that speaks God's newness into the culture of the day, so it fulfills in religious communication the role of the prophet, communicating a message of salvation, hope, and newness from the divine to the mundane, lost, secular world. However, the prophetic moving-image medium should not be confused with the words of a soothsayer or future teller, but, rather, should be considered as a collaborative voice that sends a message of the essence of a free God, who is able to bring newness to the culture to which the message is communicated.

The media occupies a large part of our everyday lives, and its influence extends into every area of communication with the audience on many different levels. The moving-image media is a dramatic reflection of, as well as a perpetrator of, the myths of the dominant culture.

For the Christian, this poses problems. What is going to determine what we think and do? Is it going to be the media, with all their powers of persuasion? Or is it going to be what God is teaching us through prayer, the Bible, and other Christians? As the world is understood through what the Bible teaches, a worldview that the audience can rationally order life by and live by will emerge. C. S. Lewis put it so profoundly when he said, "The difference between the Christian and the materialist is we hold different beliefs about the universe. They can't both be right. The one who is wrong will act in a way that simply doesn't fit the universe."[1] It is essential that producers of the moving-image media are educated and understand the weaknesses of these worldviews and why the biblical worldview is the answer, so that the truth can be presented. In the Garden of Eden, the creation covenant was established by God, telling humans to exercise dominion, till and cultivate the earth, and engage in the intellectual tasks of naming the animals. This dominion of creating as an intellectual task of humans prompts Christians, as well as Christian media, to creatively contend for the truth by portraying a Christian culture. The moving-image media must portray a lifestyle lived out of a Christian worldview, in juxtaposition to the dominant royal consciousness of secular naturalism, and in so doing glorify God in all areas of life.

A niche for film and programming and the role of the moving-image media in everyday life and popular culture will be identified. For the producer, it is necessary to understand both the dominant culture to which he or she is communicating, as well as to understand the theological perspective, if any, with which the receiver of the message is viewing the media. This solution is a complex and interdisciplinary process that will be presented and methodically analyzed in the three models that are constructed in this book. These models are presented graphically in Appendices A, B, and C to simplify the process of using media to effectively communicate a biblical worldview.

As the name Prophetic Imagination indicates, it is a prophetic theology that forms the purpose for communicating a biblical alternative consciousness as well as the strategy from which it can be developed. The first of the three models encompasses the approach that establishes the purpose and theology of a media narrative in terms of a Prophetic Imagination ministry. This forms the prophetic theological model for communication, and it is from this point that the book integrates communication techniques to format messages for Christian moving-image communication in models two and three. Model One brings to the

---

1. Quoted in Colson, *Chuck Colson*, 89.

Christian media a direction and purpose that is theologically based and relevant to the cultural context.

In the first model, Brueggemann's Prophetic Imagination terminology offers a perspective from which to formulate a biblical message to locate final cultural topics effectively (see chapter 8) and for use in telling faith-filled stories through the contemporary moving-image media. The first component of the model is *Bible*, a "counterscript"[2] or "providence,"[3] as Brueggemann terms it. Frederick Buechner describes it as the "comedy of the unforeseeable grace of God."[4] The second component is *Life,* a "countercontext"[5] understood by Brueggemann as "power."[6] Buechner calls it the dark side of truth, the tragedy of the human condition as life is lived in a world where God is visibly absent and good and bad alike go down in defeat.[7] A unique interplay of these two components determines the third, the portrayal of the *Lifestyle of a Believer,* a "counterlife"[8] or "personality."[9] Buechner describes this interaction as the formation of a fairy-tale, stating, "It might be more accurate to say that the world of the fairy tale found them and found them in the midst of their everyday lives in the everyday world."[10] This so-called fairy-tale lifestyle (or Pygmalion story) is based on a relationship with the Almighty through his Son, Jesus, and is extrapolated from the *Bible.* For a discussion of these components in the theology Model One, see below.

The task of the second model is to communicate these elements and the Prophetic Imagination purpose that undergirds them for the socio-political, religious, and technological milieu of our present audiences. Socio-rhetorical criticism is used as the methodology throughout the three models to reach the ideological texture in Model Three. Extrapolated from the theological analysis of the book of Jonah and integrated with communication techniques in the book of Jonah, a theology of communication purpose is translated into an informative, directive model for

2. Brueggemann, *Cadences,* 36.

3. Brueggemann, *Power.*

4. Buechner, *Telling the Truth,* 57.

5. Brueggemann, *Cadences,* 36.

6. Brueggemann, *Power.*

7. Buechner, *Telling the Truth,* 53.

8. Brueggemann, *Cadences,* 36.

9. Brueggemann, *Power.*

10. Buechner, *Telling the Truth,* 77.

an effective narrative communicative form that is discussed in Chapter 11 (see Appendix C). Brueggemann explains, "I believe there are crucial implications for exegesis, for theological education, and for ministry in seeing how these stories render reality as an artistic alternative."[11]

It is the possibilities that these stories present for making available an alternative reality using the three pivotal components in the models that, used for analysis, result in crucial implications for moving-image media in the dominant royal culture. These three models, once integrated, present a purpose and model for a format to allow for the transmission of biblical truths to educate the viewer through a medium of entertainment that can seize the audience's imagination. The golden thread in all three models is to understand the audience and its cultural postmodern worldview; an artistic rendering of an alternative realm of reality is then made available through the interpretation of biblical texts using the models based on a Prophetic Imagination worldview.

---

11. Brueggemann, *Power*, 20.

CHAPTER 5

Model One: Prophetic Theology

INTRODUCTION

CHRISTIAN TELEVISION AND FILM is a field that needs to be tackled with theological sensitivity in its development. In order to meet this objective, this book proposes a theological model (as the first of three interdisciplinary models), integrating theological and communicative perspectives to establish the purpose and format model for religious, i.e., biblically based, moving-image communication (see appendices A, B, and C). It is vital that audiences are presented with an interdenominational Christian message that is theologically based, relevant, topical, and of a competitive standard with secular programming. In Christian moving-image programming, it is thus theology that plays the most important role in determining how religion is communicated and received. It is necessary for Christian television and film producers to understand religion, the belief in the divine presence, and to communicate it effectively to a diverse audience via the modern moving-image media, using as starting point a theology that is appropriate to this task.

Both the ancient writers of the Bible and today's "makers of meaning" who use as their tools the moving-image media to communicate the message of the Bible, are the creators of the stories and images that form symbolic worlds in the minds of the audience. These symbolic worlds embody the values and beliefs of a people through their power to capture the imagination. The power that controls the culture's faith lies in the understanding of the function of the imagination to articulate and shape beliefs through visual forms. Czeslaw Milosz, a Christian and Nobel Prize winning poet, has said of the imagination that it "can fashion the world into a homeland as well as into a prison or a place of battle. Nobody lives in the objective world, only in a world filtered through the imagination."[1] From this follows the belief that religious imagination can be the shaping force of the world in which we really live. The rationalism of the Enlightenment, coupled with an education system that is imagination-deficient in the West, has spawned the naïve idea that the world is nothing but space and time without God or values. Christian ministries today need to address the imagination as the mental tool for connecting the visible to the invisible and in so doing encourage faith in God. The first model, Prophetic Theology, presents the theological paradigm of Prophetic Imagination from which a producer needs to approach the formulation and/or analysis of Christian programming and film.

THEOLOGY

Theology and religion are two very closely related concepts; however, in establishing the purpose and format proposed for Christian television and film, the distinction needs to be clearly defined. Gabler's persuasion was that religion's concern is fundamentally that which is divine and unchanging, whereas theology is concerned with that which is human and constantly changing.[2] The cultural context of people reveals and determines their understanding of God and thus determines their theology. An infinite God remains all-powerful and the same yesterday, today, and forever. Religion acknowledges this unchanging, divine being that must be worshipped. As finite human beings go through history and cultural contexts and understandings of the world change, so does our understanding, and thus our knowledge, of God in communication with his people. Theology thus reveals to us more of *who* it is that we know.

As Cox puts it so well, "Theology is that activity by which human beings relate their faith in God (theos) to the patterns of meaning that prevail in any historical period or culture (logos)."[3] A theological paradigm is therefore needed, from which producers of moving-image programming can draw to create with the Creator what he desires to communicate of himself to a particular audience in a particular culture. What

1. Quoted in Peterson, *Subversive*, 133.

2. Boers, *New Testament*, 30.

3. Cox, 1984:176.

Brueggemann calls "a discipline of readiness"[4] is called for as producers compose God's message in the making of meaning for our Western society. Each participant needs to serve together in a team, as a body of believers united by the Spirit to perform a function, as instruments with the powerful backing of God, to be a voice in modern society similar to the Old Testament prophets. In order for an alternative consciousness to be adopted by a society, biblical theology must be a fresh, imaginative work, taking full account of the church's new cultural situation. Independent, however, from a particular church dogma, the producers of Christian moving-image media programming must recognize that the rhetoric of the "mainline" churches is no longer part of the dominant public rhetoric of our society, but is instead at odds with and alien to it. Thus, the role of Christian producers is as interpreters of God's offer of newness to a diverse audience in a culturally foreign land. God's sovereignty needs to be feared, but intellectual assumptions must also be made in order to tailor the message for the audience. Theologically, Brueggemann's (1997) analogy and biblical interpretation of our positioning is as a culture in exile, and the call for readiness for a new imaginative response from preachers is what will be translated into a theological model for Christian communication. This will be further explored in chapters 8 and 9, where the model applied to the book of Jonah illustrates and illumines the elements of imagination necessary for a new rhetoric in preaching the message of God among exiles.

The transmission of data can be a simple task, but the communication of spiritual knowledge and the creation of shared religious understanding that together co-create a Christian cultural context amongst viewers is what needs to be achieved through biblical moving-image messages. The mythos of the electronic church frequently attempts to present this communication revolution as another Pentecost. (The media will transform the people through religious broadcasting). This is the transmission view of communication, which dominates much of American communication study. The roots of this type of cause-effect approach to communication by European and, later, American Protestants, for the purpose of evangelizing people and performing the work of missionary rhetoric, predate the development of formal communication scholarship of the early 1920s. This simplistic bullet theory tends toward marketing selectivity instead of

4. Brueggemann, *Cadences*, 119.

toward universal humanity. It emphasizes short-term impact over long-term understanding and common belief.

The media will only effectively reach and convert the world to Christ if questions of theological strategy in terms of Prophetic Imagination are applied in a manner similar to the biblical prophets of the Old Testament, who told stories immersed in symbolism aimed at capturing the universal human condition. The media and the stories they tell are influential tools in the shaping and molding of society and culture. Prophetic Imagination performs the function described by Schultze: "All media technologies require specific institutional arrangements that specify how the technologies will be used, by whom, and for what purpose."[5] The media can serve as prophetic voices not only to illuminate what is wrong with the cultural world portrayed in the moving-image media in terms of God's truth, but also to provide alternative narratives wrought through the imagination only, as Ellul states, "under the illumination of the Holy Spirit."[6] It is therefore the role of *theology* in the Theological Model to direct understanding, education, and revelation of God's truth, as the fundamental building block for the purpose and format of Christian television and film that will be constructed in this book.

MODEL ONE: PROPHETIC THEOLOGY

The Prophetic Theological Model (see Appendix A) guides the producer of moving-image media to deliver the Word of God through this medium for a time in the Christian cultural milieu and universal human condition that is typified by a very definite set of needs. The cultural setting of our time and where we can find biblical guides for preaching truth to the numbed consciousness of those who are being assimilated into the culture as fast as technology is relaying the message, are the focuses of this model. To communicate the Word of God as ultimate truth, providing the rationale in terms of which believers can order their lives in a hostile cultural environment, is what scholar Walter Brueggemann calls for as a new rhetoric: "Ways for the survival of an alternative imagination in an alternative community call(ing) for new strategies."[7]

---

5. Schultze 1986:258.

6. Ellul, *Presence*, 87.

7. Brueggemann, *Cadences*, 109.

The theological premise is that the Old Testament experience of and reflection upon exile is a helpful metaphor for understanding the current faith situation in the U.S. church, as well as a model for pondering new forms of ecclesiology. Having read Walter Brueggemann's work extensively and met with him at various intervals over the past fourteen years, I have developed the following work and vision for a theological model for Christian video, film, and TV ministry upon the metaphor he uses of a Christianity in exile. The metaphor as a theological strategy to understand and deal with the current faith situation among Christians is what Daniel L. Smith (1989) and Walter Brueggemann (1997) call the "exile" of a "deported people." The exiled Jews of the Old Testament were of course geographically displaced; however, the loss of a structured and reliable world, where treasured symbols of meaning are mocked and dismissed, is a pertinent point of contact between those ancient texts and our present situation.

This is the proposed problematic theological condition, and how we respond is the essence of a fresh imaginative look at old theological traditions and recasting them in a manner appropriate to the new faith situation. The prophetic theological model presents a paradigm within which producers can search and study God's word to engage audiences of our culture by ministering in a new way through the moving-image media that is appropriate for the condition of our culture. Brueggemann observes, "Israel's artistic rendering, which takes seriously power, providence and personality, is narrative that does not claim to be a descriptive report on social reality, that does not claim to be eyewitness to personalities in dialogue, and that does not claim to speak directly about God. Israel's settlement on narrative as its preferred mode of discourse is a remarkable decision about the revelation and about the texture of social reality."[8]

As already discussed in Chapter 2, in the Exodus narrative Moses is portrayed as a paradigmatic prophet who leads the people of Israel out of their enslaved, exiled situation to freedom by the hope he offers in a living God and a promised land. Deutero-Isaiah (Isaiah 40–55) reflects a similar scenario: the situation of Israel in exile.[9] The exilic period was a time of crisis and hopelessness, as the symbols of Israel's faith and identity, their land, and the temple in Jerusalem, are destroyed. It is through the

8. Brueggemann, *Power*, 18.
9. Prinsloo, *Tweegesprek*, 98.

prophets' announcement of faith, hope, and salvation that God focuses his people on a new, more intimate knowledge of himself. Vriezen, for example, shows that in Isaiah 46 this eschatological hope is nothing less than a newness comparable to the deliverance out of Egypt.[10] This has important implications with regard to the establishing of faith, both in Deutero-Isaiah and for ministries today. Westermann emphasizes that when the prophet in Deutero-Isaiah "summons his audience to put their faith in the message of salvation he does not mean a 'strong faith' which they now needed to bring into play as something achieved by themselves. Rather, the call to have faith means bringing the nation's experience with God in history to bear upon the present."[11] It is the mental tool of the imagination—which functions to bridge the gap between the past and what God can do in the present, the visible and the invisible, heaven and earth—that needs to be employed as the Christian "exile's" faith is challenged.

The situation in Western culture today, where the faith claims of believers are at odds with the dominant consciousness and values, is a battle of two great world views. Cultural commentator Chuck Colson describes the conflict thus: "The dominant mindset in America and much of the West today is *secular* in that it is of "this age" as opposed to being eternal, which is the Christian perspective. It is *naturalistic*, meaning that it claims that there is a naturalistic explanation for everything."[12] Thus, secular naturalism is the antithesis of a biblical worldview that says God is sovereign and holy and that he is the author of all truth, since secular naturalism espouses the moral relativism and pragmatism of this age.

The interface of the circumstance of exile and the scriptural resources that grew from and address the faith crisis in new imaginative form is where television and film ministry needs to turn. "For faith does not come through the weight of power, but through the hope of glory," as Colson writes.[13] Practically, the Prophetic Theology Model, provides for the user the first step towards bridging the content of ancient literature of the Bible into effective Christian messages for the twenty-first century.

10. Vriezen, *Hoofdlijnen*, 487.

11. Westermann, *Isaiah*, 184–85.

12. Colson, *Chuck Colson*, 88.

13. Ibid., 7.

LIFE AS A COMPONENT OF PROPHETIC THEOLOGY

Prophetic literature incorporates stories of chosen persons of God who struggle against all odds in faith to deliver a people in despair to hope in a God of love and freedom. The reality of oppression and the power of God to save were realized by Moses in leading the people out of Egypt, as well as by the covenant relationship of Israel's God that was fulfilled by the life, death, and resurrection of Jesus, bringing salvation to a lost world.

The *Life* component in the Prophetic Theological Model (see Appendix A) is defined as a sense of belonging to a culture, of being in an environment and adhering to the values of the community and its vocation. This component in the Prophetic Theology Model becomes important as it points the focus to integrate the service of ascetical theology to the message in a prophetic context. Theologian Eugene Peterson describes the poignant result of an interface of culture and theology as "Ascetical theology: How does the human condition shape our understanding and response to God?"[14] This theological dimension must be at the heart of any Christian message for it to be received effectively. Sooner or later the producers of Christian messages, as preachers, realize as the prophet Jeremiah did that it is not enough to communicate the message truly and well but that all the faculties of human receptivity and response must be engaged. The function of hearing, as in Old Testament oral/aural culture, is again being emphasized, with electronic media dominating the communications scene today. Peterson describes the implications of this development: "That means that contemporary humanity is closer in terms of communications experience to the first century than to the nineteenth. And that is good news for the Christian communicator who is now able to share a milieu with biblical humanity which is important in discovering and interpreting the biblical message."[15] The source material of most preachers as producers of biblical messages is the Bible, and as oral text this has been sufficient to understand the processes of composition and transmission.

However, Marshall McLuhan, an interpreter of the communication media, has been known in communication studies for showing the overwhelming effect that the communication medium has on interpretation. His main insight that the "medium is the message" conveys to scholars of

14. Peterson, *Subversive*, 80.

15. Ibid., 91.

contemporary electronic oral/aural culture and to the creators of meaning in the contemporary milieu that the form of a message has a greater effect on the person and the culture than the content. The biblical communities of oral culture were established in pre-literate and non-literate societies. The present day cultural setting, also an oral/aural culture, has much in common with such societies and can learn from the format of biblical texts the techniques used to impact the dominant consciousness with a radically alternative consciousness.

Oral mediums of communication similar to that of biblical texts and the moving-image medium tend to create holistic cultures. This type of society reflects an intensely participatory consciousness, with all the senses heightened and matured by constant use. In an oral culture, individualism is a rarity; people are governed by community and experience events as wholes.

The power of this *Life* component is termed "royal consciousness" in this book (see Chapter 2 and Appendix A), described by Brueggemann in its contemporary form as a "flow of social forces which include the raw power of technology and the relentless, shameless pressure of ideology"[16] established by the ruling authority. In narratives throughout the Bible the forces of this royal consciousness dominate and attempt to make subjects of those they influence, as they still do through the contemporary oral mediums of the moving-image media today.

It is important, as narratives are constructed for communicating an alternative consciousness in this time and space, that the biblical texts are consulted using Robbins' socio-rhetorical criticism as a methodology to distinguish the dominant royal consciousness that the texts are speaking out against. All the while, the Prophetic Imagination purpose of bringing hearers to fresh insight and hope and holiness in their position in the culture must be considered in format and message. Doing so will provide clear points of reference for translating the message of an alternative consciousness in terms of current dominant cultural struggles. It is the books of the exilic and post-exilic period, particularly the narrative texts, that are critically relevant. The textures of these texts are recognized and interpreted using the socio-rhetorical approach of Robbins (1996) and the other two paradigmatic models that will be discussed to show models for presenting hope and faith.

16. Brueggemann, *Power*, 13.

Brueggemann insightfully uses the Prophetic Imagination paradigm to bring the theological stages of the biblical account of ancient Israel's journey to and in exile to bear upon the faith journey of modern Western culture. Brueggemann (1997) compares the journey of Christianity in the West to the faith journey of the biblical narrative. Beginning with Genesis and Exodus, the people of God are without home or land, moving in trust to a new place to escape oppression and acquire new land. Next, the biblical story shows God keeping his promise—the land is reached and acquired. Acquisition of the land decisively transforms Israel. They organize great cities and armies and forget the source of these gifts: "Greed overcame gratitude, selfishness displaced compassion. Covenant was reduced to control and exploitation. . . . In the end mismanaged power would hurt and destroy. . . . Mismanaged security would evaporate and mismanaged promises would fail."[17] The third stage of the journey is land loss, displacement, exile, and life became exiled in an alien environment.

These three stages can be traced in the American journey of faith by the following: The white European story evolved into the American story of moving to a new land to find religious freedom and escape from an oppressive situation. The second stage is marked by an incredible account of prosperity. Brueggemann writes, "In the long run, however, impatience outran compassion and insensitivity overrode inclusiveness. Our public institutions are mainly shaped to serve the center and neglect the margin."[18] The institutions fueling prosperity and security found ways of discounting the religious roots and realities of the founding fathers and gave theological legitimacy to that which contradicts our faith, in the attempt to expand the economy.

Along with Brueggemann (1997), this book proposes that the inhabitants of the Western world live the *Life* component in metaphoric stage three, where exile has taken the form of brutality and cynicism, and despair shows up as various kinds of abuse. An absence of God is evident in the secularization of society, and *secular naturalism* (as described above) has become the dominant worldview. The dominant royal consciousness manages seemingly well without God, and there are scarcely prophetic voices that will daringly and imaginatively speak the truth and hope in an increasingly unwelcome and indifferent environment. The *Life* in exile

17. Brueggemann, *Cadences*, 111.
18. Ibid., 113.

that Christian audiences are experiencing today is a liturgical, cultural, spiritual condition of despair, in which one may be in exile while being geographically at home.

BIBLE AS A COMPONENT OF PROPHETIC THEOLOGY

The *Bible* component can be understood as referring to the holiness of God, having reached down to humankind, to be aspired to by humans. Brueggemann says this is presented through the biblical stories as a "set of models of reality made up of images situated and contextualized by narratives." He adds:

> These narrative renderings of reality in the Bible are not factual re-portage, but are inevitably artistic constructs that stand a distance from any 'fact' and are filtered through interests of a political kind. . . . The Bible in its several models is an artistic, rhetorical proposal of reality that seeks to persuade (convert) to an alternative sense of God, world, neighbor and self.[19]

"Holy" is a term used in almost every culture, yet it seems that no adequate definitions exist to describe this word. In Western culture the quest for the holy grail, the cup from which Jesus drank and which represents his promise and command to drink the holy life he gives through his death and resurrection, has been a recurring story. These quest stories have become secularized, but the search for something other than and more than money and power keeps reappearing in contemporary narratives. Peterson accounts for this, saying, "We're after a God-originated and God-shaped life: a Holy life."[20]

"The Holy Scriptures" are the authoritative source for the holy, and in the center of Holy Scripture, Isaiah worships and glorifies God in the temple. However, to understand the context of this worship, it is necessary to look at the biblical narratives, beginning with Moses' encounters with God and ending with John's revelation. The common denominator of these men is that while both were in exile—Moses in Midian and John on the prison island of Patmos—God revealed Himself in his holiness. Moses was out of his comfort zone, without books, temples or servants, having been reared in luxury in Pharaoh's palace. Precisely here (Exod 3:1–12), God chose to call Moses from a burning bush and gave him a

19. Ibid., 30.
20. Peterson, *Subversive*, 67.

job to do. Like Moses, John was in prison in an austere environment in exile when God revealed to him the holy vision of Jesus that we know as Revelation, whose words the Holy Spirit would use to encourage faithfulness from holy people in unholy times. Moses in Midian and John on Patmos frame the backdrop for Isaiah's representation of the holy in Isaiah 6. "Holy, Holy, Holy is the Lord of Hosts, the whole earth is full of his glory." It was as King Uzziah died that Isaiah worshipped in these austere conditions for Judaic society and culture and was given a holy vision–a seeing of the invisible.

In reading Israel's historical reality, a new orientation is wrought by aspects of worship through poetry and from the memory of God's intervention in the past. These liturgical forms consist of three metaphors, as illustrated in Second Isaiah (Isa 40–55).

The passage in Isaiah 40:1–11 is frequently reckoned as a *call narrative*[21] and is the supreme example of liberated poetic imagination in the Old Testament. A new circumstance is brought to speech as Israel is invited to sing a "new song" (doxology) to replace the anthem of the empire (42:10). The prophet/poet has been commissioned to speak in the face of pretenders about the real power of Yahweh as the real king, i.e. an alternative vision of social reality (compare 1 Kings 22:19–23). Brevard S. Childs describes the importance of this commission: "Although the Old Testament is unconcerned with the historical origins of prophetism, it is deeply interested in the origins of the prophet's own history with God. For this reason the Prophetic call or commission plays a significant role."[22] In Prophetic Imagination terms, the prophet in Deutero-Isaiah calls the community (*Life* or popular culture) of the royal consciousness of Israel to a new orientation, an alternative consciousness, based on a more intimate relationship with God.

The following three metaphoric concepts in Isaiah 40–55, collectively termed *poetic imagination,* encapsulate the prophet's role in establishing an alternative consciousness and can guide the producer and filmmaker.

Babylon refers to a concentration of power and value that is dominant and finally hostile to the covenant faith of the community with an alternative consciousness. The empire regularly seeks to domesticate such a community with a special vocation, which characteristically ends

21. Brueggemann, *Prophetic,* 106.
22. Childs, 1985:122.

in oppression. For example, Isaiah was living in Judah at the time King Uzziah became full of pride and anger and took over the temple for his own purposes, ultimately desecrating it. Having turned leprous, the king lived the rest of his life isolated both from the community of holy people and the holy temple. As such, Judaic culture and society at the time Isaiah received the holy vision from God was oppressed and defiled by the evil king, whose leprosy—a disease that had come to symbolize sin to the Hebrew people—finally gave public visibility to their inward profanity. It was under the shadow of the leprous king that Judah was as barren as Midian, as austere as Patmos.

Exile is practiced among those who do not accept assimilation into the royal consciousness. Overwhelmed by the holy, Isaiah recognized the circumstance of oppression and exile in the leprously defiled temple in Judah. Peterson describes Isaiah's alternative perspective: "Isaiah was there worshipping because he knew that the temple was not defined by Uzziah; the times were not defined by Uzziah; the culture did not take its impress from Uzziah."[23] The poetry of Isaiah is a summons away from such assimilation.

The third element of the prophet's role is *homecoming,* described by Brueggemann as "a dramatic decision to break with imperial rationality and to embrace a place called home where covenantal values have currency and credibility."[24] It is through worship that the spiritually exiled are given the most accessible means for orienting themselves in the invisibilities, in God where their home truly resides. Homecoming is realized as communicators become aware that if worship is absent or marginal to their agenda the communication becomes dominated by the visible. Most of reality is invisible—inaccessible to the five senses and the thoughts, dreams, hopes, purpose, character, and beliefs of a person. The essence of physical existence, such as molecules and atoms, the air we breathe, angels that protect us, ancestors who precede us, and God, are beyond our unassisted senses. To be rooted in the invisible is to incorporate worship as the centrality of any communication, directing the community to a homecoming.

Exile, Babylon, and *homecoming* comprise not only the poetry of Second Isaiah, but also a relational covenantal reality of God with his

---

23. Peterson, *Subversive,* 72.

24. Brueggemann, *Prophetic,* 107.

people that is not bound by geographical or spatial possibilities. The discipline of readiness for an alternative consciousness involves a language of hope—worship that is brought to reality in doxology or poetic format—as in Isaiah 40–55. The practice of such Poetic Imagination is the most subversive, redemptive act that a leader of a faith community can undertake in the midst of exiles. The work of Poetic Imagination holds the potential for unleashing a community of power and action that will not be contained by imperial restrictions or definitions of reality.

For example, *exile* in the geographic sense means "deported," "displaced," or "transplanted," but the term is also a theological metaphor. In Appendix A, exile articulates that the present reality is not home and never can be. After two generations, the Babylonian Jews needed to be "converted" into exiles to persuade these displaced people that Babylon was still not their home. The theological attractiveness of a home in Jerusalem had to be stated against the social, economic, and political benefits of Babylon, which felt more concretely like home. Babylon (the royal consciousness) desired to establish itself as absolute and wanted its present arrangement to appear eternal—"as it was in the past so it will be in the future"—so that after awhile one could not remember what circumstances were different, which would foster the belief that there was no real alternative available. The alternative consciousness was a threat to the empire because it asserted not only that circumstances used to be different, but that they could be different in the future.[25]

The poem of Second Isaiah proceeds as an act of passion, obedience, hope, and subversion. The alternative referred to is rooted in memory, a quite specific one of the narrative memory of Israel, which is articulated in this text in concise credo, liberated song and poetry, liturgical recital, and the more expansive reflective literature of the Torah. The Israelite Torah tradition is a threat to the claims of Babylon (the royal consciousness), because in these narrative enactments another history is made available, a history governed in different ways by the very different God, Yahweh, who has no imperial ambition or pretension. Memory of biblical narratives, e.g. accounts of Abraham and Sarah, Noah, and David, provides a critical basis for imagination that has not been co-opted by a numbed royal consciousness. To apply this to the *Lifestyle of the Believer* is, for example, to reflect on the message of barren Sarah to remind us that the

---

25. Brueggemann, *Prophetic.*

future is not limited to imperial definitions of reality and possibility, because there is at work another One who strangely does impossible things on our behalf. Similarly, the memory of the Noah tradition affirms that an experience of chaos (flood), real as it is, is not the ultimate word because there is One who presides over the chaos.

LIFESTYLE OF THE BELIEVER AS A COMPONENT OF PROPHETIC THEOLOGY

In the canonical Israelite narratives, the Prophetic Theology Model consists of a third component, the *Lifestyle of the Believer*. This is theologically motivated by what Brueggemann terms "personality,"[26] recognizable in, for example, the Samuel narratives. The personalities of Samuel, Saul, and David are presented in their brilliance, courage, foolishness, shamelessness, and infidelity. The characters take on a variety of roles in the narratives, functioning as literary constructs of personalities that are models for the reader. The role of the Prophetic Theology Model is to discern those characters, the *eirons,* that display the alternative consciousness and trust in God's providence. These characters become the medium for displaying the message. Throughout Scripture, it is the lives of people—from Moses to Jesus—that became the message of hope that contained and communicated the transcendent reality.

Good writes of *irony* as the conflict between the characters of the *alazon,* the imposter, and the *eiron,* the ironical man. "The alazon is the pompous fool, the pretender who affects more than he actually is. The eiron, his antagonist, is the sly shrewd dissimulator, who poses as less than he is. The conflict ends, of course, in the pricking of the alazon's bubble, the triumph of the eiron."[27]

In the context of the narrative, the character of the *alazon* identifies the dominant consciousness, and the *eiron* is present in the roles of the character who demonstrates the alternative consciousness as the hope for the *Lifestyle of the Believer*. In a literary genre, these personalities portray the hope of a homecoming to the reader in exile. In the book of Jonah, Jonah exemplifies the *alazon*. The sailors and Ninevites who repent and are accepted by God are acting as the human *eirons* to Jonah, illuminating the qualities of the character of God for the reader or listener. However, the

---

26. Brueggemann, *Power*, 16.
27. Good, *Irony*, 14.

character of God, who is the ultimate *eiron* to all mankind and necessarily present in all Christian narratives, becomes the epitome of one who is presented as less than he is in the narrative. He surprises all characters, as well as the audience, and specifically highlights (and in so doing criticizes) the dominant consciousness, which the *alazon* represents. The rationale for the *Lifestyle of the Believer* is not communicated on a linear level but in an entertaining and enlightening manner as it relates to the struggles of a cultural setting that is numbed by enculturation. Newness has sprung into being, and the transcendent reality made available through the interaction of characters has created a theological portrait of hope relevant to the audience.

Brueggemann writes, "The most remarkable observation one can make about this interface of *exilic circumstance* and *scriptural resources* is this: Exile did not lead Jews in the Old Testament to abandon faith or to settle for abdicating despair, nor to retreat to privatistic religion. On the contrary, exile evoked the most brilliant literature and most daring theological articulation in the Old Testament."[28]

Through the personalities of the biblical heroes, the component of "providence" is evident in the narratives. The narrator does not directly describe God's intervention but makes available certain memories, facts, and traditions that he discloses to the readers via artistic rendering. Ritualistic narratives filled with ironic hope provide meaning and a means to cope in an alien environment. Narrative specificity is the means by which biblical theology and Israelite thinking are retold. The narrator does not make broad generalized claims but presents the theological case one episode at a time. In the David narrative, the narrator does not claim that God is with David but uses narrative specificity to demonstrate that in the midst of unfavorable circumstances, David is strangely kept safe and even gains success and power. The reader is permitted to watch the providence of God operate through the *Lifestyle of the Believer* in the narratives. The variables of providence, personality, and power are indeed inextricably linked in the narratives.

As Christian standards and the Christian lifestyle are threatened in the Babylon of the technological age of the twenty-first century, the sureness about God recorded for us in the narrative constructs of the people and personalities in Scripture should be a challenge and an inspiration.

---

28. Brueggemann, *Cadences*, 3.

Christian producers of the moving-image media, as the prophetic voice of faith to a people in exile, will need to communicate, via new visionary media and with a buoyant theological imagination, the testimonies of lives of believers so that the good news of hope will be received and an alternative consciousness adopted.

A CONTINUUM FOR THE *LIFESTYLE OF THE BELIEVER* COMPONENT

The two positions on the Prophetic Imagination Theological continuum (see Appendix A) are *Bible* and *Life* experiences. While a Christian fundamentalist reading takes biblical narratives and transposes them directly onto experiences in life, the skeptical philosopher takes life experiences to interpret or justify biblical narratives. However, metaphorically, as described from a Prophetic Imagination perspective, biblical narratives as models of an alternative consciousness may be integrated in terms of non-geographic aspects to reflect the alternative of living by faith in the contemporary world. Good writes, "Faith to which the Old Testament bears witness is not a body of doctrines or a set of ideas, but a kind and context of life. The context of the life of faith is the covenant, the bond in history between God and Israel. Israel's faith relates her to a God who comes to be known in his acts."[29] The covenant faith as a relationship with God, not merely an idea about God, is indicative of life for Israel and leads to the imperative context of an actual *Lifestyle of the Believer* in the Old Testament. Similarly, for contemporary biblical life, narratives without an absolute truth as the indicative in the narrative imperative have no ground except arbitrary law. Without the imperative, however, the relationship of the Christian with God becomes a context but not a life lived in terms of the divine claim of specific obedience. In a discussion of film theory and cultural communication theory in the following chapter, both these aspects—life experiences and aspects of transcendence—are incorporated. Based on the Prophetic Theological Model, a broader purpose for Christian moving-image media leads to some guidelines to tailoring a genre for Christian film and television with the imperative message of living a *Lifestyle of the Believer*.

29. Good 1950:241.

CONCLUSION

The Prophetic Imagination paradigm (see Chapter 2) suggests purpose or authorial *intent* as the driving force behind the *form* and *style* of *content*. In the current chapter the impact of a Christian message to an audience in a metaphoric exile has been discussed in terms of prophetic theological elements. This process of creating or analyzing a message to be communicated from a theological perspective for the moving-image media is practically presented in the Prophetic Theology Model One, which integrates the Prophetic Imagination paradigm (see Appendix A). Reflecting on biblical texts, particularly of the exilic and post-exilic period, Model One outlines how the theological aspects form the core of any biblically based message. This is then arranged in terms of the three components, namely *Bible, Life,* and the *Lifestyle of the Believer,* that link the three models (see appendices A, B, and C). Particular emphasis is placed on the *Lifestyle of the Believer* component, which is described in terms of a continuum. This continuum is important to ensure that, as the prophetic theology is applied and worked in and through the message, balance is discerned and neither a fundamentalist reading nor skepticism results from the portrayal of the transcendental elements in the message. Instead, it is required of the prophetic minister through moving-image media to tell stories with consummate artistry, based on sound biblical theology, that will invite audiences to experience God's power as a reality to be reckoned with, communicating an alternative *Lifestyle of the Believer.*

CHAPTER 6

A Case Study in Prophetic Theology

The Book of Jonah

INTRODUCTION

B Y APPLYING THE FIRST model and the principles of socio-rhetorical criticism, educating the audience regarding the biblical message is understood. This formulates the Education variable of Model Three. The authorial *intent* and purpose of the canonical book of Jonah, the first missionary to a foreign culture, leads to the development of a biblically based purpose in the production of moving picture narratives.

It is purpose that drives a message into a format that will communicate with impact and persuasion to achieve a specific set of objectives. Model One (Appendix A) develops steps toward a theological imagination to compose a message in a format for moving-image biblical communication. The first question is to establish how God will be immanent in the message. It is therefore imperative to analyze the message from the approach of educating the viewer in some capacity about God. The purpose of the message is to deepen the viewer's understanding of God's attributes and how that influences the relationship that they have with and to God, as well as the impact of such on their consciousness within the dominant reality of their contextual culture.

When applied to Jonah, the inner texture and intertexture principles set out by Robbins in his socio-rhetorical interpretation of biblical texts, *Exploring the Texture of Texts,* provide a starting point for analyzing how the author achieves this Prophetic Imagination purpose. The analysis will direct our attention to the three components of the first model (see Appendix A) that can serve to construct imaginative, didactic narratives

63

for communicating God and a Prophetic Imagination purpose to our culture via the moving-image narratives of our time. This act of biblical imagination for contemporary storytelling will be termed *imagineering*, henceforth. As the textures of Jonah are analyzed, we will highlight those elements that are foundational for renewing the culture with biblical truth, as a cultural approach to communication that will be examined in Chapter 7. These elements can translate as the theologically critical thread connecting the other two models (see appendices B and C) to achieve the defined purpose of a Prophetic Imagination.

INNER TEXTURE OF THE BOOK OF JONAH

Robbins's definition of inner texture determines the "relationships among word-phrase and narrational patterns that produce argumentative and aesthetic patterns in texts."[1] The intermingling of the five patterns, namely, (1) repetitive-progressive, (2) opening-middle-closing, (3) narrational, (4) argumentative, and (5) aesthetic, provides the context for what Robbins terms the "network of significance" in the biblical text. These inner elements of a text itself are important for understanding the narrative character and, consequently, the purpose of the discourse.

Thus, this book considers defining the purpose and genre of the prose narrative of the book of Jonah, which is a much debated and disputed topic among scholars and a difficult one to determine conclusively. Jonah has been designated as a midrash, prophet's biography, legend, parable, and satire, among many other forms. This book will first show that the purpose of Jonah is that of a Prophetic Imagination, concluding that this purpose drives the prose and poetry of the narrative into a unique format, in agreement with Old Testament Scholar Hans Walter Wolff's analysis of the genre of the book Jonah:

> The problems are due mainly to the protean character of the material and traditions that go to make up the book. Here we find learned theology side by side with original experiences, sacred texts beside dramatic stories, contemporary material flanked by the fabric of tradition. The narrator takes the risk of linking thrilling episodes from tales of the sea, such as are current coin in seaports with an acknowledgment of faith in Yahweh as the creator of sea and land (1:9). He takes the name of a historical prophet and tells things about his behavior, with which we are familiar in the stories

1. Robbins, *Tapestry*, 46.

about Elijah or Jeremiah—or which are deliberately contrasted with these. He introduces great liturgical texts (4:2) and theological precepts (3:8–10), only to interpret them the next moment in a completely new way through some fantastic happening.[2]

In the true sense, then, of postmodernism, this book must not be regarded as characterizing only one aspect of literary technique but as a combination of several stylized artistic formats of biblical and extra-biblical storytelling, resulting in a highly potent genre for unleashing the imagination in a new sense, prophetically.

REPETITIVE-PROGRESSIVE TEXTURE: *ON A MACRO LEVEL*

In 1:1–2 God instructs Jonah, who reacts to such counsel in a negative manner. In 3:1–2 the same instruction is repeated, but this time Jonah reacts positively. This is an example of not only repetition but also progression in the text.

1. In Chapter 1 Jonah is reluctant and passive, whereas in Chapter 3 he is aggressive and active.

2. In Chapter 1 Jonah is very passive, going downwards to flee from his assignment: from Jerusalem (probably) to Joppa, then onto the boat and into the chaos of the sea, then down into the boat, then fast asleep, then *passively* thrown into the sea. In Chapter 2 this descending trend continues until Jonah finds himself at the foundations of the mountains under the sea. In the belly of the fish, he then becomes *actively* involved in prayer. In Chapter 3, Jonah again does not show great enthusiasm for God's instruction, as he walks only partially through the city to which God has called him. Jonah's sermon is very abrupt and negative, without any references to God's mercy (the narrator does not give us the contents of God's message to Jonah). In Chapter 4, Jonah sits passively waiting for God's wrath to destroy the Ninevites. And then Jonah really unleashes his fury against God in Chapter 4. Where in Chapter 1 Jonah was a meek and mild person without aggression, in Chapter 4 he shows himself to be quite an aggressive person, reluctant to share his God with pagans. Exactly the opposite can be said of God. In Chapter 1, he is the God of wrath, while in chapters 3 and 4 he is the God of mercy.

2. Wolff, *Obadiah*, 75.

3. The book of Jonah is also full of *tension* related to repetition and progression, as discussed below.

Having been in the belly of a fish, and having done much wrong himself,
Jonah is situated to warn people who serve other gods (2:8). In 2:9, he contrasts himself with such people as the good guy, a clear example of *irony*.

It is important to note that form and message were inextricably
linked for the biblical writers. They understood that the medium is the
message. Often in analysis of the structure of biblical texts, the shape of
what is said will be seen to highlight the themes and ideas that the text
wants to convey. In the structure and repetition that is evident (see below) in the book of Jonah, structure seems to emerge as important to
the author of Jonah. As Allen pertinently notes, "The book of Jonah is a
model of literary artistry, marked by symmetry and balance."[3] The strik-
ing repetition of the first three verses of Chapter 1, which are replicated
almost identically in 3:1–3 and serve as an introduction to the second half
of the book, must be examined. God essentially gives Jonah the identical
call to go and prophesy to Nineveh a second time, and it is in this call
and response of Jonah, as a man of faith, to God, that the key themes of
the book are introduced. The main theme, which the book explores, is
the relationship between God and mankind. The two chapters subsequent
to chapters 1 and 3 are also developed in a similar manner structurally,
with regard to the sequence of events, as Old Testament Scholar Terence
Fretheim identifies: After the response of Jonah, comes the "response
from the group as a whole, the leader (captain, king) emerges, and efforts
are made to avert disaster. Both chapters end in deliverance."[4]

The following repetitive structure taken from Fretheim accentuates
the development of the thought of the author:

A) 1:1–3   Introduction   a
B) 1:4–16   Focus on the sailors   b
C) 1:17–2:10   Focus on Jonah   c
D) 3:1–3a   Recapitulation of the introduction   a
E) 3:3b–10   Focus on Nineveh   b
F) 4:1–11   Focus on Jonah   c[5]

3. Allen, *Joel*, 197.

4. Fretheim, *Message*, 105.

5. Ibid., 55.

Other than the two introductory sections of A and D, the remaining four parts are self-contained units that do not repeat or reflect on each other. Sections B and C also do not anticipate segments E and F, but in the repetition of a pattern indicated above as abcabc, the author reinforces the main theme of the book: God's deliverance and merciful acceptance into a relationship with him of all those who by faith sincerely come to repentance. It also explores the relationship of the faith of a man of God, a believer, an Israelite, and prophet, to issues of theological conflict, self-centeredness, and complacency, to which he has become assimilated as part of the dominant consciousness of his culture. Jonah is therefore both the subject and object of the message, as he forms part of the audience to whom the book is addressed and whom it critiques. Thus, the didactic aspect supported by structural parallel elements is God's deliverance, in which he sovereignly chooses to act mercifully for a just outcome as the Creator God who is in control of our circumstances beyond our finite ability to comprehend.

In the text of the book of Jonah, exegesis of the inner texture points the implied reader immediately to the interactions between the characters through repetition. Contrary to Douglas Stuart's view that the repetition of vocabulary in Jonah originates in the "desire for simplicity,"[6] Johan Coetzee stresses that this repetition demonstrates the importance of stylistic techniques for the narrator.[7] Using the fear motif in Jonah Chapter 1 as example, Coetzee shows the narrator's aim of contrasting Jonah's conduct to that of the sailors.[8] The narrator employs, through repetition and progression, contrast as a stylistic convention to create tension and surprise, ensuring a vibrant interactive relationship between the implied author and implied reader of the text. This technique also establishes the basis for *irony*, as will be discussed.

REPETITION OF GOD'S NAME

The name of Yahweh is repeatedly and progressively used in the book of Jonah in four different variations, namely *Yahweh*; *Elohim*; *Ha-Elohim*; and *Yahweh, the God of Heaven*. These variations emphasize the developing relationship and knowledge of God exemplified by the book's

6. Stuart, *Hosea-Jonah*, 457, quoted in Coetzee, "Fear Motif," 1.

7. Coetzee, "Fear Motif," 2.

8. Coetzee, "Fear Motif," 6.

different characters. The name *Yahweh*, God's covenant name, is used primarily when God is interacting with his prophet Jonah. The sailors and Ninevites pray and believe in God, namely, *Elohim*. The captain and king of Nineveh seek the mercy of *Ha-Elohim* to save them. However, Jonah professes his faith in *Yahweh, the God of Heaven,* whom he serves. This results in the sailors' praying to Jonah's God, finally calling him *Yahweh*. Throughout the text of the first three chapters, the name Yahweh points repeatedly to the developing relationship that the characters have with the covenant God of Israel. The name changes from *Elohim* or *Ha Elohim* to *Yahweh*, highlighting the progression and change of the characters' knowledge and consequent relationship to God as he is experienced in the narrative. Wolff describes this progression:

> The result is that they come to "fear Yahweh." In Chapter 3 neither the gods of Nineveh nor Jonah's God are specifically named. Here "belief in God" comes into being as the people turn from their wickedness and put their hope in the one who sent Jonah. An already existing train of theological ideas, not mentioned in Chapter 1, shapes the description of the path to salvation.[9]

J. Magonet describes a pattern of use of the four names of God in Chapter 4. *Yahweh* is used when the focus is on the mercifulness of God, while *Elohim* and *Ha-Elohim* are used when God instructs Jonah about his grace in a disciplinary context. These name repetitions and progressions have been used by scholars such as Magonet (1983) and Wolff (1986) to draw conclusions regarding source material and literary growth of the book of Jonah. Such conclusions have proved laborious and are peripheral to this book.

It is important to note that in defining the author's main themes, structure enhances and subtly reinforces the message of Jonah. In varied forms, God's attributes construct a round and central character in the plot. In all Prophetic Imagination messages, God's attributes as a power to be reckoned with and known in the *Lifestyle of the Believer* must be the essence of the communication. The manner in which God is immanent in the message can be overt, directly naming him in the plot of the narrative, or subversive, letting the structure and pattern illuminate characteristics and actions that will highlight faith and God's presence in all of creation. In the book of Jonah God's presence is evident in the

9. Wolff, *Obadiah*, 79.

explicit characterization of him but also in the implicit structure of the text, revealing the laws of God's nature in relation to humans through patterned structure of action and repetition of word phrases and the use of different names for God.

NARRATIONAL AND OPENING-MIDDLE-CLOSING TEXTURES

In the text of Jonah it is Yahweh who has the first (1:1f.) and the last (4:10f.) word. It is the opening words in the text that, as Robbins points out, "automatically presuppose (that) a narrator is speaking the words."[10] Thus, Yahweh speaks in this text with the same voice and position as the narrator. The narrator of Jonah takes on an omniscient posture, knowing the happenings on board the ship and in downtown Nineveh and hearing the words spoken between God and Jonah, including those uttered under water. The narrator's understanding also extends to knowledge of all the characters' feelings, as well as of God's thoughts regarding Nineveh's repentance. The narrator of Jonah is, according to Sternberg, well within the known scriptural narrative convention. It is thus interesting to notice how the author uses even this accepted convention of omniscience in biblical texts to surprise the audience when trying to bring home his criticism of contemporaneous doctrines or institutions.

The following unexpected thought of Jonah is omitted from the opening of the text: "Please Lord, this certainly was my opinion (or my word), while yet in my homeland; accordingly I planned to flee toward Tarshish because I realized then that you are a gracious and compassionate God, very patient and abundantly benevolent, who would also relent from bringing disaster" (4:2). Then it is sprung into the text near the end of the story. This indicates not only a justification of Jonah's actions, but also ". . . conveys sentiments of major importance to Israel's theology."[11] The narrator conceals the thought from a conventionally all-knowing God in the scriptures and, in so doing, leaves something that should have made up part of the opening after 1:2 until the closing 4:2. In so doing, interference is introduced into the flow of the whole narrative. If the piece were to be put in its chronological position, with Jonah foretelling that God would relent, this would make Jonah communicate condescendingly,

---

10. Robbins, *Texture*, 15.

11. Sasson, *Jonah*, 329.

placing authorial omniscience above God's freedom to dispense mercy to whom he pleases, as the all-powerful, Creator God.

In Chapter 5, a critical element of God's presence is demonstrated through inner texture elements. God is not spoken about but becomes an integral figure via the texture, pacing and progressing the narration. As the repetitive texture highlights, God develops relationships with the characters throughout the narrative. There is no communication with God by the characters that is effective other than the expression of worship. Theologically, this points the composition of a format for biblically based moving-image media messages toward realizing the importance of worship as an element for powerfully providing access to the Prophetic Imagination, thereby ushering in the alternative consciousness. This is particularly evident in the author's placing of the psalm of worship at the center of the book, where Jonah has reached his furthest point of physical and emotional descent in an attempt to get away from God. Structurally, this reinforces the *intent* of the message of Jonah: God rules everywhere and is able to save all.

Peterson describes the importance of worship:

> The reality of the human condition is that we are determined (as Jonah exemplifies) to rule and save (ourselves) and that we make a total mess of it every time we do. . . . We have, it is quite true, a part in the ruling and saving, but it is strictly an obeying and believing part. And the only way in which we can stay alert to the reality of God in Christ ruling and saving is in the act of worship. The only way we can be trusted to say anything about God that is close to true, to do anything for God that is halfway right, is by repeated singing and praying.[12]

It is at the point of such praying and singing to God in worship, even if it is only liturgical formulae in the form of a thanksgiving psalm, that Jonah receives deliverance and a second chance to obey God's call and become effective for him. God's presence and power allow Jonah a second chance to overcome his sinful nature. However, again, Jonah's reluctant attempt to preach to Nineveh shows his skewed theology, which creates his self-centered complacency and denial of the very nature of God's love for the lost.

---

12. Peterson, *Subversive*, 89.

ARGUMENTATIVE TEXTURE

The interplay between the logical and qualitative progression in the argumentative texture of the book of Jonah focuses this book's attention on an element of narrative assertions that create specific expectations within the interpretive framework of the reader. When, as in Jonah for example, many of the assertions are fulfilled within a short span of text, the reader expects a logical progression. As the intertexture reveals, the progression of a prophetic call is often hindered by the prophet's hesitation or denial of that call. It is, therefore, in the logical progression that follows, not surprising that the reader of the book would expect the final outcome to be as follows:

Jonah a prophet is called by God to speak against Nineveh.

Jonah refuses.

God calls Jonah again.

Jonah obeys.

God destroys Nineveh as the prophet has announced (the reader's expectation of the final outcome).

As Robbins identifies it, the qualitative rhetorical progression of the argumentative texture occurs when an attribute of speech or action occurs that the reader had no reason to expect on the basis of previous assertions. In the second half of the narrative, the narrator in Jonah—emerging in relation to one or more characters in the narrative—uses this technique when all expectations are trumped by the unexpected:

Nineveh repents.

God forgives.

Jonah is mad.

In each case the narrator, through the use of qualitative rhetorical progression in relation to the logical rhetorical argumentation in the first half of the discourse, surprises the reader and thus amplifies the account with a resulting didactic sensational function of the narrative. Robbins writes that "ancient rhetoricians (who) observed that stories as well as speeches used argumentative devices to persuade the reader to think and act in one way rather than another."[13] Jonah concludes his wrestling

---

13. Robbins, *Texture*, 21.

with God in a theological conflict of a complexly interwoven matrix of activity, passivity, speech, emotion, and will. This mimetically enacts the challenge for an alternative sensory-aesthetic mode of action and speech in the world, which becomes, as discussed in Chapter 7, the *Lifestyle of the Believer*.

SENSORY/AESTHETIC TEXTURE

In the conclusion of the book, God employs Jonah's senses to teach Jonah about God through the shade's comfort, the heat's discomfort, and Jonah's resulting thirst. The narrator emphasizes God as a person to know and have a relationship with because he cares for Jonah, symbolizing his concern and care for creation. God reveals himself in terms of human senses and feelings in order to make himself available for relationship. This is represented in the narrative by the contrast between Jonah's character and God's character. The words and actions in the text reveal God's feelings, mercy, care, and forgiveness. Three times in Jonah, God acts mercifully and is forgiving when humans rebel. He desires a reconciled relationship with those he has created. In Matthew, Jesus uses the message of Jonah as a prophetic sign of God's will and redemption for mankind, saying, "As Jonah was in the belly of the fish for three days so the son of man will die and be resurrected in three days." This will happen as an act of God's character of love and mercy for his creation, even when it rebels.

The message that God will judge evil and that death will be the consequence, as would have been the outcome for the Ninevites, is superseded by God's display of mercy because of his will to deliver his created beings. This is exemplified by God's actions toward the Ninevites' repentance. The portrayal of God's merciful character as part of his judgment is conveyed to Jonah through the open-ended question in Chapter 4. Through appealing to all of Jonah's senses, God makes the point didactically to Jonah, as well as to the reader, that God's ultimate will to deliver mercifully shall yet be fulfilled and can be waited for expectantly. Chapter 4 becomes somewhat of a prophetic vision in and of itself, as culmination of a Prophetic Imagination purpose with an invitation from God to have faith and believe.

In Jonah, we see God taking on human attributes, waiting for and wanting a relationship with Jonah and caring about him enough to give him a second and even a third chance to learn about God and his true nature. It is, however, only finally in the incarnation of God as man, in the life of Jesus, that God can truly exemplify what the book of Jonah communicates prophetically in the minds and imaginations of the readers. God's mercy and care for his creation translates into a willingness to forgive, no matter how evil or alien the repentant sinner.

Jonah might not change, and so the Jews or Gentiles, despite God's merciful desire to save all of mankind, may not accept the deliverance God has made available to them. Precisely because the Jews were waiting on a political savior, they did not accept Jesus the Messiah. Like Jonah, they were not willing to change their theology to incorporate God's mercy.

INTERTEXTURE OF THE BOOK OF JONAH

Julia Kristeva introduced the term "intertexture," which Robbins has appropriated for use in socio-rhetorical criticism, and consequently refers to texts as a "mosaic of quotations."[14] This builds on Mikhail Bakhtin's explanation of the "literary word" as "an intersection of textual surfaces rather than a point (a fixed meaning), as a dialogue among several writings: that of the writer, the addressee (or the character) and the contemporary or earlier cultural context."[15] The issue here is to analyze and understand intertexture as the *Life* component of the Theology Model of Appendix A. To understand the references in a biblical text in terms of the cultural context of the text is a key element when analyzing the crafting of the meaning of the message to achieve an intended effect. That effect of an alternative message being spiritually "heard" by the dominant consciousness of a particular time will be exemplified in the intertextual analysis of the book of Jonah.

The artistic rendering of the story of Jonah as a prophetic narrative is highlighted by the apparent echoing of experiences or statements of prophets in a different manner from their original usage in other texts. Jonah is portrayed in 4:4, 8 as reacting in a despondent way, similar to that of Elijah (1 Kgs 19:4), using the words of Elijah without the excuse of Elijah, thereby showing himself inferior to the model of a prophet that Elijah exemplified. This literary creativity serves the author's *intent* to illustrate Jonah as a parody of Elijah. The intertexture of the hearer's contemporary understanding and knowledge of existing texts regarding a

---

14. Kristeva, *Kristeva Reader*, 36, quoted in Robbins, *Tapestry*.

15. Quoted in Reed, *Dialogues*.

prophet's role is used in the text to reflect on the character of Jonah and his relationship with God, thereby creating the meaning of *Life* in terms of the context of the message received. In Jonah 3:9 and 4:2, a similar technique is used, as the text closely resembles post-exilic Joel 2:13, 14—as has been implied by several scholars and likely intended by the writer. This passage, an accepted passage in the cultural context of Jonah's audience, is applied to a non-Israelite situation in the book of Jonah, thus revealing that the love of God for Israel also extends to pagans. Communication of this truth to a nationalistic community of Jews was probably not well received, as this audience was dominated by the royal consciousness of that day. So the author had to teach inspired truth using established thought in a provocative new way, using creative literary techniques within a narrative format to educate and establish the alternative consciousness wrought by a Prophetic Imagination.

A third instance of an intertextual reference to support the Prophetic Imagination purpose of the meaning and message of the book of Jonah is found in Jonah 3:9, 10, which is dependent on Jeremiah 18. Peterson terms Jeremiah an ascetical theologian,[16] referring to Jeremiah 17:5–10 to support this description. This text refers to the deceit of the human heart and the need for repentance, describing those who trust in the Lord as a well-watered tree bearing fruit near a river and those who turn away from the Lord and trust in humankind and its idols as bushes thirsting in the desert. God here says that he tests human minds and hearts. The same aspects are illustrated in Jonah 4: Jonah receives comfort from a plant's shade, but when God takes it away and allows heat and wind to overcome Jonah, he is catapulted into despair. This message is similar to that which is illustrated by the Jeremiah passage; this plant is used by God to test Jonah's mind and heart. Peterson writes that in Jonah, as in the passage in Jeremiah 17:5–10, "The presumption here is that the kinds of lives we lead, who we are, not just what we do, are huge factors influencing our access to truth, any truth, but especially Truth that is God."[17] As in the interpretation of Jeremiah, Jonah cannot be understood merely as an analysis of good or bad behavior of the characters or a checklist for moral conduct, or the point will be surely missed. Instead of emphasizing moralism, the ascetical theologian engages the hearer as an "organ"

---

16. Peterson, *Subversive*, 80.

17. Ibid., 81.

that must be adequate to the thing to be known, which is, above all else, God. Throughout Scripture, the intricacies, properties, and conditions of humanity as flesh and bone, mind and emotion, and explanation and imagination are portrayed as instruments designed to respond to God. This fact makes the last chapters of Jonah come alive, as the purpose of the *Life* component of the character, Jonah, begins to resemble God's searching of the hearts and minds—the complete organism of each of his children—in service of the Prophetic Imagination purpose. God communicates knowledgeably with his created beings as he does with Jonah, wisely dealing with our fallen nature that must be prepared, cultivated, and corrected if we are to respond with repentance to the revelation of God with an alternative consciousness. God is the central character in the story, as the author satirically renders the character of Jonah in juxtaposition to the mystery of God's mercy and grace. The author portrays the prophet in order to ridicule him and to reject all that the figure of Jonah represents as the *Life* of the royal consciousness (see also Chapter 10). The intertext between Jonah 1:1, with the negative message Jonah is preaching to the Ninevites, and 2 Kings 14:25, where King Jeroboam received a very positive message from God through the prophet Jonah, son of Amittai, contrasts the two scenarios. This is also a parody on the conduct of the prophets of old, suggesting that the book is more than a didactic narrative or a loose parable, but instead achieves ascetical theology through ironic satire. The author of the book of Jonah employs the three elements critical to *irony* as defined by Good: a stance in truth, a method of suggestion depending on the hearer or reader for recognition, and a form of classical protest testifying in favor of one thing over against another.[18]

> With ironic patience, Yahweh's final speech lays bare the absurdity of Jonah's position. The plant means nothing to Jonah except shade from sun. It is sheer luxury. He has had neither responsibility nor governance over it. "You feel sorry . . . But I, I am not to feel sorry." Jonah, unable to take seriously either of his confessions of Yahweh, "the God who made the sea and the dry land" (1:9), "a God gracious and merciful, slow to anger and great of grace, and one who repents of evil" (4:2), is the personification of the arrogant isolationism that holds the God of heaven and earth in its pocket, all the while making pious noises about the breadth of His compassion. But the author of the book of Jonah challenges this

18. Good, *Irony*, 32.

isolationism to consider the implications of such a reign and such compassion. In that sense, we may see Jonah as representative of Israel. Such an untenable understanding about God's ways with man as that held by Jonah was a persistent notion in Israel. Jesus was battling with the same pattern of belief when he said to the chief priests and elders, "The tax collectors and harlots go into the kingdom of God before you." (Matt 21:31)[19]

PROPHETIC THEOLOGICAL PURPOSE IN THE BOOK OF JONAH

Believers today need to be heeding the same warning as that evidenced in Jonah. This type of isolationism—the idea that God only acts in church circles, keeping faith and God's dealings with believers exclusive—is a danger for our souls. God is God of all, but in threatening times (e.g., as Christianity is exiled, as this book proposes) God's people, who should be acting as prophetic ministers of an alternative consciousness of God's saving grace to all mankind, often withdraw and become inwardly focused on maintaining their pious identity.

On the other hand, secular culture, as the *Life* component of the Theology Model, puts the notion of a Creator God on the back burner, in exchange for a more inclusive concept of god that refers to whatever a person believes has power. Often it is the persons themselves who are the defenders of their relative truth and tolerance and who act as if they are gods in their own created worldviews. So the message of Jonah regarding the relationship of the Creator God of the universe to all people's *Life*, claiming responsibility for and governance of all created things, is even more relevant in the midst of contemporary culture's positivism and relativism. The book of Jonah's references to the extraordinary—such as the fish delivering Jonah, the storm calming after Jonah is hurled overboard, and all of nature reacting to the word of God in Chapter 4, challenges the faith of those who view God's power and glory in terms of their limited human understanding. Jonah speaks out in narrative format against the secular naturalism that pervades contemporary culture. The introduction of subjectivity as a means of knowing reality that developed into the Enlightenment passion for a person's rights had as its basis the idea that humankind does not need God to explain creation

19. Ibid., 53, 54.

and that God is irrelevant for moral formulation. This led to naturalism, which, on the heels of Kant and Nietzsche's thought systems, claimed, if it could not be empirically proved, that God does not exist. Faith is therefore dead and irrelevant, and God is nothing more than a relative subjective truth for those living in the twentieth century. Chuck Colson wrote that C. S. Lewis, a keen prophet of the twentieth century, saw that naturalism would usurp supernaturalism for a time, and thus the Western world would become led by "elite controllers who would tell us what was good for us and take away our human dignity, instituting the kind of soft despotism Tocqueville wrote about. And Lewis saw that ultimately this would produce tyranny."[20] It is this dominant consciousness of power as the *Life* component of the secular worldview that the producers of biblical worldview media messages must seek to address. It is with the power of the imagination that truth, not only propositionally to the mind but alternatively to all of the aesthetic senses (as the ascetical theologians and people like C. S. Lewis understood), must be presented and affect the way we ultimately think. This concept of truth delivered in the book of Jonah remains relevant today, as faith in a transcendent reality and the God of creation is in question.

CONCLUSION

The analysis of inner and intertexture of the book of Jonah in this chapter shows how the author achieves a Prophetic Imagination purpose. This indicates how format and purpose are inextricably linked in the biblical narratives. The biblical authors understood the medium as the message. The book of Jonah is used to illustrate this concept as the socio-rhetorical methodology is applied and the aspects comprising the inner and inter-textures are identified. The presence of these textures provides evidence for the hypothesis of this book that the Prophetic Imagination paradigm could indicate a common purpose between ancient writers of the Bible and today's makers of meaning. In the book of Jonah the portrayal of God's immanence in the message illustrates the elements of theology interwoven in the message. At times this is as overt as naming him in the plot of the narrative; at other times it is subversive, letting the structure of the pattern and progression illuminate characteristics and actions that will highlight faith and God's presence in all of creation. The intertexture

20. Colson, *Chuck Colson*, 111.

highlights the creatively crafted communication of the book of Jonah, capturing the imagination of the audience with ironical *style* to bring about an alternative consciousness in a particular cultural setting. Therefore, for the book's goal of developing a format for Christian moving–image media, much is gained from this analysis of the structural elements that communicate a Prophetic Imagination purpose in biblical texts.

The book of Jonah is communicating a message of revelation of an alternative lifestyle relevant for both believers and gentiles, educating the secular, post-modern audiences of today as well as the ancient audience. This is an essential dimension required of contemporary Christian media messages. Essential to the task of being an effective communicator is to bear an audience's spiritual readiness, as well as its varied positions and cultural preconceptions, in mind. This is critical as the producer attempts to relate the biblical *intent* to the audience, so that the lifestyle of the hearer is affected and transformed from a dominant ideology to a biblically based alternative made available through a Prophetic Imagination; this creative act is termed *imagineering* (see Chapter 9).

CHAPTER 7

Model Two: Managing Messages

Communication Theory

Christianity, Culture, and Communication

INTRODUCTION

THIS CHAPTER WILL IDENTIFY communication based theory. The theory can be used concurrently with the social and cultural texture of rhetorical criticism to give insight regarding the *content* of narratives. This will achieve the goal of establishing effective Prophetic Imagination television and film narratives as outlined in Model Two.

The term "communication," from the Latin root *communicare*, which means "to share" or, literally, "to make common," is the meaning of the role of Christian moving-image media in this book as *to create and share a Christian culture on earth*. The process of communicating via Christian moving-image media enables God's image bearers to share the images and message of truth as agents of God's "common grace." Colson and Pearcey define *common grace* as "carrying out God's work of maintaining creation by promoting righteousness and restraining evil"[1] and thus fulfilling the cultural commission.

With its root being "cult," the term "culture," in its most basic meaning, indicates a system of religious worship. To communicate through the moving-image media employing the prophetic theology of Model One has the potential, when in the spirit of worship, to glorify God (see Chapter 11, "Disciplines of Readiness"), to redeem culture by displaying a dynamic spiritual order of an alternative consciousness in terms of

---

1. Colson and Pearcey, *How Now Shall We Live?*, 33–34.

the dominant belief systems of the secular empire. As Rossouw explains, "Culture is the interpretative and coping mechanism of society. It is the way in which people understand themselves, their world and the appropriate interaction with one another and with the world they live in."[2] It requires producers and directors of moving-image media messages to become a "culture-creating cult, men and women of another type arrayed for the great battle of principle against principle,"[3] in order to address the *Life* of the dominant consciousness of the secular worldview. If the moving-image media, through a prophetic theological purpose discussed in Chapter 2, portrays the *Bible* as defining all of *Life*, a *Lifestyle of the Believer* can be presented in and through the viewing of these narratives. This "sharing" of and "making common" the communication process could be instrumental in affecting culture in terms of biblically based truth. As political philosopher Russell Kirk wrote, "When belief in the cult has been wretchedly enfeebled, the culture will decay swiftly. . . . The material order rests on the spiritual order."[4] It is necessary when formulating the *content* of messages for biblical moving-image media to understand the decay of the material order of the culture. The cultural shift (*Life* component) from a modern to a postmodern (or late-modern, as some prefer to call it) culture brought a new understanding of self and the world.

POSTMODERNISM

In order to translate the revelation of God into the language of the world, a study of the development of the relationship between faith and reason must be made as it translates into postmodernism. According to Colson and Pearcey, "*Postmodernism* rejects any notion of a universal overarching truth and reduces all ideas to social constructions shaped by class, gender, and ethnicity."[5] An understanding of postmodernism presupposes an understanding of the rationality behind modernism. First, however, it is important to note that the rationality of the medieval times' fundamental distinction between the transcendent and the immanent emphasized the Transcendent. Faith defined every dimension of society and was considered to be part of God's divine plan. The church and its officials were

2. Rossouw, "Theology," 804.

3. Colson and Pearcey, *How Now Shall We Live?*, 37.

4. Quoted in Colson and Pearcey, *How Now Shall We Live?*, 37.

5. Colson and Pearcey, *How Now Shall We Live?*, 23.

regarded as representing God and were vested with authority, i.e. the dominant consciousness of that period.

The modern culture that replaced medieval culture rejected the medieval notion of rationality because of its basic distinction between subjective and objective thought. The interpretation of reality came to be understood not in terms of what is external, objective, and transcendent, but in terms of truth as it is perceived by the individual or group. With no biblical meta-narrative, truth became subjective. The Enlightenment emphasized that the rights of man made God irrelevant in explaining the world and therefore also irrelevant for moral formulation. With Kant and Nietzsche came the idea that unless something can be empirically validated, it cannot be known or proven to exist. This notion stimulated the development of science and technology, but these successes were often accompanied by human alienation. It was considered impossible to incorporate values, ultimate ends, or the meaning of life with the requirements of objective evidence. Discourses on these matters were rejected as mere utterances of emotions and were regarded as no longer binding. Colson describes the result: "Relativism, the idea that all propositions are morally equal and that there is no binding, objective transcendent truth, and naturalism (or materialism), the idea that there is a naturalistic explanation for everything, have become the dominant consciousness of today's post modern culture."[6]

A broader rationality including both non-rational (in terms of modernist rationality) and non-mechanical dimensions of life is needed for holding on to the ultimate truth of God's Word. This is necessary for the electronic mass media ministry, which has to communicate through a technological medium a transcendent, theological message that is relevant to the center stage of the modern world and not restricted to the domain of personal relations.

Shriver analyzes the current situation: "Theologians tried to build a belief system in which deductions were made in a logically consistent way, resulting in a rationalistic and theological exercise that was *timeless* and irrelevant for the culture in which it was practiced. Many, if not most, have been disempowered by the exclusion imposed on them by modernist rationality."[7]

---

6. Colson, *Chuck Colson*, 113.

7. Shriver, "Business Managers," 124.

The implication of training and re-training producers of biblical storytelling in using television or film in contemporary culture and employing the skills needed for a proper ethical analysis of *content* presents an opportunity that should be seized. New styles of leadership and communication are critical elements in the production process, especially for the tapping of resources. The challenge is for the producers to abandon a style of communication that aims at downloading religious information on its audience, adopting instead a style of communication that involves the experiences and expectations of its viewers (see www.jonahre.com, "Receiver and Channel Research"). C. S. Lewis put it so well: "We don't need Christian writers; we need writers who are Christians; we need writers who get that redemptive message into people's minds and imaginations."[8] This process of identity and character formation is not a merely intellectual process that can be discussed by a panel, but is a comprehensive process of socialization within a community of believers, i.e., a *Lifestyle of the Believer*. The moving-image medium must portray life lived according to the truth of the biblical worldview, persuading viewers that this worldview provides a more rational way to order life. The aim of Christian programming is not to eliminate the theological expertise of theologians involved in the production process, but to merge it with the experiences and expectations of the non-theologian and non-clergy believers in a way that is consistent with a biblical understanding of reality.

Much Christian moving-image communication is limited to its own interpretive community; it is hegemonic for its own in-group, and one is inclined to believe that it is unable to speak much beyond that community. However, with a biblically based theology for communicating biblical truth as a means of revealing a kingdom view of the world, coupled with an attitude of worship, God's Spirit becomes a power to be reckoned with in and through the communication in any community. For thousands of years, biblical narratives have conveyed the message of truth inspired by God, providing cross-cultural audiences from various religious backgrounds with a way to orientate themselves to the world. Mel Gibson's portrayal of Jesus' crucifixion in the "Passion of the Christ" (2004), made from a Roman Catholic viewpoint, has communicated to Christian audiences across various denominations. Its power to communicate truth came through the portrayal of the alternative consciousness

8. Quoted in Colson, *Chuck Colson*, 99.

that Jesus took to the cross and Jesus' self-sacrificial testimony. This was echoed by the fact that Mel Gibson, in producing the film, demonstrated a self-sacrificial heart by using his own money for the movie and putting his reputation as an actor and director on the line to make a biblically based film. However, despite criticism, the very passion of the man making this film to communicate biblically based truth allowed the Spirit of God to use him and to portray the truth as a vehicle that would transcend the audience to a kingdom reality. As Mel says, "The Holy Spirit was working through me in this film, and I was just directing traffic."[9] This is testimony to the fact that God's power is available through the presence of the Holy Spirit to believers, as producers and directors, when their productions are carried out as worship unto him. God can use these moving-image productions as vehicles of *common grace* to establish an alternative consciousness through the portrayal of *content* with prophetic theological *intent* (see Appendix A).

Model Two relies on the consistency of biblical truth that must be based in the prophetic theological purpose of Model One, as well as on a biblical worldview, to establish an alternative consciousness within the *Life* component that is variable and culture specific, thereby illuminating the *Lifestyle of the Believer* in a post-modernist culture. This demands that the authoritarian with a dominant consciousness (in the production process) step down from a dominating position and become a fellow player in the search for a meaningful biblical life to be portrayed in contemporary culture. Williams elaborates: "Closely related to this is a shift from the emphasis in spiritual formation from 'What do we believe?' to 'Who are we?'"[10] Part of that understanding is that Christians develop a strong identity and character through their faith in God. It is thus that Christianity, as a biblical lifestyle with an ultimate standard of truth, can illuminate an *alternative consciousness* to Western deconstructionism.

TWO WORLDVIEWS

The root of the struggle today is between conflicting worldviews about questions of ultimate reality and the source of all things. C. S. Lewis called himself a "supernaturalist," seeing supernaturalism as a view of the world in terms of absolute truth defined by God's sovereignty as Creator. This

9. Rogers, "*Passion*," 241.

10. Williams, *New Communication*, 473.

worldview is in conflict with its antithesis, naturalism, that is overthrowing the moral order in the Western world. As the Christian worldview is in exile, it is not, however, a time of despair for Christian communicators but a time to go back to the creation covenant and be *energized* by the truth that the Bible is the only rational explanation for reality. It is a time to boldly offer hope in an alternative consciousness as the world looks and surveys the shambles of the modern experiment. A cultural approach to communication needs to be examined to understand how managing the *content* of messages in moving-image productions can affect and transform culture.

THEORETICAL STEPS TOWARD A CULTURAL APPROACH

In the early 1970s, two scholars, namely, Raymond Williams from Jesus College, Cambridge, and Stuart Hall, then director of the Center for the Study of Contemporary Culture at Birmingham University, voiced objections to the term "mass communication" or "communication," respectively, as a name for the field of study. Williams and Hall both believed that these labels limit scholars' studies, isolating them substantively and the parameters placed on communication as a field of study have isolated it. To integrate it with other disciplines like theology and theological methodology could advance its understanding and application, as this book suggests. The relationship of Christianity to culture and the relationship of communication to culture are proposed as the theoretical point of convergence for the disciplines of communication and theology. The theory of culture as developed by anthropologist Clifford Geertz in a set of essays, *The Interpretation of Culture* (1973), has been used by scholars of theology and communication independently. As communication scholar James Carey writes of Geertz's work, "To read . . . (it) is to witness the development of an increasingly precise and powerful theory of culture and one that progressively becomes a theory of communication as well."[11] Religion professor Vernon Robbins draws upon Geertz in forming the bases of developing a methodology of exegesis for biblical texts, namely, socio-rhetorical criticism, to understand the relationship of Christianity to culture.[12] Here socio-rhetorical criticism is used as a hermeneutic for recovering truth in biblical texts. As Robbins writes:

11. Carey, *Communication*, 40.
12. Robbins, *Tapestry*, 35.

A number of anthropologists and sociologists have been helping us to find the terminology with which to investigate and describe Christianity as a cultural phenomenon. The work of an anthropologist like Clifford Geertz helps us to understand that some form of Christianity is 'the primary culture' in which many people live (1973). Also his work helps us to understand the function of 'local cultures' and their relation to national and international cultures (1983).[13]

Therefore, in agreement with Walter Fisher and the narrative paradigm (see Chapter 10), this book considers rhetoric, traditionally, as more than a form of discourse. Rhetoric is considered as theory that forms the basis of a methodology for critique, which, in Fisher's words, "is the purpose of the concept of narrative rationality. Calvin O. Schrag makes the case for hermeneutic critique in his *Communicative Praxis and the Space of Subjectivity*. He specifically cites the narrative paradigm and narrative rationality as useful in moving hermeneutics to a critical stance."[14]

As this book explores the use of moving-image media as an effective means of Christian communication to create a shared alternative community of believers, described theologically as an alternative cultural consciousness, to the dominant secular culture of the twenty-first century, two precepts are necessary.

First, Christianity (as a worldview) needs to be understood in terms of a cultural phenomenon; secondly, communication cannot be understood comprehensively apart from the context of culture.

Communication scholar Clifford Christians argues similarly that, "Without a cultural center, articulated from an evangelical worldview, communication falls apart, driven largely by 'passionate intensity.'"[15]

Hall develops the argument for the cultural aspect of communication as follows:

The word "culture," which in its anthropological sense directs us toward the study of an entire way of life, is replaced by the word "communication" which directs us to the study of one isolated segment of existence. Methodologically, the word "communication" isolates us from an entire body of critical, interpretive and com-

---

13. Ibid., 5.
14. Fisher, *Human Communication*, 95.
15. Christians, "Redemptive Media," 331.

parative methodology that has been at the heart of anthropology and the study of literature as well as modern Marxism.[16]

Insight into the nature of culture and its relation to communication can be gained from describing the two categories of interpretation that are prevalent in communication studies.

Communication is a term that some describe scientifically and others describe humanistically. These two streams of thought reflect the division that exists in communication theory: the scientific perspective versus the humanistic perspective. The scientific techniques are comprised of experiments and survey research that result in quantitative methodology and hold a transmission view of culture. This methodology is applied by behavioral scientists. "The study of communication in the United States has been dominated by the attempts to create a behavioral science and to elucidate laws or functions of behavior."[17] This approach has been predominantly used by the Protestants, who adopted a scientific view of communication in tune with their own theological tendencies toward manipulation and control of culture. In the process, they established the models of communication later adopted by mass marketers.

The humanist techniques constitute textual analysis and ethnography, which provide qualitative interpretations employed by rhetoricians. This historically Christian view of communication, tied to meaning and ritual, lost ground to the transmission view. This ritual view of communication understands communication to be a process through which shared culture is created, modified, and transformed. This book argues that further analysis of the cultural view of communication will allow biblical texts and theology to be translated into a mass communication medium message that can co-create Christian culture and be relevant in terms of the dominant consciousness. "If a transmission view centers on the extension of messages across geography for purposes of control, a ritual view centers on the sacred ceremony that draws persons together in fellowship and commonality."[18]

16. Carey, *Communication*, 42.

17. Ibid., 49.

18. Ibid., 42.

COMMUNICATION THEORY CLASSIFICATION

A useful way to organize communication theories for understanding the nuances and contributions of each is to group them by genre. Although this system does not perfectly classify the diversity of the theories, the similarities and differences will be apparent, and it will capture some important philosophical trends. The system of five classifications, reflecting Littlejohn's (1996) ideas, includes structural and functional theories, cognitive and behavioral theories, interactionist theories, interpretive theories, and critical theories.

Structural and Functional Theories

Littlejohn's classification of theories is based on "the belief that social structures are real and function in ways that can be observed objectively."[19] This is a concept that would be critical to a behavioral scientist coming primarily from the scientific perspective of research. Going back to at least Plato and Aristotle, subjectivity and consciousness have been widely mistrusted, and knowledge has been thought to be discovered through careful observation and classification.

According to these theories, communication is a process in which individuals use language and symbol systems to convey meaning. The focus is mainly on the unintended consequences of action, rather than purposeful outcomes. These ideas have been described as anti-human and have influenced communication scholars in the U.S. considerably. Today such notions are under scrutiny, and other theories are thought to offer more important perspectives.

Cognitive and Behavioral Theories

These theories differ from the aforementioned in that they focus on the individual, as opposed to social and cultural structures. The cognitivists are interested in how people think. Falling more toward the scientific perspective, this "variable-analytic" approach seeks to learn how information impacts the individual and how people evaluate the credibility, organization, and argumentation of a message.

19. Littlejohn, *Theories*, 14.

Interactionist Theories

This set of theories considers social life to be a product, and not a determinant, of interaction. The use of language is to create social structures such as organizations, groups, families, and institutions. Language is understood to be both maintained and changed as a result of its use.

Interpretive Theories

Littlejohn writes that "This genre includes theories that try to discover meaning in actions and texts, from ancient scrolls to the behavior of teenagers."[20] These theories are predominantly interpretive from a rhetorical humanist perspective. Encouraging subjectivism and individual experience, the process attempts to uncover the way people understand and make meaning of their experiences without looking to a moral or biblical compass. This tends to become an exercise in subjectivism and relativism, with no discernible purpose if no link to the creation of culture is inferred.

Critical Theories

The critical theories rooted in Marxism are concerned with the quality of communication and human life. Criticizing and not merely observing, these theories analyze "the conflict of interests in society and the ways communication perpetuates domination of one group over another."[21] Having advanced well beyond original Marxist thought, critical theories encompass much of the other genres discussed. Functional and cognitive theories are largely rejected, but as most of the research is based on the underlying social structures that affect relations in society, a strong structural orientation does exist. The importance of culture and its changes through interaction is recognized in these theories, which therefore borrow from the interactionists.

According to Littlejohn, "Critical theories share with interpretive approaches the central concern for language and for the way language affects experience."[22] Relying heavily on the interpretive method, one of the theories' important contributions is the premise that communication

20. Ibid., 16.
21. Ibid., 17.
22. Ibid., 17.

defines culture. In this book's attempt to bridge the gap between the purpose of communication of ancient biblical texts and that of communication via Christian modern moving-image media, the final cultural topics of socio-rhetorical criticism bring the interpreter closer to understanding cultural contexts in terms of different kinds of cultural rhetoric.

It is in the realm of critical theory combined with rhetoric that this book chose socio-rhetorical criticism as its methodology, "to explore a text in a systematic, broad manner that leads to a rich environment of interpretation and dialogue. Underlying the method is a presupposition that words themselves work in very complicated ways to communicate meanings . . . informative about life and the world in which we live."[23] This is important, as Robbins's final cultural topics are inherent in the biblical texts' communication and become a view into translating these texts' understanding of *Life* into moving-image communication with a Prophetic Imagination perspective. In Robbins's final cultural categories, taken from Aristotle's "final topics" in his *Art of Rhetoric,* the manner in which propositions, arguments, and reasons are presented offers insight into different cultural rhetoric. Cultural studies from a sociological perspective, such as Stuart Hall's British Cultural Studies, have probably been among the most influential. Hall identifies an ideology as "a set of ideas that structure a group's reality, a system of representations or a code of meanings governing how individuals and groups see the world."[24] It is ideology that forms culture's meanings that is important as it relates to social and cultural texture.

Ideological Theories

Louis Althusser contributed an ideological point of view to Third Cinema using the term "interpellation" to describe the position of the subject, which is manipulated by the mechanisms of ideological discourse.

Reading Strategies

To understand ideological discourse, the following must he explained. British Cultural Studies, for example, considers culture to be a way of living within an industrial society that encompasses all the messages of that social experience. This understanding has implications for the media.

23. Robbins, *Texture*, 132.
24. Quoted in Littlejohn, *Theories*, 228.

Hall postulated three common *reading strategies,* or responses to an ideo-logical message produced by the dominant consciousness, depending on the social and cultural milieu of the audience: The *dominant, negotiated,* and *antagonistic reading.*

I The *dominant reading* is that of the viewer who accepts the dominant ideology (royal consciousness of Prophetic Imagination) and agrees with the subjective *content.*

II The *negotiated reading* is that of the viewer who in general identifies with the dominant ideology but considers his or her own social posi-tion first. This reading strategy implies conflict.

III Finally, there is the *antagonistic reading* of the person whose social and cultural background puts him or her in conflict with the domi-nant ideology.

(See also Chapter 8, where Robbins's "final cultural categories [topics]" that "most decisively identify one's cultural location" are discussed.[25])

Cultural studies hypothesize that a capitalist society is a split soci-ety. At first class difference was considered the main ideological divider, but others have been identified: race (e.g., the South African situation), age, religion (as in Christian denominational differences), occupation, education, political convictions, gender, etc. The society is not an organic whole but a developed network of groups, each with different interests, but linked by a relationship of power with the dominant class (the royal consciousness). Social relationships are defined by power in a structure of those with power and those subordinate to that power. This is never a static relationship, but a constant struggle, as occurs in a negotiated reading. In cultural studies, the dominant class attempts to naturalize meaning in the society. This, however, is not done on a conscious level, as culture's ideology is rooted in a class and its members' consciousness.

Communities of interpretation also play a role in dictating or shap-ing the "readings" of texts. Historically, the church provides such a com-munity. Contemporary society is riddled with conflicting interpretive communities. In other words, dominant readings are negotiated among various parties.

25. Robbins, *Texture,* 65.

Model Two: Managing Messages

Ideological State Apparatuses

Althusser considers ideology not as a static set of beliefs that is enforced on subordinates, but as a dynamic process that is being formed in practice and that determines a person's belief system, behavior, and relationship to society. Althusser's theory centers around "ideological state apparatuses" (ISAs), e.g. social institutions such as family, education systems, language, political structure and the media.

In a post-modern society, the ISAs are autonomous, without any connection to the system of law and are not explicitly linked to the school system or the media, but they all do have the same ideology. The dominant consciousness of society today is patriarchal, trying to gain material riches, and reinforces individuality and power dominance. ISAs, however, postulate social neutrality and the idea that the institutions of law, media, and education, for example, all have static sets of principles and treat all individuals equally. However, their definitions of equality and justice have been proven to serve the interests of white, middle class, male persons.

Althusser's theory of over-determination develops the idea that institutions are all linked by a common ideology, and a network of inter-relationships determines the ideology of any institution. Ideology is thus not a static idea, but a process that continually reproduces itself in ISAs. It works on a macro-level (institutions), because it functions in the same way on a micro-level (the individual). To understand this concept, the individual is considered to be a "subject" formed by culture. Althusser believes that all persons are ideological subjects formed by ISAs and that naturalized ideology does not only form our worldview but also our image of self. In other words, our identity and our relationship with other human beings and society are shaped in this manner. The "subject'" is therefore a social and not a natural creation (e.g., a biological female can think like a male as a result of patriarchal ideology, and a member of the black working class can be influenced by white, middle class subjectivity). The important implications of these concepts are reflected in what Brueggemann terms Prophetic Imagination. In outlining the correlation with the British Cultural Studies in Chapter 5, the use and purpose of this conceptual ideological framework becomes relevant when evaluating interpretations of *Life* to communicate through Christian moving-image media messages designed to affect the creation of culture.

THEORETICAL CONSIDERATIONS FOR MODEL TWO

(See Appendix B)

The critical theorists are essentially correct that some groups in society have more symbolic power, that communication is often hegemonic (permitting one group to dominate another group) and that economic interests are always significant in mass communication. The cultural view focuses on understanding the culture and creating and maintaining through ritual the culture's own meaning. The problem, however, with this theory lies in determining which culture's meaning must be created and maintained. For Christian programming, this meaning lies in the producer's communication of what is ultimately true, a biblical standard of truth as a moral compass. However, cultural theory does not claim this worldview and does not address or incorporate it; thus, this theory is marked by the same pitfalls that currently draw our culture away from faith in a miracle-working God toward subjective relativism and naturalism. What is needed is a theory of communication that is able to merge with a theology for communication (a biblically based prophetic theology that is the clear *intent* of the production). In this book, the cultural approach lends a context for the intention of biblically based texts and communication that have a clearly defined purpose of communicating a Christian worldview. This message brings forth meaning, as coherent truth is communicated through the text of the *Bible* to establish an alternative consciousness in terms of the *Life* of the dominant consciousness of the audience. Thus, this book argues for a kind of biblical anthropology—for a definition of communication grounded in our created humanness. This view of communication makes possible integration of the constant truth of God's Word with constantly changing meanings as new circumstances arise in the culture. This approach makes certain that the audience identifies with the message, the golden rule of effective communication.

The definition of communication provided by scholars Lawrence Frey, Carl Botan, Paul Friedman, and Gary Kreps brings together the essence of the theories discussed: "Communication is the management of messages for the purpose of creating meaning."[26] For the purposes of this book, the definition provides a broad framework, which incorporates various strands of communication theory that regard communication as

---

26. Griffin, *Communication Theory*, 19.

an intentional cultural approach, while not ruling out accidental out-comes, including both verbal and non-verbal symbols.

The study of communication from a cultural approach uniquely contributes what Geertz calls, "the creation of a theory of fictions" by allowing various "meanings that others have placed on experience to build up a veridical record of what has been said at other times, in other places, and in other ways; to enlarge the human conversation by comprehending what others are saying."[27] A failure of moving-image media communication theory entrenched in the modern social sciences is that it imposes meanings on other cultures instead of conversing with them. The making of a "theory of fiction" can thus be considered as a construction of cultural forms. The technological moving-image media messages are cultural forms through which reality based on the principles of the Word of God can be created. Grounded in the theological paradigm, which puts the cultural mandate at the center of all human communication to redeem culture, results in a response to the religious message that Clifford Geertz says, "creates a kind of culture that gives meanings, values, traditions, convictions, rituals, beliefs and actions to people."[28]

European scholarship gives particular attention to the matter of creating and understanding culture through expressive artistic forms. British sociologist Tom Burns acknowledges that the theoretical communication paradigm should be considered as an integrated approach to communication that draws upon different fields of study (e.g., spiritual, literary, sociological, cultural, or historical) relating to humanity.[29] That is precisely the goal of this book's proposition of a Communication Model (in Appendix B) to set out a paradigm from which many interrelated fields can interact and lend to an understanding of the cultural context for creating biblical moving-image media messages. It connects with the Biblical Theology Model One and the Contemporary *Edutainment* Model Three to bridge the gap in creatively communicating the truth as revealed through biblical interpretations of life to a modern context with modern technological tools.

American studies have been preoccupied with communication study as a behavioral science, attempting to find the particular psychological

27. Quoted in Carey, *Communication*, 62.
28. Quoted in Robbins, *Texture*, 72.
29. Quoted in Carey, *Communication*, 44.

and sociological environment in which to elucidate laws and functions of attitude and behavioral change for the transmission of messages to control the outcome. The role of expressive forms using communication technologies in American studies is considered intellectually, and economic gain or political control is the desired outcome. However, the role of mass media messages, as Carey states, "in creating a general culture—a way of life and a pattern of significance—never is entertained seriously.[30]

The biblical text as literature, which must be translated in its cultural context and communicated in terms of the contemporary culture's expressive forms, is what Burns addresses. Burns observed that the literary critic's task to find meaning and interpretation of the presentation of life and how it relates to a historical audience's sense of life (as done by Appendix A) is the same process by which the contemporary Christian communicator must artistically render and make sense of cultural forms that define meaning for life (appendices B and C).[31]

The task, then, of the Christian communicator, from the perspective of a biblical worldview, is to interpret the interpretations of life in a postmodern culture before artistically and imaginatively rendering to the audience a meaning suited to their context. Burns then notes in the communication situation, as explicated in Model B, that there is on the one hand there is a *Life-Audience* component, "existence, experience, and behavior," and on the other hand are attempts to find "the meaning and significance in this experience and behavior,"[32] translated in Model B as the *Bible-Context* component. Theology Model A becomes a critical practical step for elaborating the *Bible* component, as the biblical text is consulted for a biblical worldview in a historical *Life* setting. Biblical culture is thus, according to this reading and for the purposes of this book, the meaning and significance particular people discover, in this case the Christian producer and/or the director, in their pursuit to order and render experience comprehensible and charged with affect as it is imaginatively communicated. In agreement with Burns, this book claims that "what is called the study of culture also can be called the study of communications, for what we are studying in this context are the ways in which experience *(Life)* is

30. Ibid., 45.

31. Quoted in Carey, *Communication*, 44.

32. Carey, *Communication*, 44.

worked into understanding *(Bible)* and then disseminated and celebrated *(Lifestyle of the Believer)*" (italics mine) in an expressive form.[33]

INTEGRATING SOCIAL AND CULTURAL TEXTURE TO CREATE AND APPLY MODEL TWO

Drawing from the cultural and anthropological trends in communication theory, in congruence with the social and cultural texture of socio-rhetorical criticism, provides insight into the goal of effectively communicating through the Christian moving-image media. In formulating a biblical Prophetic Imagination message for television and film, "Social and cultural texture . . . concerns the capacities of the text to support social reform, withdrawal or opposition and to evoke cultural perception of dominance, subordinance, difference or exclusion."[34] These aspects are incorporated in the three components of formulating the context for the *content* of the message in Model Two.

Bible-Content Component Applied to The Lamb
(See Appendix B)

The first aspect is the specific social topics in the text to be considered. For a text to have a substantive religious texture, specific ways of talking about the world must be considered in the communication model. These reveal the author's considerations of what the context of the religious response to the world should be in the discourse. These specific social topics for biblical lifestyle productions come from the biblical text as a resource "for changing people or social practices, for destroying or recreating social order, for withdrawing from present society to create one's own social order, or for coping with the world by transforming one's own perception of it."[35] How to live in the world with its dominant consciousness—or how to change—becomes the consideration of the author of a biblical worldview message. As anthropologist Clifford Geertz maintains, each response of the audience participating in the message then creates a kind of culture that gives meanings, values, traditions, rituals, beliefs, and actions to people in the discourse. Therefore, the producer or communicator formulating a message for Christian moving-image media must come

33. Ibid.
34. Robbins, *Texture*, 3.
35. Ibid.

to realize that the *Bible-Content* component incorporated in the rhetoric will nurture different types of biblical culture. Each type of social rhetoric in biblical texts will result in different types of social responses critical to evoking a Prophetic Imagination response.

The seven types of responses are as follows and is verbatim wording taken from Robbins:

1. Conversionist

   The conversionist response is characterized by a view that the world is corrupt. If people can be changed, the world will be changed. Salvation is considered to be available not through objective agencies but only by a profound and supernaturally wrought transformation of the self. The world itself will not change, but the presence of a new subjective orientation to it will itself be salvation.

2. Revolutionist

   The revolutionist response declares that only the destruction of the world—the natural world but also, more specifically, the social order—will be sufficient to save people. Supernatural powers must perform the destruction, because people lack the power, if not to destroy the world, then certainly to re-create it. Believers may themselves feel called upon to participate in the process of overturning the world, but they do no more than assist greater powers and give testimony of faith by their words and deeds.

3. Introversionist

   The introversionist response views the world as irredeemably evil and considers salvation to be attainable only by the fullest withdrawal from it. The self may be purified by denouncing the world and leaving it. This might be an individual response, of course, but as the response of a social movement it leads to the establishment of a separated community preoccupied with its own holiness and its means of insulation from the wider society.

4. Gnostic-Manipulation

   The gnostic-manipulation response seeks only a transformed set of relationships—a transformed method of coping with evil. Whereas the foregoing orientations reject the goals of society as well as the institutionalized means of attaining them and the existing facilities by which people might be saved, the gnostic-manipulationist rejects only the means and the facilities. Salvation is possible in the world, and evil may be overcome if people learn the right means, improved techniques, to deal with their problems.

5. Thaumatugical

The thaumaturgical response focuses on the individual's concern for relief from the present and specific ills by special dispensations. The request for supernatural help is personal and local, and its operation is magical. Salvation takes the form of healing, assuagement of grief, restoration after loss, reassurance, the foresight and avoidance of calamity, and the guarantee of eternal (or at least continuing) life after death.

6. Reformist

The reformist response views the world as corrupt because its social structures are corrupt. If the structures can be changed so that the behaviors they sanction are changed, then salvation will be present in the world. This response, then, assumes that evil may be dealt with according to supernaturally given insights about the ways in which social organization should be amended. Investigation of the ways of the world and recommendations for amending it are the essential orientation. The specific alterations to be made are revealed to people whose hearts and minds are open to supernatural influence.

7. Utopian

The utopian response seeks to reconstruct the entire social world according to the divinely given principles, rather than simply to amend it from a reformist position. The goal of a utopian response is to establish a new social organization that will eliminate evil. It is much more radical than the reformist response because it insists on complete replacement of the present social organization. The utopian response differs from the revolutionist response by insisting that people themselves remake the world rather than that a divine power destroy this present world and re-create another. In turn, a utopian response is more active and constructive than an introversionist response of simply withdrawing from the world.[36]

For assessing how the biblical *content* in a cultural context results in these specific responses, the *content* of the moving-image production *The Lamb* will be analyzed in terms of a specific cultural topic. Although there might be others, the dominant consciousness that is primarily addressed in the movie as a specific cultural topic is the biblically based theme of religiosity. The dominant culture that is being addressed consists of those who belong to some religious group who don't have a living,

---

36. Robbins, *Texture*, 72–73.

real relationship with God because they have hardened their hearts and cannot see or understand his salvation work.

In *The Lamb* Mattias, a good orthodox Jew, turns away from God when tragedy overwhelms him. He blames God, and his religion does not stand up to the test of his faith. The result is that he hardens his heart toward God. A similar theme is found in the biblical book of Jonah: When Jonah's understanding of God and his religion fails, he hardens his heart to the salvation God is bringing. In both cases, the rhetoric is a dramatic portrayal of a conversionist response in the dominant context, where the view is that the world will not change but the presence of a new subjective orientation to it will itself bring salvation. This is worked out in the storyline, as Mattias and his son witness the crucifixion of Jesus. Along with father and son, the viewer is invited to undergo transformation to a new reality, resulting in a conversionist response.[37] In the book of Jonah, Jonah's conversion in the final chapter is uncertain, but he is left with God's compelling final illustration in Chapter 4 of his great love for his creation and his desire for all who repent to be saved. The invitation for a conversionist response is again inherent in the specific cultural rhetoric in the text.[38] Therefore, it can be said that this aspect of the *content* of *The Lamb* (see www.thelambmovie.com) is biblically based and conversionist, in that it evokes a specific cultural response of the dominant consciousness to an alternative lifestyle based in truth.[39]

Life-Audience Component

(See Appendix B)

The common social and cultural topics are those values, patterns, and codes of behavior that are consciously or unconsciously internalized by those living in a particular time and environment. Therefore the *Life-Audience* component in the communication transaction translates into the ability of the audience to recognize their own context—the world in which they live—in the "text." Geertz pointed out that the cockfights of the Balinese people (see further discussion below) were a means of expression and a participatory ritual that entertained because they relayed an image to the spectators and, metaphorically, their own stories

37. Ibid., 72.
38. Ibid.
39. Ibid.

to themselves. In recognizing their own status, relationships, and characteristics of brutality and jealousy, they were entertained. However, it is not enough to be entertained by ourselves; we need truth to educate us of the "more" to life.

The *Bible-Content* component with its biblical worldview engages the *Life-Audience* component through the moving-image narrative media in "a challenge-response" type of social communication, as Robbins terms it. "The channels are always public, and the publicity of the message guarantees that the receiving individual will react in some way, since even his nonaction is publicly interpreted as a response."[40]

Considering Audience and Content

Careful analysis of tactic, strategy, and audience demographics is imperative when structuring and deciding on *content* for the effective communication of moving-image media messages in a cultural context. For the purposes of Christian moving-image media, this has, however, been a point of contention, as Christian communicators have been accused of being "sellers of Christianity" and compromising the transcendent aspect of faith in a living God in order to suit a "waiting constituency" (see Chapter 1). On the other side of the coin, Christians have long been guilty of an if-it's-not-religious, it's-not-relevant approach. With a few brave exceptions there is still little evidence in most Christian programming that God might ever work outside the church or that his presence is ever felt without the approval and prior arrangement of a synod, evangelist, or church council. Bluck writes, "To do justice to the wholeness of the Gospel in the media requires that we see the way we communicate in its wholeness as well."[41]

Effective communication of the Word of God demands a skillfully analyzed process that has incorporated the two golden rules of communication, which affects the purpose of Christian visual media.

Golden Rule Number One is that the audience must identify with the content of the program, building on the Prophetic Imagination components of Theology Model One (see Appendix A, discussed in Chapter 5).

40. Robbins, *Texture*, 80.
41. Bluck, *Neutrality*, 29.

Golden Rule Number Two is that a suitable format must be chosen for the content, developed in the *Edutainment* Model Three (see Appendix C discussed in chapters 9 and 10).

To be effective, communication of the Bible's content necessitates, as does any other communicated message, that the audience identifies with the content. The *Bible-Content* component in Model Two (Appendix B) incorporates the whole Prophetic Theology as explicated in Model One (Appendix A). It is important to understand the message and relevant biblical concepts in the text, which the Prophetic Theology Model helps to discern and which the producer intends to communicate in terms of biblical worldview. Christian television or film may have as content a single biblical truth or moral topic—or a series of such—with which the audience must identify. These truths must first be analyzed in the context of the biblical reader. Theological research thus needs to be done particularly with regard to the meaning of the content in terms of the royal dominant consciousness of a particular biblical era, how the alternative consciousness is established through biblical *memory,* and where in the Bible there are examples. Then this content must be brought into context with the contemporary *Life*-Audience variable. This enables the essence of the content to become accessible, so that it may be effectively used in the moving-image message to transcend the audience toward an alternative worldview.

This is an extensive collaborative process with various "chains" and stages, as can be read about on www.jonahre.com under "Receiver and Channel" research. Finally, the *Lifestyle of the Believer* can be effectively portrayed as an alternative to the dominant consciousness.

Having been involved in the production process of Christian Network in South Africa (CNW) and then with an international Christian broadcasting network in the United States (the "700 Club"), I gained personal insight into these "chains," or stages of production and the relevance of content to the establishment of an alternative consciousness in a society that has been numbed by the royal dominant consciousness of our enculturation. Currently, the production of the movie *The Lamb*—scheduled for release in 2009, will be the first of a trilogy of films that will be made according to the process of biblical imagineering in storytelling, called a *Jonahre* film. The film series *Narnia*, with *The Lion, the Witch and the Wardrobe* (2005) and *Prince Caspian* (2008) completed, is also proving a success. As the theological imagination of C. S. Lewis is under the microscope in books such as *Planet Narnia* (2008), by Michael Ward, to reveal new insights into composing such narratives, the relevance of these arguments for biblically-based moving-image media messages that communicate truth in narrative is critical.

The *Life-Audience* variable incorporates the demographics of the modern day viewer of Christian television and film from which the enculturation of the society can be established. Each different age, language, gender, and denomination makes different demands on the biblical content communicated. Charis Productions is an example of a production company that has based its mission statement on impacting the lives of the dominant culture with the truth of God's Word. They state in "Our Mission" that "It is our hope that their (the movie-goers') experience will stay with them forever and have a lasting impact on their lives"[42] (insertion mine). *The Lamb,* the first movie that Charis Productions will produce, serves as an example of story content to which the theology of communication theory developed in the three-phase models in this thesis can be applied. Director Regardt van den Bergh states, "*The Lamb* will speak to the secular movie going audiences because it deals with real people, real tragedies and circumstances that happen to all of us at some stage in our lives."[43, 44] Charis Productions' mission explicitly states that they are not trying to make a one-hit movie but "to establish a mold for the development, financing, production, and distribution of films with similar content and vision, starting with the sequel to *The Lamb, Deo Volente,* the story of Saul of Tarsus."[45] In achieving this end, the production team has done thorough, documented market research on U.S. domestic markets, international markets, and religious markets, applying sound receiver research of target audiences in terms of content, phases of release, and analysis of the demand for biblically based films.[46]

42. "*The Lamb* Business Plan," www.jonahre.com.

43. Ibid., "The Vision."

44. Permission has been granted for this book to incorporate all aspects of the movie *The Lamb* for applying the theory and academic pursuits of this book in developing a biblically based genre for the moving-image media (see Appendix H).

45. "*The Lamb* Business Plan," www.jonahre.com.

46. Ibid., 12–13, 41–45, 24–25.

Lifestyle of the Believer Component

(See Appendix B)

Language, as identified by Brueggemann in *Prophetic Imagination* as well as by the media, plays an important role in forming subjects. "Speech or 'the ministry of language' is one of the few available resources for exile."[47] Althusser speaks of "interpellation" (interpellate means to question formally, as an executive officer, concerning an official action or policy or personal conduct) and "hailing" (to hail means to summon the attention of the hearer). This process of communication is important to understand when attempting to communicate an alternative consciousness effectively. Those who want to communicate with someone else first have to "hail" the other person. In order to react, the receivers must first accept that they are being spoken to. The receivers' recognition of the message flows from their decoding of the message (e.g., children, adults, men, women, or servants are spoken to in a particular manner). If the receivers react "cooperatively," they acknowledge the social position constructed by the hailing of the communicator. In a similar way, social consciousness and relationships can be established by different kinds of culture rhetoric (both verbal and non-verbal) within a text.

It is the work of Geertz (1983) by which this convergence of culture and communication takes place unobtrusively and independently in the fields of both communication studies and biblical studies. His work explores contexts that language evokes and creates to form social and cultural locations. Clifford Geertz's Balinese cockfight study gave him much insight, from which he drew important conclusions on culture and communication. This book also postulates that it is reasonable to consider formats of communication in our cultural locations as important aspects that will influence the impact of the message. As an anthropologist, Geertz became part of the culture of the Balinese people, living in Bali in order to understand the meaning of this elaborate cockfight ritual in terms of that culture's form of expression. The cockfights start in the late afternoon, before which time men enter the ring with their birds and seek out opponents. When two birds are paired, the opponent attaches steel spurs to each cock's feet when the men have left the ring. The two cocks are left in the ring, and in the words of Geertz, "a wing- beating, head-thrusting, leg-kicking explosion of animal fury so pure and absolute and in its own way

47. Brueggemann, *Cadences*, 23.

so beautiful as to almost abstract a Platonic concept of hate" is demonstrated.[48] The audience watches intently with silent applause in the form of various hand and body motions. As Geertz concluded, this enactment is an expressive form for the Balinese people, taking on a ritual practice by which this image, model, or metaphor, as it can be termed, is more than entertainment, rendering the people a reading of their own lifestyles and enacting status relationships.

Our moving-image media formats—television and film—are expressive forms of our lives as a cultural enactment, relaying status relationships of the dominant consciousness. Therefore, the need to consider the moving-image media as more than entertainment for those who ritualistically participate in the event is reinforced by the study of the cockfight. It seems to indicate that stories portrayed become the story the participants tell themselves, thereby affecting and co-creating a shared culture. This then affects the *Lifestyle of the Believer* in the text and the *Lifestyle of the Audience* participating in the story. It most decisively serves to identify the cultural topics that appear in the form of different cultural rhetoric. In the Christian moving-image context, this relates to the *Lifestyle of the Believer* in terms of the dominant and alternative consciousness. Robbins writes that in the text of the moving-image media, the "cultural locations in contrast to social location, concern the manner in which people present their propositions, reasons and arguments both to themselves and to other people. These topics separate people in terms of dominant culture, subculture, counterculture, contraculture and liminal culture"[49] (see Chapter 8).

First, the cultural locations are described in this model as a necessary part of the cultural context of the *Lifestyle of the Believer* in the script that must be analyzed and then formulated in terms of meaning. The next model addresses how these locations, through the moving-image media format, create and communicate meaning. In this Communication Model Two (see Appendix B), rhetoric functions as hermeneutic, which, together with the form and *style* of discourse in *Edutainment* Model Three (see Appendix C), determines locations of ideology. Thus, *Edutainment*

---

48. Quoted in Schultze, *Communicating*, 54.
49. Robbins, *Texture*, 86.

Model Three is an expansion of Communication Model Two, using the theory of "The Narrative Paradigm" for human communication.[50]

As the media influences the twenty-first century audience, the Christian must be aware of the powers of rhetoric as persuasion and their ability to co-create culture and establish cultural locations via both the message and medium. The architects of biblical moving-image media messages, on the other hand, need to understand and research these influences on culture and demographics. The business plan of *The Lamb* exemplifies such research, as documented for the biblically based film by Charis Productions. This is an important phase in any production that has a mission to communicate effectively, defining principled *Bible-Content* with a theologically formulated *intent* in a context that must consider the dominant worldview of the *Life-Audience* component as part of a postmodern culture.

CONCLUSION

The first golden rule of communication is that the audience must identify with the *content*. This implies a cultural dimension to the field of communication study as discussed in the current chapter. Therefore, having defined communication as creating and sharing or making common, the role of Christian moving-image communication thus is to fulfill the cultural mandate by creating and sharing a Christian culture on earth. The postmodern worldview is considered the dominant consciousness of the current world, into which a biblically based alternative consciousness needs to be communicated. This requires for communication to be loosed from its understanding as an isolated category of study and to become integrated with other disciplines that can advance its application. In this book the relationship between Christianity and culture and the relationship between communication and culture are proposed as the theoretical point of convergence for the disciplines of communication and theology. The work of anthropologist Clifford Geertz (1973) is discussed as used by Vernon Robbins (1996), Carey (1989), and other communication scholars, as well as by theologian Walter Brueggemann (1997), to poignantly show the overlaps in these disciplines and how they are complementary to the development of a theology of communication as the goal of this book. The critique, however, with the cultural approach to communica-

50. Fisher, *Human Communication*.

tion exclusively, as outlined in this chapter, is that it does not overcome the pitfalls in society of subjective relativism and naturalism. This thesis thus argues for a type of biblical anthropology, a view of communication that makes possible the constant truth of God's Word with constantly changing meaning as new circumstances arise in the culture. This is illustrated using Communication Model Two, as communication theory is related to Prophetic Theology Model One and practically made viable in the *Edutainment* Model Three (see appendices B, A, and C respectively).

CHAPTER 8

Toward a Message

The Socio-Cultural Context of the Book of Jonah

T HE SECOND MODEL AND the social and cultural texture of socio-rhetorical criticism distinguish the core elements of the *entertainment* component of Model Three. The meaning of the message of the Jonah narrative is analyzed in terms of its entertainment elements, using irony, hyperbole, comedy, and surprise, while educating the culture of that context in terms of biblical truth. Important social and cultural criteria in communicating truth-filled messages are highlighted. Storytelling techniques with Prophetic Imagination *intent* are appropriated for film and television messages that must entertain while educating the popular culture.

INTRODUCTION

In order to present the message to the audience of Jonah, the Theological Model One (see Appendix A) applies the intertexture analysis to the text so that the occurrence of certain core theologies, such as ascetical theology and creation theology and the use of satiric *irony*, can be recognized (see chapter 5). This book proposes finding common ground between the culture and context of the implied author of Jonah and today's readers of the book, as well as determining how such variables affect consciousness. To understand the challenges and theological difficulties of the original audience of the book would require dating the manuscript. It is in the circumstances of the first readers of Jonah and the contemporary audience of mass media ministry that there exists a parallel, as has been highlighted. In a postmodern, also referred to as post-Christian era, Christians today find their worldview to be in the same circumstance of exile as that of the Jews in late exilic or post-exilic Israel in the text of Jonah. Robbins's approach to exploring the intertexture of the book of Jonah can be applied to reach some insight on the audience of the book of Jonah in reconstructing the socio-cultural context.

Another advantage that closes the gap between ancient audiences of the Bible and modern viewers is that contemporary culture has become more aural/oral in nature. The moving-image media rely on storytelling and strong master images to reveal the message as entertaining and educational like never before. Today's film technologies can make mythological creatures like those of *Narnia* come alive from the imagination onto the screen. In Chapter 7 the contemporary cultural setting was explored from a communication theory perspective. This chapter, through inter-textural analysis as well as socio-cultural text analysis of the book of Jonah, presents background to the message that has implications for format and, combined with further exegetical efforts, points to theological and practical relevance in communicating the Word of God effectively among "exiles" in an aural/oral culture.

THE HISTORICAL CONTEXT OF THE BOOK OF JONAH

Dating the book of Jonah has always been an uncertain and inconclusive endeavor; however, even without definitive answers, intertextual study permits determination of the framework relevant for understanding the message in the historical context of the audience and for relating the biblical message to a modern setting.

The composition of the canon clearly indicates that the book of Jonah was written before the beginning of the second century BC. However, many features point to a late, even post-exilic, date rather than to a pre-exilic period like that of the historical Jonah in 2 Kings 14:25. Intertextually, then, it can be said that, apart from his being mentioned in 2 Kings 14:25 as a nationalistic court prophet who predicted the expansion of the frontiers of the Northern Kingdom during the reign of King Jeroboam II in the eighth century BC, nothing is known about Jonah. The figure of Jonah as a vehicle to criticize and impress the wrongs of an incorrect theology like religious nationalism in the original hearers' context was an ideal choice for the book's author. Jonah would serve as both the object and subject of the critique of the dominant culture's marginalized faith and fortress mentality. As already evidenced in the Judean audience of that period, the nationalistic sentiment of Jonah would have prejudiced the hearer against the prophet's words in favor of the words of God, to which the audience would give respectful credence. Thus, tension is established early on through the choice of characters and what they represent within the cultural context of the hearers. This important aspect should be at the forefront of an author's or producer's mind when composing a message designed not only to educate but also to entertain a contemporary audience. From such tensions and dissonance stem format styles such *irony*, satire, and even *comedy*, all which are present in the book of Jonah. The composition of Jonah reflects the integration of these natural sentiments and socio-cultural issues of the hearer into the plot of the narrative such that tension is created and a response is provoked. This tension as it relates to *irony* (parody) will be explored with regard to characterization in Chapter 10.

In regard to dating, Wolff writes, "How far removed the narrator is from the historical realities of the preexilic era is shown by the uninhibited way he combines historical names."[1] The author of Jonah makes Jonah speak his message to Nineveh, but the city only becomes significant to Israel when it became the capital of the Neo-Assyrian Empire in the seventh century and not in the eighth century when Jonah lived, during the reign of Jeroboam II, the historical person. Joppa is also an unusual choice for the author, as it was not a port well accessible for a Galilean in the eighth century, though it did become of interest to the cultural context of post-exilic Israel. Further, thematically, intertextual analysis highlights certain ideas and phraseology regarding a theology of repentance; Deuteronomistic and Jeremian perception was that the word of judgment would result in a conversionist response. Thus, this theology of repentance was being stretched boldly by the narrator to apply to Nineveh, a foreign people, in the book of Jonah. A correlation to elements in the Elijah narratives is also an indication that the author is familiar with these ideas and uses similar formulations that could very well have influenced him (e.g., the ravens, the broom tree, the cave, and the number of days involved). Jonah is most probably also picking up and echoing the book of Joel. The developing reflection on the proclamations of judgments to Gentiles in the book of Jonah is, however, still unknown in the book of Joel; therefore, a dating later than Joel can be assigned. This gives the indication, as Day

---

1. Wolff, *Obadiah*, 77.

suggests, that "Its message is directed at the proto-apocalyptic prophets (cf. Joel) who looked with longing for the coming of God's judgment on the hated foreign nations . . . and Yahweh's sparing of Nineveh is an object lesson that his mercy extends to the gentile nations too."[2] It would then be deduced that Jonah could not have been written before the middle of the fourth century, perhaps influenced to some degree by the universalistic theology in Psalm 145. The non-biblical sea motifs, such as the "great sea monster" and "being swallowed and vomited up" and the "lots cast by the seamen in the storm," are all likely inspired by Greek saga material that emerged after the campaigns of Alexander the Great in the fourth century. Even a later dating could be suggested by the book's Hellenistic mentality, close to the early Stoa, recognizable as a "narrated dogmatics." All these intertextual cues, however, point to a more likely dating in the early Hellenistic period than in the late Persian era, but no conclusive evidence to support even this dating can be found. We are thus provided with a general notion of a timeline to direct consideration of the cultural and thus spiritual issues that were present and of concern to the author, who most probably lived in the exilic and post-exilic period.

SPECIFIC SOCIAL TOPICS: AN AUDIENCE IN EXILE

In order to understand the elements which the author chose to construct the narrative of Jonah, the specific social topics of the political structure of exilic and post-exilic Jewry must be explored. When Judah was taken into exile in 586 BC some Israelites were left behind. Those who remained viewed those taken into exile as the guilty ones who were being punished, while regarding themselves as the *righteous remnant* of which the prophets had spoken. This remnant was awaiting the re-establishment of the Davidic dynasty from amongst themselves in order again to rule from Damascus to the Dead Sea. Professor Jacques R. Kriel explains, "They were equally understandably upset when Ezra and Nehemiah pitched up and started acting as if the prophetic promises were applicable to them."[3]

Similarly, there was a *nationalistic group* in exile in Babylon who considered the Babylonian exile to be a temporary punishment from God. The Davidic dynasty would again be established and, in Kriel's words, "Israel would again rule the nations and revenge herself on her

2. Day, "Problems," 47.

3. Kriel, "Jonah," 15.

enemies and would become a super-power that would rise above all her oppressors."[4]

However, a second exilic group, a strong force to which the major exilic prophets belonged, developed the most profound insight into the nature of God and humankind that the world has ever known. As Brueggemann observes, "Exile evoked the most brilliant literature and the most daring theological articulation in the Old Testament."[5] Different from the other groups' ideologies regarding what the exile meant for this minority group, this second group believed that "The exile did not mean that God's plan had failed, but actually created a unique opportunity to witness to God's *power, love,* and *mercy.* Even in exile they could be a light to the nations so that his *salvation* may reach the ends of the earth (Isaiah 49:6)"[6] (italics mine).

In the books written during the exile and for the exiles, it becomes evident that the exilic audience suffered tremendously and that certain theological themes such as hope for the destitute in an estranged land amidst difficult circumstances became prominent. In Lamentations 3 for example, the poet reveals the major foundation for his hope, as well as his method for resolving the pain and sorrow he feels in exilic circumstances. It is not the particular specific covenant traditions of Israel but the *merciful character of God* that the poet recalls and that comforts him: "Yahweh's mercies never come to an end, and his pity is never exhausted" (v. 22). This can be compared to the often-used cultic formula that appears also in Jonah: "Yahweh, Yahweh, a God merciful and gracious, slow to anger and abounding in steadfast love and faithfulness" (Exod 34:6; Num 14:18; Neh 9:17,31; Ps 86:15; 103:8; 145:8; Jer 32:18; Joel 2:13; Jonah 4:2). Klein writes of the poet, "In his hope he waits on God and submits to suffering, trusting that God always replaces affliction with mercy or at least that it is part of his sovereign freedom to do so."[7] The crying of the paradigmatic lament in Lamentations (3:1–39) is, however, not enough; it must be followed by self-examination and sincere repentance (vv. 40–41), to which the people respond in v. 42 by confessing their sins. This is also a theological pattern of the message in the book of Jonah and serves as a poignant example for

4. Ibid.

5. Brueggemann, *Cadences*, 3.

6. Ibid.

7. Klein, *Israel*, 16.

the moving-image media and biblically based communication. Despite seeing God's merciful character displayed through repeated deliverance of the Ninevites, the sailors, and himself, through the vehicle of the fish, Jonah offers a lament to God in poetic format in Chapter 4, which must be followed by self-examination and ultimately repentance, as God stands ready to forgive. This is the message implicit in the storied form that is didactic as it entertains with the purpose of inviting a response from Israel in the context of the original hearers. It serves as an example of the creative potential of stories that the moving-image media can and must unlock, as the essence of biblically based Prophetic Imagination messages. A conversionist response (see Robbins's categories in Chapter 7) inviting self-examination and ultimately repentance is the result.

Jonah also parallels the theological concerns of Second Isaiah (also dated as an exilic writing), outlined in a series of disputations showing and refuting mistaken notions of God. The message emphasizes God's sovereignty and ability to save in order to permit a joyful acceptance of his announced *salvation*. In Isaiah 40:12–17, God is portrayed as a giant (a superman figure) for whom *creation* was mere child's play. God's stature and wisdom is above all great, and all else—including Israel's enemies—is nothing in comparison. This decidedly disputed any notions Israel might have had that their God was not able to deliver them. In Jonah this same theme is emphasized in an entertaining manner through hyperbole, when God creates a massive storm and sends a giant fish to deliver Jonah safely to land, thus giving him a second chance to respond to God's call. This scene in the belly of the sea creature and Jonah's deliverance is referred to by Jesus in Matthew in a similar message to the Jews, eliciting a joyful acceptance of God's prophetically announced salvation.

Isaiah 40:18–26 answers the question of who can be compared to God. The conclusion is that God is sovereign. In contrast to the astral deities of Babylon, Yahweh is pointed to as the only sovereign God who has displayed his sovereignty and *power* in *creating* also the stars and assigning them their proper function.

Finally, Isaiah 40:27–31 disputes the complaint that God disregarded them and was not willing to deliver them. The following four reasons are given for such an objection:

- Yahweh is everlasting now, then, and forever.

- As *Creator* of the universe, his power is without limits.

- *Sovereign* over time and space, God never grows weary.
- God's all-knowing and all-understanding nature affirms that he will act when the time is ripe to *deliver* his people.

In Jonah, these disputations are addressed in the same way as in Isaiah's appeal to Yahweh's *creative* power and dominion over all, leaving no question that he is willing and *able to save* his people. "Nevertheless," Klein writes, "his decision to deliver Israel via the pagan Cyrus (41:2–3:25) evoked indignant reactions in Second Isaiah's audience."[8] Jonah, having experienced God's Sovereignty over his creation in the storm, in the fish, and then demonstratively with the plant and worm in Chapter 4, was given a display of God's creative power similar to that of the Israelites in Second Isaiah. However, in the midst of the exile, Israel, in Second Isaiah, met the disputations with the same disdain Jonah did when God chose to deliver the Ninevites. God's ability and willingness to *deliver, forgive,* and *show grace* is the message of hope in both these passages. This is a fitting message for the exilic and post-exilic audiences, who hopelessly questioned God's presence and sovereign purposes for them. The storyteller in Jonah used the subject matter that was immediately evident within the social and cultural setting to entertain the audience through imaginative elements of storytelling, thereby delivering the same message as Isaiah did via a poetic format to an audience struggling with God's presence among foreign gods. This is a work of Prophetic Imagination; through these socio-cultural imaginative constructs of the book of Jonah, the audience of Jonah, like ourselves, "are able to make breakthroughs and exercise criticism against thought patterns which rule our own thinking."[9]

SPECIFIC SOCIAL TOPICS

Having considered the audience in exile and discerned corresponding specific social and cultural topics and concerns of those in exile through theological parallels in messages of Lamentations and Second Isaiah, the response of the audience in exile is demonstrated to create a kind of culture. Robbins describes the process: "In the terms of an anthropologist like Clifford Geertz, each kind of response creates a kind of culture that gives meanings, values, traditions, convictions, rituals, beliefs, and actions

8. Klein, *Israel*, 105.
9. Van Heerden, "Imagination," 357.

to people."[10] For this book, therefore, it is important to identify the social rhetoric in these comparable texts, which were likely written to exilic or post-exilic audiences, to understand the kinds of social responses that they elicit. These in turn create established meanings, and as chapters 7 and 10 of this book identify, there is strong theory that supports the link between communication and the creation of culture. Chapter 7 lists the seven types of responses that Robbins outlines.[11] How these apply to the text of Jonah is relevant to establishing the response and culture of those in exile that the author is interested in creating.

The author of Jonah is portraying a response within the text that becomes a form of rhetoric, through which he wants to elicit a seemingly different response from the audience. Jonah, in conversation and in reacting to Yahweh, responds in an *introversionist* manner, in terms of Robbins's categorization. This response "views the world as irredeemably evil and considers salvation to be attainable by . . . withdrawal from it."[12] As Jonah is commanded to go to Nineveh—the archenemy of Israel as part of the Assyrian empire and the epitome of evil in that day—he responds in a typical *introversionist* way, as the audience of that day would possibly have done or expected of him. Thus, he tries to avoid his call and runs from God. His avoidance of going to or wanting to associate with this evil nation is a response that on the surface was easily identifiable for the typical Israelite, who considered Gentile nations to be irredeemably evil.

However, in this response lies the *irony,* the criticism, and the surprise all wrapped up in one. The author wants to reveal the problem with the dominant culture's theology and ideology and to invite a different response from the audience. The nature of Jonah's character is revealed when in the final chapter of the narrative his lament towards God is that he knew God would be merciful to the lost who repent—as Nineveh did. He was angry with God for not judging these Gentile sinners, who according to his social, cultural, and theological persuasions are irredeemably evil and must be punished. It is precisely these incongruencies in Jonah's character, as he moves from a typical to a round character, that are displayed in the final rhetoric between Jonah and God, where the miracle of the plant and worm are used as didactic images and symbols by God

10. Robbins, *Texture*, 72.

11. Ibid., 72–74.

12. Ibid., 73.

(and the author). Jonah wants comfort and shade from God and is miserable when the worm that God sends eats the tree that provided shade.

Through the words God speaks, the author challenges Jonah's conceptions of God and Jonah's social, cultural, and theological response to his circumstances. The author wishes to illicit a *conversionist* response from the audience, however, to create a new type of culture using the character of Jonah to expose the essence of the dominant theological issues. The *conversionist* response is, as Robbins writes, "that the world is corrupt because people are corrupt. If people can be changed, the world will be changed. Salvation is considered to be available not through objective agencies but only by a profound and supernaturally wrought transformation of the self. The world itself will not change, but the presence of a new subjective orientation to it will itself be salvation."[13] This is what the author of the book of Jonah wishes to accomplish with the stubborn people of Israel.

A narrative that entertains, while like the book of Jonah, inviting self-examination and ultimately repentance, must confront the audience with the God who awaits his creation's recognition of his sovereign salvation, power, mercy, love, and readiness to forgive. In the socio-cultural texture of exilic or post-exilic circumstances, Kriel writes that the message of Jonah is "the story of a very human man with all his prejudices and his God; the story of his response to a demand for change."[14] This ultimately illuminates the audience's response to the world in light of the nature of God.

FINAL CULTURAL TOPICS

By reflecting on the dominant culture in his rhetoric, the intent of the author of the book of Jonah is, in Robbins's words, to bring to light "the manner in which people (in this instance Israel) present their propositions, reasons, and arguments both to themselves and to other people"[15] (insertion mine). The author wants to expose to public contempt the negative dominant culture and theological thinking and to introduce a counterculture or alternative theological thinking. Robbins adds:

13. Ibid., 72.
14. Kriel, "Jonah," 16.
15. Robbins, *Texture*, 86.

> *Dominant culture rhetoric* presents system of attitudes, values, dis-
> positions, and norms that the speaker either presupposes or asserts
> are supported by social structures vested with power to impose
> its goals on people in a significantly broad territorial region. . . .
> *Alternative culture rhetoric* rejects *explicit* and *mutable* character-
> istics of the dominant or subculture rhetoric to which it responds
> . . . a culturally heretical rhetoric that evokes "a new future."[16]

It is clear from the contents of the book of Jonah that the dominant
culture in Israel reflects a specific theological outlook, namely that God
is seated in Jerusalem (the temple), and that he is Israel's God, whom
they are not willing to share with pagan nations. In response to this theological view, the rhetoric of the author of the book of Jonah propagates,
as Robbins describes it, "'a new future,' not an alien rhetoric that evokes
the preservation of an 'old culture.'"[17] The author wants to introduce an
alternative and hopes that the dominant society will open their eyes to see
that Yahweh is a universal God who seeks the conversion of all people on
earth. His undertone is that of "*hope* of voluntary reform by the dominant
society in accord with a different model of 'the good life.'"[18] While Israel
is convinced that their theological thinking is the only correct and good
model, the author of the book of Jonah wants to persuade them of a different good model.

In this book, Brueggemann's Prophetic Imagination classification of
dominant and alternative consciousnesses, described in chapters 2 and
5, correlates with these topics in a theological context and with regard to
Christian moving-image media messages. These topics are integrated to
form the social and cultural texture and considerations of the production
in the Communication Model Two (see Appendix B and Chapter 7).

THE CONTEMPORARY AUDIENCE AND THE COMMUNICATION MODEL TWO

(See Appendix B)

The starting point for most cultural studies of communication is illuminated by the following words of Geertz: "Believing with Max Weber,
that man is an animal suspended in webs of significance he himself has

---

16. Ibid., 86–87.

17. Ibid., 87.

18. Ibid.

spun, I take culture to be these webs, and the analysis of it to be therefore not an experimental science in search of law, but an interpretive one in search of meaning."[19] Therefore, the cultural science of communication views human behavior, and in effect human action, similarly to the way in which Robbins views the biblical text. The key to translating meaning from the biblical text to the cultural science of communication (that affects the behavior of humans) lies in realizing that both are texts, and the task is to construct a reading of these texts and interpret the interpretations. As Carey so insightfully writes about Geertz's use of the text as a metaphor for human action, "The metaphor emphasizes that the task of the cultural scientist is closer to that of a literary critic or a scriptural scholar."[20] This emphasizes the notion that expressive art forms such as contemporary film and television media are comparable to that of biblical narratives such as Jonah in ancient cultures. This is true precisely because, as Peterson writes, "Hearing is once again the primary means of communication. For long centuries, learning was dominated by the printed word; and the characteristic experience with the word was of something seen, not heard. But electronic media dominate the communications scene today."[21] These electronic media are primarily oral/aural again, with little knowledge gained from literature. The prevalence of hearing and seeing the words spoken through the visual aspect of the moving-image media means stories are absorbed, told visually around the television and film. This situation is essentially how communications took place in oral/aural cultures when stories were told around campfires or meals as the biblical material was in formation. Peterson celebrates this, saying, "That means that contemporary humanity is closer in terms of communications experience to the first century than to the nineteenth. And that is good news for the Christian communicator who is now able to share a milieu with biblical humanity, which is important in discovering and interpreting the biblical message."[22]

As authors seek to alter and challenge the dominant thought patterns and behavior of listeners, they use oral/aural and literary techniques to, through didactic entertainment, provide an alternative consciousness in

19. Geertz, *Interpretation*, 5, quoted in Carey, *Communication*, 56.

20. Carey, *Communication*, 60.

21. Peterson, *Subversive*, 91.

22. Ibid., 91.

the minds and actions of the hearer. The first model (see Appendix A) uses the inner textures and intertextures of Robbins to extract meaning exegetically so that Truth is communicated. Next, as this chapter demonstrates, the second model (see Appendix B) adds the socio-cultural textures of Robbins and the biblically specific "cultural" approach of Brueggemann to translate the main topics of concern for the author of the biblical text as they relate to the contemporary *Life* context *of the audience*. Keep in mind that the three components identified in the biblical text—namely *Bible, Life,* and *Lifestyle of the Believer* of the first model—will serve as golden threads to connect the models and will be used to exemplify the elements of the Prophetic Imagination purpose and message in narrative format. The three components will be evident throughout the book as the socio-rhetorical methodology is applied through the various textures of texts (i.e. written and moving-image texts).

The *Life–Audience* component, described by Brueggemann as the "*Power*" component of the dominant consciousness of the culture behind the text,[23] is demonstrated by Jonah's worldview and likely that of scattered Israel during and after the exile, who comprised the primary audience of the text. The secondary audience is those readers who have, subsequent to the writing of the book, read or heard the story as unbelievers, constituting an integral part of the secular culture of their day. The *Bible–Content* component in the model, also termed "*Providence,*"[24] relates to the way the contents of the narrative itself tell that God mobilizes people and creation to get the character's (Jonah's) attention as relevant to the primary audience. The inclusion of the sailors' and Nineveh's repentance serves to address the universalistic salvation and mercy of God, evangelistically, to the secondary Gentile audience and, prophetically, to inform both Jews and Gentiles of what is to come precisely because of the nature of God. The "*Personality*"[25] or *Lifestyle of the Believer* component is elicited through the literary *style* of *irony*, surprise, and humor (see also chapters 10 and 11). This stylistic functioning of the book of Jonah culminates in the final chapter of Jonah, when God in dialogue with Jonah attempts to illuminate the personality of Jonah and to elicit changes in it. The ascetical theology lesson in Chapter 4 entertains while,

---

23. Brueggemann, *Power*, 13.

24. Ibid., 15.

25. Ibid., 16.

via an open-ended conclusion, didactically providing hope for Jonah and the Gentile of a true homecoming and right relationship with God by correcting their misconceptions of God. Thus, when communicating truth to the believer as the primary audience, in the characterization of Jonah and construction of the narrative, a metaphor of "exilic circumstance" according to Brueggemann's Prophetic Imagination can be recognized. Jonah's actions reveal the influence of *power* of the Jewish religious empire on his understanding and conduct, which is contrary to God's will and direction. The book of Jonah exemplifies the dominant consciousness of the audience that the message addresses and seeks to demonstrate an alternative consciousness by using storytelling techniques, for example, *irony*, surprise, hyperbole, and misdirection (see also Chapter 10). The book of Jonah thus:

> Wants to tell us that Israel had learnt that God is a God of compassion and mercy and forgiveness who can and wants to forgive and transform even a repentant Nineveh. It tell us that fun and laughter are legitimate responses to the presence of God, rather than serious debates and solemn sermons—as Chesterton remarked "we have sinned and grown old and our God is younger than we." But it also wants to tell us something about ourselves and our response to the world in the light of the nature of God. It is the story of a very human man with all his prejudices and his God: the story of his response to a demand for change.[26]

A right relationship with God requires the *Lifestyle of the Believer* and not just obedient action. In the dialogue in the last chapter God affirms his grace and mercy to Jonah in forgiving all. However, the matter of Jonah's heart, and thus the authenticity of the *Lifestyle of the Believer*, is left as a final challenge to all who read the book.

The book of Jonah addresses two audiences. The primary audience includes those believers belonging to Israel, who draw upon their righteous and nationalistic theology in an attempt to keep God exclusive and to understand him in a narrow theological, social and cultural context. The secondary audience is that of the Gentile and unbeliever, to whom the character of God as merciful and forgiving must be communicated evangelistically. God is ready to embrace those who have sinned, no matter to what extent, when they are repentant and turn from their wicked ways to embrace him as their God. The theme of universalism is emphasized to

26. Kriel, "Jonah," 17–18.

communicate God's salvation for all, even those who enforce the exilic circumstance of the believer.

In contemporary moving-image media ministry messages, these same two audiences are relevant. On the one hand, the believer in exile, as Brueggemann metaphorically indicates, must be addressed and warned against becoming complacent and self-centered and regarding Christianity as exclusive amongst those who are like-minded, which can lead to its own theological pitfalls. On the other hand, any popular media message must also address the unbeliever with the good news of an opportunity to be in relationship with the God of truth who has revealed a comprehensive framework for right living. The two-prong approach in media messaging requires the evangelical thrust of the Great Commission to be presented, as in Jonah, so that the cultural stereotypes of what God means to those on the outside are used in terms of social and cultural norms. Elements such as surprise and an unexpected twist in characterization or open-ended invitation at the conclusion of the narrative are techniques that can entertainingly provide new insights into stereotypes of both primary and secondary audiences. The message becomes accessible to both these audiences in a familiar social and cultural milieu, allowing the Holy Spirit to work in their lives to open up their hearts to God's voice.

CONCLUSION

When the book of Jonah is examined in this chapter in terms of its socio-cultural context, it becomes evident in terms of the exilic and post-exilic circumstance that the author is communicating an alternative consciousness. This is exemplified by identification of the exclusive religious milieu of the Jewish community of that time. Also, the artistic rendering through story and plot of certain characteristics of the characters, Jonah and God, direct the audience's attention to the development of point of view by the author. The connection between form and content and background becomes apparent as the author of Jonah uses social and cultural topics to educate, using entertaining styles like surprise, *irony,* and parody. The insight of Marshal McLuhan that "the medium is the message" is clearly illustrated by the above analysis, which brings together *style* and message as introduced by the author of the book of Jonah. Form, content, and a socio-cultural background in a medium are used effectively to penetrate the consciousness of the audience in a dramatic, gripping manner to reveal an alternative to the dominant consciousness. Final cultural topics highlight the different group identification and what is clearly the dominant rhetoric in the popular culture. While Israel is convinced that their theological thinking as dominant rhetoric is the only correct and good model, the author of the book of Jonah wants to persuade them of a different good model as an alternative rhetoric.

In the Communication Model Two this artistic rendering of the author incorporating the dynamic socio-cultural environment fits well with current cultural communication theory, which takes as pivotal criteria the audience in their context identifying with the message. The study of the biblical author of the book of Jonah in the current chapter clearly shows the focus of the storyteller to relate content with audience in an appropriate form to communicate an alternative rhetoric of a Prophetic Imagination. This will be explored from both a communication and a theological perspective in terms of the genre that communicates the meaning of biblical moving-image messages in the following chapters.

CHAPTER 9

Edutainment

Ideological and Sacred Elements in the Book of Jonah

INTRODUCTION

JONAH IS ANALYZED USING the ideological and sacred textures of socio-rhetorical criticism to formulate the *edutainment* variable of Model Three. Examples of Prophetic Imagination in modern television programming and film narratives are examined. *Edutainment* is shown to be the element that identifies the redemptive theological qualities practically in these popular stories. This indicates a new form that defines a distinctive quality for biblical moving picture formats.

In Chapter 11 *Jonahre* will be introduced as the term to describe the genre that communicates with a Prophetic Imagination intent, a form of *edutainment* as *content,* and an ironic *style.* The current chapter will focus on the need for a specified form and define the term *"edutainment."*

IDEOLOGICAL TEXTURE IN JONAH

By understanding ideologies that are part of the author's framework, insight is provided into the way that symbols, master images, and imagination are employed in the narrative to become effective communication that accomplishes the purposes of a Prophetic Imagination narrative.

As identified in Chapter 8 via mention of specific social categories, the setting of Jonah most likely found the Jews in exile or post-exilic circumstance. They belonged to two similar groups: those who were left behind in Israel (who believed they were the righteous remnant) and those in exile (a nationalistic group who awaited their return to Israel). As God's

121

chosen people, both believed he would in his sovereignty usher in and establish the Davidic dynasty and punish their enemies. These ideologies were in contrast to a third group in exile who believed that God's salvation could reach the ends of the earth and who felt that they were uniquely situated to witness God's power, mercy, and love to their enemies.[1]

It is against these ideological backgrounds that the author of the book of Jonah communicates this story. This was the ideology of a historic tradition that the author displays in the formulation of a narrative with the *intent* to ideologically entertain. Through the sacred texture of the narrative, he educates through symbols to incite holy transformation of the Israelite expectations, which stemmed from an exclusivist, nationalistic, and self-centered understanding of God. In this sphere of the author's ideological social and cultural location, he constructs a narrative in which the ideology "represents the points where power impacts upon certain utterances and inscribes itself tacitly within them."[2] The competing ideologies of the author and the audience are powerfully at work to affect the belief systems and points of view of the reader through various narrative techniques. The author of Jonah, for example, uses the prophetic call narrative ironically as parody. The institutionalized stereotypical religious clique of which prophets were part is criticized through, in Robbins's terms, a "system of differentiates."[3]

As Jonah's character represents the dominant consciousness of the religious believer and prophet in terms of Israel's dominant ideology, the misdirection and surprise elements in the narrative—with regard to all that is expected from a prophet like Jonah—serve to expose the self-serving ideology of certain dominant Israelite beliefs. It also invites the audience to adopt an alternative consciousness, to which end the author *imagineered* the narrative. It is also Nineveh, the epitome of evil in terms of Israel's ideology, and the pagan sailors' worship of other deities that set up the exposition of and contrast to the "empire," the ideological sphere of Jonah. These ideologies involve a tension and conflict for what they represent as typified master images.

It is the open-ended resolution in Jonah Chapter 4, where God wrestles with Jonah's ideology, and where surprising twists in characterization

---

1. Kriel, "Jonah," 15.

2. Eagleton, *Ideology*, 223, quoted in Robbins, *Texture*, 110.

3. Robbins, *Texture*, 113.

are introduced, that provides opportunity for the transformation of the ideology of altruistic power represented by Jonah and his culture. If this ideological shift through the dramatic portrayal of Jonah can inspire symbolic identity, the audience is called to choice and action. Achievement of the author's *intent*—to make available the alternative of political salvation to his audience—could usher in the fulfillment, in spite of loss of political power, as Kriel describes:

> Israel becomes the suffering servant of her God, suffering so that the whole world would learn that God is merciful, filled with compassion, that he forgives, that he can disperse hatred and turn enemies into brothers, that he desires the salvation not only of Israel, but of all people that God can deliver and save from even the most degrading of circumstances.[4]

The *intent* and message of the book of Jonah can thus be seen as a Prophetic Imagination proclaiming God's justice, which stands in service of his love for his entire creation. This is in contrast to the vengeful theology of God's judgment for Israel's enemies as propagated by the elite. This was an alternative that was not popular but the truth of a reality God intended for humankind to know. These shifts and corrections in our empire-dominated realities are a necessary part of the renewal of culture, a mandate in which narratives must challenge the ideologies of the world via God's revelation in the Bible as the source of all truth and a comprehensive framework for all of life. This is transferable and relevant today in many milieus, as Colson and Pearcey assert in their book "How Now Shall We Live" (1999), which exhorts believers to equip themselves to present Christianity as an alternative consciousness and worldview, a life system to transform and build a new Christian culture. That is the mandate, challenge, and prophetic call for which the form of *edutainment* is proposed. As biblically based vehicles of truth, the moving-image media's *edutainment* narratives must become effective agents of God's common grace by communicating the alternative consciousness of the kingdom of God, that of Christians living *the Lifestyle of the Believer*.

SACRED TEXTURE IN JONAH: THEOLOGY

As the two components of *Bible* and *Life* are funneled into the *Lifestyle of the Believer* component and the sacred texture of the text is analyzed in

4. Kriel, "Jonah," 15–16.

the narrative of Jonah, the *edutainment* format is recognized and incorporated in Model Three (see Appendix C). It is this *edutainment* format as the component integrated in the third model that establishes the sacred texture. When evidenced in the portrayal in the moving-image media narrative, this *edutainment* format challenges the power of secular empires. Robbins writes that to talk of the sacred is to talk at once of "theology . . . the nature of God, and God's action and revelation,"[5] and "the relation of human life to the divine in the text."[6]

The format in which the sacred can be incorporated in moving-image media narratives as a powerful transformative presence can be found in the format of *edutainment* exemplified in the biblical narrative of Jonah. These *sacred elements of life* translate the transcendental as truth and reality through the *edutainment* format via an imagination paradigm, namely *the presence of Holiness.* Peterson describes the relationship between holiness and life: "Holiness is the most attractive quality, the most intense experience we ever get of sheer *life*—authentic, firsthand living, not life looked at or enjoyed from a distance. We find ourselves in on the operations of God himself."[7]

As Isaiah writes of the Holy in Isaiah 6, the following elements depict how God's holiness is experienced and transforms an individual. In each case, this is how such experience and transformation took place in the narrative of Jonah and how they still take place in the stories of God's presence in our lives:

- *Tragedy*—abandonment of self-sufficiency
- *Comedy*—experience of mercy and forgiveness
- *Command-content*
- *Fairy Tale*—an invitation to respond in faith and obedience

All of these elements play out in the *context of a living God.*

Through the moving-image media form of *edutainment,* the formation of these elements informs a *counterscript* containing an alternative consciousness that becomes the life-giving narrative of the kingdom, inviting an audience to a *countercontext* and can usher in a *counterlife* of holiness. These elements will now be implemented to discuss how God is

5. Robbins, *Texture*, 120.

6. Ibid., 123.

7. Peterson, *Subversive*, 73.

experienced and the lives and the culture of people are transformed in the book of Jonah, while applying it to moving-image media.

THE TRAGEDY

Abandoning Self-Sufficiency

The tragedy of the experience in which life is played out without the biblical character and purposes of God as central truth is the deficit of *Life*. This is the acceptance of a narrative that is destructive and has the consequence of death. Jonah's life as a prophet of God, a holy person, attempting to escape the word of God and his purposes, is such a narrative. He is thrown into despair, wishing for death in his attempt to avoid the presence of God. The Jewish concept of death is more than a physical death. A Fretheim expresses it, "The greater the distress in which a person finds himself the more the reality of death that person experiences. . . . Any form of weakness or misery suffered in life is considered to be the intrusion of death into the sphere of life."[8] The images and language used to show the depths of Jonah's distress (e.g., Sheol) indicate how death was more characteristic of him than life.

The Bible is filled with narratives of people turning to the powers that govern them and to their own self-sufficiency for comfort and security. These persons abandon a worldview of faith in God's sovereignty for what seems plausible to man with his finite perceptions, abilities, and understanding. The early Hebrews, for example, wanted to settle on the narrative of Pharaoh's enslavement; many Israelites in Babylon in 587 BC accepted the narrative of exile imposed by the Persian rulers; today Christians and non-believers are uncritically assimilated into the life portrayed by selective dissemination of images and information in the godless dominant narratives of the moving-image media. The popular news media, for example, while covering daily the escalating death toll in the war on terrorism, is quiet about the escalating number of Christians who are being martyred at a yearly rate that exceeds the cumulative number for the entire 2000 years since the birth of Christ. This is the tragedy—the absence of God which grows more overt each passing day—as the church is no longer part of the "intellectual-ideational hegemony of the culture."[9]

---

8. Fretheim, *Message*, 100.

9. Brueggemann, *Cadences*, 40.

In narrative, whether in the Bible, film, television, or literature, the unleashing of the power of God through the message is that the artists, like the prophets of old, are, as Buechner writes, "willing to appall and bless us with the tragic word—to speak out of the darkness."[10] In moving-image narrative messages the essence of the medium to display the tragic vision of truth is the beginning of the plot.

In the story of Jonah, God's glory and holiness are revealed and intensely experienced only when the messenger is willing to proclaim the tragedy to befall the depravity of Nineveh. The tragedy also befalls Jonah as individual when he sinfully disobeys God and wishes for death by asking to be thrown into the depths of the raging storm and again in Chapter 4 when not his will but God's is done.

In Herman Melville's *Moby Dick*, in which Father Mapple delivers a sermon on Jonah that, according to Buechner, "charges all preachers not to shrink from facing for themselves and proclaiming the dark side of truth,"[11] the necessity of this act of portraying the tragedy is recognized. Poignantly, when tragedy is brought into juxtaposition with the acts of a holy God, the doors of the soul are opened to the sacred, as a transcendental reality is made available and can be experienced. Only in the context of the living God and in comparison to the Holy can the abolition of self-sufficiency, inadequacy, unworthiness, and sin be accepted as the beginning of the narrative. This, then, becomes, as in the individual, the entrance to the transformative power of the sacred. The first element in the *edutainment* format of the genre, *Life*, is therefore the education of the viewer through narrative to portray the dark side of truth and life in terms of the tragedy caused by cultural assimilation (see Appendix C). Peterson describes the need for exposure to the sacred: "It is very easy to suppose we are doing just fine with our lives, thank you, if we can only insulate ourselves against the Holy, and live in comparison with our surroundings."[12]

10. Buechner, *Telling*, 47.

11. Ibid., 45.

12. Peterson, *Subversive*, 74.

THE COMEDY

Experience of Mercy and Forgiveness

The tragic is the inevitable result of our fallen world, while the comic is the unforeseeable intervention of God to provide miraculously and redeem. *Comedy* is the assurance that after the representation of catastrophe—of failed economic certitude, bewilderment about sexuality, and loss of security (as experienced worldwide post-9/11)—God is present as the one who is faithful to his covenant with his people. This is only possible by faith, as it speaks beyond perceived circumstance in order to "reconstruct, replace and redraw the threatened paradigm of meaning."[13] This task of assurance of mercy and forgiveness is made available through doxology and promise and finds itself manifest in gospel *testimony*. The communication to exiles must involve the capacity of God to bestow a newness that creates hope in and for the future, a reflection of the power of *God's* promise. In the narrative of Jonah, it is the miraculous that is used to assure the audience of the grace of God's holy presence as demonstrated through his power and might in service of his love for his creation. It is in the place of hopelessness and the desire to escape God and his call that Jonah gets thrown into the raging storm to die. Here God's miraculous actions become a vehicle for his mercy and forgiveness. The storm ceases as testimony to the pagan sailors, and the fish is sent by God to swallow Jonah.

This newness is only credible in light of the context of reality in which the storyteller has created Yahweh as a normal and indispensable character. The Enlightenment has made this an intellectual problem for the postmodern society, which does not believe that newness can come from without into the fixed, defined empirical world of rationalism. The rationalism of our age has caused many to miss the meaning of Jonah's rich text, which can provide a strong metaphoric "homecoming for the exile," as well as master images to assure of God's presence in all of life. By refusing to be entertained by the comedy of God's grace and mercy, the empirically reasoning person seeks only after evidence of a man remaining alive in the belly of a fish.

The "Babylonian gods" of our day, to which the character of Jonah's passive stubbornness speaks, command exile and are strongly contrasted to the active, attentive, true God who makes available newness through his mighty, holy presence. God wrestles (Chapter 4) with Jonah's

---

13. Mintz, *Hurban*, 2, quoted in Brueggemann, *Cadences*, 15.

assumptions about his actions and character. This communicates *comically* and *entertainingly* the possibility of a return home for the exiled believer, not because he or she deserves it but because God's mercy and forgiving character wills a relationship with his created.

The contemporary situation of privilege and satiation has made such dangerous promise and hope of an intervening God as contained in the narrative of Jonah an alien category. In fact, what is most wanted is a guarantee of the *status quo* and the preferred present tense of the empire that is empirically "real." However, producers of a Prophetic Imagination message for the moving-image media will work, in Brueggemann's words, "primarily not from visible hints and hunches precisely because hope is 'the conviction of things not seen,' a conviction rooted in the trusted character of God."[14] The *edutainment* format of the genre thus entertains by the comedy that the *Bible* is the "good tiding" (the term meaning gospel, first used in Isaiah 52:7 to bid the exiles home). The gospel truth proclaims, "Blessed is he who is not offended that no man receives what he deserves but vastly more. Blessed is he who gets that joke, who sees that miracle."[15] The truth that any biblically based moving-image media message should proclaim and make available artistically is a comedy of promise, for God did not choose to condemn us but to forgive our sin. This marvelous love, faith, and hope can be communicated as exemplified by the poet of Deutero-Isaiah, who offers utterances as a vehicle of poetic imagination that provides the Messenger within the poem. The *poetic imagination* in the biblical narrative media message is purposed by the Prophetic Imagination *intent* to provide storied, symbolic master images of comic proportions that can, as they communicate truth in life contexts, "change verdicts, change narratives and so enact an alternative existence."[16]

COMMAND-CONTENT

These messages of an alternative existence, of gospel testimony provided in and through the presentation of truth as *tragedy* and *comedy* seek not only to encourage exiles to take hold of the new world available to them but also to urge them to bear *testimony* as witnesses of the truth. A witness in a court of law always falls short of proof. He or she only hopes to

14. Brueggemann, *Cadences*, 23.

15. Buechner, *Telling*, 69.

16. Brueggemann, *Cadences*, 47.

provide a coherent, carefully framed narrative that convinces the court that this is a credible account of how the world is. As Brueggemann succinctly states, "I shall argue that in the end, most generally, all of the Bible is testimony of a new construal of reality, which lives outside imperial rationality and which cannot and does not appeal either to historical data or consensus metaphysics or answers in the back of the book."[17] This witness to evidence in the life of the believer summoned to provide *testimony* to an alternative account of reality is the work of the Prophetic Imagination message that must offer *command-content* in the process of communicating truth and holiness. To this end Peterson maintains that "The effusion, the overflow of life that is holiness, is not something that can be hoarded, but delivered, spread around, spoken and acted."[18]

This is the point of incorporating *testimony* as a mode of faith to "speak of Yahweh's mighty deeds which constitute the substance of the Gospel. That is each space of the decisive way in which this Character—credible, normal and indispensable—has made a decisive difference."[19] This can be communicated by engaging the person in the narrative or liturgy. In the example of the book of Jonah, the character of Jonah interacts with Yahweh as he invites Jonah to respond to his intervention, manifest as God's mighty deeds recorded in the narrative account. "But the testimony characteristically moves beyond those present in the proclamation and intends to address those outside the community who must also reckon with this Character (Yahweh) who comes to power in, with and under the testimony of Israel."[20] The invitation to servant work is the outcome of such "Yahweh-focused"[21] *testimony* to exiles in an attempt to communicate the Word of God through Prophetic Imagination narratives.

Brueggemann stipulates preaching for exiles as contained in the following:

- The rendering of Yahweh among exiles must be *credible,* that is, linked to real life circumstance. (See *Life* component, appendices A, B, and C.)

- The rendering of Yahweh must be *normal.* Yahweh is not some supernatural oddity that needs explanation, but an accepted assumed

17. Ibid., 45.
18. Peterson, *Subversive,* 74.
19. Brueggemann, *Cadences,* 50.
20. Ibid., 49.
21. Ibid., 43.

Character who belongs invariably and without question in the middle of the narrative. (See *Bible* component, appendices A, B, and C.)

- The rendering of Yahweh must be *indispensable*. The tale of existence offered exiles must be told so that Yahweh is seen to be a necessary character, not an extra or addendum. If one omits Yahweh from the tale, the tale collapses into nonsense. Among the exiles, it is important that Yahweh be a real key player in their existence"[22] (insertions mine). (See *Lifestyle of the Believer,* component Appendix A, B, and C.)

CONTEXT OF THE LIVING GOD

Discipline of Readiness—Worship

As the producer prepares to put into format this holiness as a testimony of God's working in the hearts and lives of people, the following injunction from Eugene Peterson must be considered:

> Nothing in our relations with God can be secularized to our expectations, or customized to our conditions or managed for our convenience. We acquire readiness and perspective for this by worshipping God and practicing the posture and rudiments of worship wherever we find ourselves . . . there is more and the more is God revealing himself in Jesus by the Spirit, the *Holy* Spirit.[23]

It is therefore that the "disciplines of readiness," as the posture of the producer of Prophetic Imagination communication, must be considered in Chapter 11 as an intentional discipline following closely the discipline of worship in liturgy "whereby we wait for the wind,"[24] God's Spirit, to bring newness and communicate holiness.

Peterson writes, "Holiness is a furnace that transforms the men and women who get to close to it. Holy, Holy, Holy is not Christian needlepoint—it is the banner of a revolution, *the* revolution."[25]

22. Ibid., 43.
23. Peterson, *Subversive*, 75.
24. Brueggemann, *Cadences*, 134.
25. Peterson, *Subversive*, 73.

FAIRY TALE

Invitation to Respond in Faith and Obedience

The human response to nearness to God, attained through faith and obedience, is the final element in the process of communicating the Holy among exiles. The ultimate theme for the exiles is homecoming. It is through the identification of a *Lifestyle of the Believer* that the audience is able, by invitation, to enter into an alternative existence based on the premises that the narrative communicates. Such an existence is not a return to how things used to be before the empire took control, but a yearning for a new home arena where God's good intention is decisive, where the term "kingdom of God" is used. Brueggemann writes:

> It is no stretch to link *homecoming* to *gospel* to *kingdom*. The linkage is already made in Isaiah 40–55 and in Ezekiel 37:1–14. . . . It is my intention to suggest that the metaphor of exile/homecoming that Barth handles Christologically, and that Buber handles philosophically, be understood among us ecclesiologically with reference to the concrete realities of economics, politics and social relations.[26]

Jacques Ellul describes the presence of the kingdom also in terms of "the creation of a new style of life." He continues:

> This is the "missing link." There used to be a style of life peculiar to the Middle Ages. In the sixteenth century, there was a style of life carried on by the Reformed Church Christians, and it is extremely interesting to note where it was opposed to the style of life of the Renaissance. There is a bourgeois style of life, which has no spiritual quality at all; there is the Communist style of life; there is no longer a Christian style of life. To speak quite frankly, without beating around the bush, a doctrine only has power (apart from that which God gives it) to the extent in which it is adopted, believed, and accepted by men who have a style of life that is in harmony with it.[27]

God doing concrete acts of transformation that the world judges as impossible is how the Bible portrays the images of the kingdom of God, using as tool narratives full of miracle and wonder. "The 'Kingdom' is a time and place and context in which God's 'impossibilities' for life, joy,

26. Brueggemann, *Cadences*, 14.

27. Ellul, *Presence*, 121.

and wholeness are all possible and available."[28] This is the *fairy tale* element that the Prophetic Imagination narrative communicates as an invitation to *a new Lifestyle of the Believer*, not through coercion but via a shift in consciousness to which the audience has the freedom to respond either yes or no. This does not mean that the believer must withdraw from the dominant consciousness into exile, in the presence of "Babylonians." Brueggemann writes that the believer's identity is a style of life "intended for full participation in the life of the dominant culture, albeit with a sense of subversiveness that gives unnerving freedom."[29] Jeremiah wrote to the exiles in Babylon about the dangers of withdrawal from the empire, expressing their *Lifestyle as Believers* in terms of *Shalom,* an ancient Hebrew concept, in the following excerpt:

"But seek the welfare (*shalom*) of the city where I have sent you into exile, and pray to the Lord on its behalf, for in its welfare (*shalom*) you will find your welfare (*shalom*)" (Jer 29:7 ESV).

"There is no 'separate peace' for exiles, no private deals with God, no permitted withdrawal from the affairs of the empire."[30] Jeremiah's letter, however, clarifies to the Jews in exile that the impact of *Shalom* on Babylon through their active involvement and prayer can only happen as the community is aware that it is not Babylon. The *Lifestyle of the Believer* must result in *communities of Shalom* indicative of the presence of God in everyday relationships that can indeed impact the dominant culture, shattering the existing paradigms of meaning. This is God's kingdom on earth, as it will be established.

EDUTAINMENT

From the biblical text, describing the elements of holiness translated as *tragedy, comedy* and *fairy tale* above, the format of a new genre for narrative communication in terms of a Prophetic Imagination purpose for the moving-image media may be characterized as *edutainment*. To educate to a *new Lifestyle of the Believer*, the narrative as in the biblical text must first entertain to capture the element of play of the imagination (developed by Gadamerian theory in the following chapter), as referred to by the fairy-tale element of Buechner (1977). Through this element, the senses

28. Klein, *Israel*, quoted in Brueggemann, *Cadences*, 14.

29. Brueggemann, *Cadences*, 13.

30. Ibid.

and consciousness and *Lifestyle of the Believer* can be developed by the symbols that cultivate entertainingly and educationally the faith, hope and love of an alternative consciousness.

In the following chapter, narrative and imagination theory will be analyzed from a communication perspective to develop how narration theoretically and ontologically works, in terms of format integrated with *style*, *content*, and *intent*, to make available an expression of social reality as alternative consciousness. The integration of these narrative and imagination theories with the theological paradigm and cultural communication theory occurs in a discussion of the Narrative Paradigm in the following chapter. Then, *edutainment* as a biblically based format is appropriated with communication theory to explain its function as part of the new genre for moving-image media communication.

CONCLUSION

It was the goal of this chapter to have identified a biblically based format—*edutainment*—using the ideological and holy textures in the story of Jonah, as well as the theological paradigm of Prophetic Imagination applied to the book of Jonah. This format, once theoretically grounded in a communication paradigm of narration, will become the basis of the form for a genre consisting of *format* and *style* that results in facilitation through moving-image media of the *Lifestyle of the Believer*, as communities of *Shalom*, God's kingdom on earth.

CHAPTER 10

Model Three: Communicating Transcendental Meaning by Telling Stories

Narrative and Imagination

INTRODUCTION

TELLING STORIES IS THE means by which biblical truth is predominantly communicated in the canonical texts, and the book of Jonah is no exception. In continuing with this case study focused on the book of Jonah, biblically based story elements of a new genre comprising the *form edutainment* and *style* of *irony* in the communication process, are identified theologically. This storytelling format is shown to employ Prophetic Imagination theology and to transform culture from a pragmatic and theoretical perspective. This creates a narrative message with transcendental meaning. The elements for communicating a Prophetic Imagination are linked to the construction of a new narrative faith model for film and television that would appropriately communicate meaning through its *form* and *content*. This is examined in the following chapter.

According to the cultural communication theory of Chapter 7, the second golden rule for communicating effectively is insisting that the medium be suited to the *content*. It is the medium (*format* and *style*) of the message that Model Three addresses (see Appendix C) while developing an understanding of meaning in terms of communication as storytelling.

This book has argued that the purpose of moving-image media, as is the purpose of the biblical narratives in the Bible, is to establish a Prophetic Imagination (biblical worldview) against and in the dominant culture (secular worldview.) However "the medium is the message," and therefore the *format* and *style* (together with the medium) are just as important for containing and communicating the message of another type of consciousness, the *Lifestyle of the Believer*. Having dealt with narrative and imagination theologically in the book of Jonah, it is possible to focus on the working of narrative theory and imagination theory that will carry the message of a Prophetic Imagination (biblical worldview) such that meaning is created. This will then provide a communication theology for the medium (*format* and *style*) that will fit the message (*content* and *intent*) that has been discussed culturally and theologically in the preceding chapters. However, to arrive at a new understanding of a genre (medium and message) for biblical moving-image media (developed in Chapter 11), the following now addresses popular culture and the adage "the medium is the message."

POPULAR CULTURE FORMS AND STYLES

As the popular culture becomes more pervasive in the face of modern communication technologies, it is perhaps easily understood that immoral *content* can have a negative effect on the individual. However, few may realize that the *format* in which *content* is communicated also dramatically affects the culture. "The medium is the message," as communication scholar Marshal McLuhan (1967) is famous for saying, means that *what* is said is as important as *how* it is said when it comes to communicating meaning.

Various forms of popular culture, such as the moving-image media, have, as it has been said, become "cotton candy for the mind," intended *not* to let the audience think deeply. Striving for simplicity and entertainment that offers instant gratification, these forms of media are negatively affecting our mental processes and fostering an addiction to comfort, as Neil Postman (1985) concluded in *Amusing Ourselves to Death*. Postman equates print with linear rational thinking and television with disjointed emotional responses. Recent studies have been published reporting the deleterious effects of television on children and links to higher occurrences of Attention Deficit Disorder (ADD) in youths with higher exposures to the moving-image media.

Chuck Colson and Nancy Pearcey have highlighted two classic works of literature—Aldous Huxley's *A Brave New World* and George Orwell's *1984*—to underscore the manner in which the stories we are exposed to and the entertainment we enjoy have a dramatic impact on our very manner of being in the world.

> Orwell warned of a communist government that would ban books; Huxley warned of a Western government that wouldn't need to ban them—because no one would read serious books anymore. Orwell predicted a society deprived of information by government censors; Huxley predicted a society oversaturated by information from electronic media—until people lost the ability to analyze what they saw and heard. Orwell feared a system that concealed the truth under government propaganda and lies; Huxley feared a system where people stopped caring about the truth and cared only about being entertained. Orwell described a world where people were controlled by inflicting pain; Huxley imagined a world where people were controlled by inflicting pleasure. Both novels have proven to be uncannily accurate—Orwell describing the totalitarian plague of our century, Huxley the sickness of affluent free societies.[1]

This soft oppression by the popular cultural forms can be linked to the history of *logos*, which will be examined in the next section. It is when science claimed the only path to truth and knowledge that expressive forms were demoted as merely the result of subjective imagination. This rebellion of art and art forms such as occurred in the mediums of music and painting migrated from Europe to America, infiltrating folk culture and attacking mainstream values. This anti-establishment movement, however, has now escalated to the point of glorifying death and destructive behavior. These forms of popular culture belong to no specific ethnic group but have invaded all cultures, having destructive effects on culture everywhere. The question that is posed in this chapter is: Can these popular cultural forms—if Christian *content* is superimposed on them—redeem a culture that has largely been created by the mainstream secular media of the popular culture? Colson and Pearcey make the following very important point, which also agrees with the principles set out in the development of *Jonahre*: "Are we creating a genuinely Christian culture, or are we simply creating a parallel culture with a Christian veneer? Are we imposing Christian content onto an already existing form? For the form and style always send a message of their own. . . . We should cultivate something

---

1. Colson and Pearcey, *How Now Shall We Live?*, 268–69.

distinctly Christian in both content and form."[2] They suggest, as this book proposes, that worldview is at the core of this problem, stating, "We must learn how to identify the worldviews expressed in various art forms in order to critique them and craft an alternative that is soundly biblical."[3] This is the purpose of the Prophetic Imagination analysis of the dominant and alternative consciousness based on a biblical worldview. *Jonahre* as genre is the culmination of this book's proposal for a biblically based *format, style,* and consequently medium/form of narrative communication that allows a truly alternative *Lifestyle of the Believer* to be manifested through the popular culture of the moving-image media.

NARRATIVE ELEMENTS

Christian communication as a cultural mandate presupposes a covenant of God with his created and "To speak of covenant's inception is impossible without adopting narrative form."[4] Covenant relationship reveals itself in story and through story form. In order to identify the structural elements of narrative, the biblical account of creation where the relationship between God and humans begins will be consulted.

In Genesis the *temporal, spatial,* and *rhetorical* elements are introduced in the Priestly text of the first creation story. The *temporal element* in the narrative occurs in the form of days, as the story begins and is subsequently ordered. With creation the *spatiality of narrative* is made available, as the earth becomes the story's place. This creation text, likely written in exile, carries the distinctive voice of God, welcomed by those in a situation of lament and hopelessness as *God becomes a rhetorical presence* among humans and in their narratives. The Yahwist tradition introduces the second (though earlier) creation account, and the additional rich elements of biblical narrative are identified as *plot, character, setting,* and *tone* of the narrative. To use moving-image media "in the context of biblical faith will have a narrative form into which the ruach of God will need to breathe life."[5] In a civilization that has lost the meaning of life, it is through the Holy Spirit working in the individual and expressing himself in the words, deeds, and decisions as life is lived that the moving-image

2. Ibid., 471.

3. Ibid.

4. Eslinger, *Narrative,* 3.

5. Ibid., 5.

media message becomes an explosive force. "The entire Bible narrative addresses the past, present and future of God's relationship with human-kind. Our understanding of the world, of ourselves, of God, of virtually everything is wrapped in rich biblical narrative."[6] These stories become *meta-narratives* to negotiate interpretations of other stories.

Mundane stories clarify a person's sense of the world in the particular social and cultural milieu that shapes him or her, allowing an expression of experience in the world understood as the *Life* component in the third model. It is sacred stories that serve to create consciousness. Stephen Crites refers to them as sacred because of "their power to create the sense of meaning, of self and world"—creation stories in themselves creating a world of consciousness.[7] It is therefore in and through narrative com-munication that the biblical texts achieve an alternative consciousness. So also the purpose of biblical moving-image media messages as defined in Chapter 5 is to establish an alternative consciousness of a Prophetic Imagination that creates the *Lifestyle of the Believer*. This can find its theo-retical function and form in the Narrative Communication Paradigm.

For the biblical moving-image media to be a prophetic voice, it must express faith via the concrete forms of life portrayed in story, creating and sharing through symbolic form and media format a new form of a biblical life and using truth as an agent for sanctification in these narra-tives. In order for Christianity to have a point of contact with the world, it is necessary to create and communicate in the narrative a *Lifestyle of the Believer* sanctified by the truth: "When we seek to discover effective action for the church, owing to the necessity for its intervention in the world, it seems as though its first objective should be the creation of a style of life. . . . This problem of the style of life is absolutely central; for it is at this point that the question of the integration of Christianity into the world, or at least of its creative power, will be most fiercely tested.[8] The contours of a "Christian life system," as Chuck Colson writes in *How Now Shall We Live?* are then understood in the third model (see Appendix C) as pertaining to the *Life* of the culture encompassing the *fall* from grace, the *Bible* with its message of *creation* and *redemption* of humankind, and, finally, the *Lifestyle of the Believer* that is the *restorative* work that calls

6. Schultze, *Communicating*, 42.

7. Crites, "Narrative Quality," 296, quoted in Eslinger *Narrative*, 6.

8. Ellul, *Presence*, 121.

Christians to engage in holiness. This establishes a theological model of holiness, as was discussed in Chapter 9. "We are called to bring these principals into every area of life and create a new culture."[9]

These messages must counteract the fact that "We have lost the meaning of true action, which is the testimony of a profound life, action which comes from the heart, which is the product of faith and not of a myth, or of propaganda or of Mammon! What matters is to live and not to act. In this world, this is a revolutionary attitude, for the world only desires action, and has no desire for life."[10]

THE NARRATIVE PARADIGM

Two important criteria of stories are implied in the following observations:

1. We create meaning for ourselves by the stories we tell ourselves.

2. The form of creative discourse plays a role in the message communicated.

The Narrative Paradigm will be explored to consider the theoretical basis for such claims and to establish an understanding from a communication perspective of how we can be sure that our stories' messages create the meaning for a biblical culture's style of life.

The Narrative Paradigm understands both *logos* and *mythos* as integral to knowledge, and communication as it was commonly understood prior to Socrates, Plato, and Aristotle. This is a non-positivist view postulating that rhetoric and poetry can communicate truth, knowledge and reality and that such do not belong exclusively to the domain of scientific, philosophical discourse, as Aristotle and later Francis Bacon maintained. Walter Fisher contends for the original conception of *logos* in the narrative paradigm by stating that "Human communication in all of its forms is imbued with mythos—ideas that cannot be verified or proved in any absolute way."[11] Kenneth Burke recognizes and reinforces the idea that reason and aesthetic qualities are present in all forms of human communication.[12] However, Burke's notion of human behavior—a dramatist view assessed by presentational standards—is that people are actors in

9. Colson and Pearcey, *How Now Shall We Live?*, 36–37.

10. Ellul, *Presence*, 76.

11. Fisher, *Human Communication*, 19.

12. Burke, *Counter-statement*, 124.

stories through which they understand life.[13] This book, along with "The narrative paradigm sees people as storytellers, as authors and co-authors who creatively read and evaluate the texts of life and literature" from the perspective of a certain "logic."[14] This intrinsic logic of the narrativity, which Walter Fisher identifies as rational narration in the Narrative Paradigm, is what this study (in terms of biblically based moving-image media communication) has theologically termed a Prophetic Theology of the genre that communicates biblical truth. The narrative rationality of the Narrative Paradigm thus analyzes the *content* (biblical or not) of stories using the principles of coherence and fidelity. These principles account for how people, as full participants in the making of messages, as agents (authors), or audience members (co-authors), will, through a philosophy of reason, value, and action, come to adopt these stories. This notion implies that any *content* to be rhetorically presented will consist of symbols that are "created and communicated ultimately as stories meant to give order to human experience and to induce others to dwell in them in order to establish ways of living in common, in intellectual and spiritual communities in which there is confirmation for the story that constitutes one's life."[15] This is the *intent* of the Prophetic Imagination paradigm that describes, simultaneously, the basis of the purpose (a critique) of biblically based moving-image media discourse and the result of a form of narrative that achieves the Prophetic Imagination meaning through the rhetoric as narration. Even though a story might entertain on an aesthetic level, it will inherently also educate to a way of life as biblical truth is communicated. Therefore this book, in developing a form of discourse that will meet the criteria of entertaining and educating as seen in biblical literature, the term *edutainment* was coined, which is supplemented from a communication perspective by what Walter Fisher (1987) writes:

> There is hope in the fact that narrative as a mode of discourse is more universal and probably more efficacious than argument for non-technical forms of communication. There are several reasons why this should be true. First, narration comes closer to capturing the experience of the world, simultaneously appealing to the various senses, to reason and emotion, to intellect and imagination, and to fact and value. It does not presume intellectual contact only.

13. Fisher, *Human Communication*, 18–19.

14. Fisher, *Human Communication*, 18.

15. Ibid., 75.

> Second, one does not have to be taught narrative probability and narrative fidelity; one culturally acquires them through universal faculty and experience.[16]

However, the Prophetic Imagination paradigm of narration differs from the Narrative Paradigm in the matter of how it handles truth. The Narrative Paradigm describes the term "narrative fidelity" in terms of truth as "a matter of truth according to the doctrine of correspondence . . . truths that humanity shares in regard to reason, justice, veracity and peaceful ways to resolve social-political differences." For the purposes of biblically based narratives, this study considers truth as the view of reality from the perspective of how God communicated it through his inspired Word—it is absolute and not determined by how many people find it to correspond with their view of the basis of a good life. However, to bring into focus individuated components of stories and discern whether they represent accurate assertions in terms of a biblical worldview about social reality (i.e. values) as part of Prophetic Imagination is a useful function of the Narrative Paradigm. The procedure that tests an interpretation of a dramatic or literary work as an aesthetic experience is an application of Walter Fisher's Narrative Paradigm and contributes to this hypothesis. This procedure entails four considerations. The first three parallel the criteria for logical reasoning—fact and relevance:

> First is determining the message, the overall conclusion fostered by the work. Second is deciding whether one's determination of the message is justified by *(a)* the reliability of the narrator(s); *(b)* the words or actions of other characters; and *(c)* the descriptions of characters, scenes, and events—which are verbal in literature and both verbal and nonverbal in drama. Third is noting the outcomes of the various conflicts that make up the story, observing whose values seem most powerful and/or worthy, whether events are controlled by characters or forces outside of them. Up to this point, one's primary concern is whether or not the story rings true as a story in itself and what "truth" it makes known.[17]

This book identifies *fact* and *relevance* as indicators of truth in the Narrative Paradigm in terms of the theological paradigm of Prophetic Imagination that defines biblical truth. It identifies the elements that identify this worldview in biblical narratives of an alternative consciousness in

16. Ibid., 75.

17. Ibid., 175.

the dominant culture. Walter Fisher goes on to parallel the criteria for the narrative paradigm—*consequence, consistency,* and *transcendent issue*— with the fourth consideration of weighing this truth, which is "advanced by the story against one's own perceptions of the world to determine their fidelity. The questions are (a) Does the message accurately portray the world we live in? *(dominant consciousness of the* Life *componant in Model Three)* and (b) Does it provide a reliable guide to *our* beliefs, attitudes, values, actions? *(alternative consciousness of the* Bible *component Model Three)*"[18] (insertions and emphasis mine). These criteria imply that narratives have a way of communicating the value of values. In this study those values pertain to the Prophetic Imagination worldview in moving-image communication. The Narrative Paradigm establishes a theoretical communication paradigm that says, "A value is valuable not because it is tied to a reason or is expressed by a reasonable person per se, but because *it makes a pragmatic difference in one's life and in one's community*"[19] (italics mine). This is the work of narration, and in service of the Prophetic Imagination paradigm, this indicates that the value of values, "meaning," is bound, communicated, and formed in the context of narration to establish a *Lifestyle of the Believer* for humans as storytellers—*Homo narrans,* as exemplified in biblical literature.[20]

IMAGINATION THEORY

In a postmodern/post-liberal setting, the opportunity for Prophetic *Imagination* "is to explore the world of the text *(Bible)* and to note the interplay, tension and conflict between that world and our conventional personal and social 'worlds' *(Life)*"[21] (insertions mine). Paul Ricouer advanced imagination theory in the twentieth century to shift from merely perceptive (primarily reproductive) to productive of new meaning in the linguistic world. Ricoeur provided the definition of imagination used in this book as, "the capacity to work through images, metaphors, and narratives as a way of evoking, generating and constructing an alternative world that lies beyond and in tension with the taken for granted commonsense

18. Ibid.

19. Fisher, *Human Communication*, 111.

20. See also Fisher, *Human Communication*, 158–79, for examples of application to *The Great Gatsby* and *Death of a Salesman.*

21. Eslinger, *Narrative*, 99.

world of day to day experience."[22] Thus, for Ricoeur, reality is created as language, through metaphor, creates new meaning. For the purposes of this study, however, the interest in his work is not focused on a general theory of metaphor. Instead, it is in analyzing biblical narrative genres such as the book of Jonah, using socio-rhetorical criticism that makes Ricoeur's theoretical categories modes of practice that can illuminate narrative metaphor and its revealing power to disclose the reality of God's dominion as an exercise of imagination theory. This "permits the text community to *redescribe, reimagine and recharacterize* the world in which it lives. The symbolic world we inhabit, unless there is great intentionality, goes by default to the hegemonic definitions of the dominant powers."[23] Metaphor is, however, not the only device of indirection that has been studied in hermeneutics considering imagination theory. "Rather, there is an increasing appreciation for the role of irony in the witness of Scripture, to the point that it will need to be placed alongside metaphor as an essential vehicle for conveying the world of the text and the character of God. . . . Wayne C. Booth is right to observe that both metaphor and irony, beginning as 'minute oratorical device(s),' have risen to 'imperialistic world conqueror(s)'"[24] (see Chapter 11, "Irony"). Prophetic Imagination has claimed to identify these devices in biblical texts and to illuminate their effects in terms of subversion of the dominant cultural ideology, not only in the ancient culture of the text but also in contemporary society.

Gadamer was the next theorist who culminated imagination theory with the idea of imagination as play, blazing a trail leading to the game metaphor. His metaphor, concerning the role of the pattern of the game as a "field" that diminishes the self-consciousness of the player, speaks to the form of moving-image media. The audience becomes part of the drama, as the actors invite the audience to complete their play by participating.[25] Schiller, who complements Gadamer's theory of play, wrote: "'Man only plays when he is in the fullest sense of the word a human being, and he is only fully a human being when he plays.' Aesthetic expression, he maintained, is 'the most fruitful of all in respect of knowledge and morality.'"[26]

---

22. Brueggemann, *Cadences*, 59.

23. Ibid., 60.

24. Eslinger, *Narrative*, 117.

25. Gadamer, *Truth*, 104–8.

26. Quoted in Fisher, *Human Communication*, 12.

Both homiliticians and communication scholars have incorporated the functioning of play as part of the rhetorical transaction determining how the rules of the form of the context of play provide an experience of the text that creates meaning and action as response to *content*.

More accurately, however, this imaginative function involves a presentation of images and stories out of the lived experience of the audience as the *Life* component is communicated in terms of the message of biblical truth. "Memory as a function of imagination is the vehicle through which most of these imagined situations are typically 'brought near'"[27] (*Lifestyle of the Believer*). This makes testimony a vehicle of support for biblical truth. This leads us to the definition of *testimony* given as: "utterances by alleged first-person witnesses who offer an account of experience that depends solely upon the trustworthiness of the witnesses but that cannot appeal for verification either to agreed-upon metaphysics or to external historical data."[28] It is through these *testimonies* that transformation is anticipated and comes in the form of a new pattern of the imagination, described by Eslinger as a shift in the paradigmatic imagination (see "Testimony" in Chapter 9).

Christian media communication in narrative form involves a creative reorganization of the imagination of the audience so that they become conformed to the world of biblical narrative. Kuhn's work on scientific paradigms observes that the "decision to reject one paradigm is always simultaneously the decision to accept another."[29] Our recognition or perception can only at any one time see a single set of lines forming either, for example, a rabbit or a duck—to see the other picture the perceptions of the first must be abandoned to memory. (See duck/rabbit picture [Appendix G] to illustrate the fact that the paradigmatic imagination functions as a whole.) This illustrates the incommensurable quality of paradigms. Kuhn emphasizes that the canons of evaluation can not be extended into the world of another. Establishing the elements of a paradigm of Prophetic Imagination to communicate biblical truth and shift the dominant consciousness to an alternative consciousness must proceed in the manner illuminated by Kuhn's example of incommensurable imaginative paradigms. The symbols and images of the communication

27. Ibid., 98–99.
28. Brueggemann, *Cadences*, 44.
29. Kuhn, *Structure*, 77, quoted in Eslinger, *Narrative*, 100.

as *edutainment* will allow the recognition of *both* "rabbit" and "duck"; however, they remain discontinuous, as the whole is seen as one or the other. In the case of the moving-image media, the biblical worldview, although applicable in *Life*, cannot blend with the secular worldview, as the two must be paradigmatically communicated as discontinuous.

EDUTAINMENT AS FORMAT

The following list indicates the aspects identified by Brueggemann (1997), which script reality that becomes an evangelical imagination in terms of an audience in exile, such as the believer is in contemporary culture. The book of Jonah has exemplified the summary below of a form of communication that can be redescriptive through the format, *edutainment,* and *style, irony,* as represented in biblical narratives. Here these will be evidenced employed in the example of one of the most effective moving-image media messages of an alternative consciousness, *The Sound of Music,* which is demonstrated as redescriptive "speech."

No Monolithic Language

In the empire, oppressive certitudes and relativist reductionism are the language that is spoken by the hegemony of the dominant consciousness. The exiles live all day in the closure of the flat, monolithic rhetoric of the empire in economic and interpretive practices. In the hegemony of the apartheid in South Africa, Old Testament scholars, Brueggemann writes, "were not allowed to say of the book of Jonah that it might be fiction, that it might be satire, or *truth*, or humor. Interpretations needed to be flat, one-dimensional and on the surface in order to suggest that there is no slippage in the Bible, that is, no ground for slippage in social relations."[30] It is playful rhetoric that must be at work in moving-image communication, "seeking to maintain an *alternative identity*, an *alternative vision* of the world and an *alternative vocation* in a societal context where the main forces of culture seek to deny, discredit, or disregard that odd identity."[31] It is the methodology of socio-rhetorical criticism applied to particular texts, as this study has demonstrated using Jonah, that focuses attention on the fact that the impact of "what" is said depends largely on "how" it is said. Scripture has thus provided us with examples that this book has

30. Brueggemann, *Cadences*, 42.

31. Ibid., 42.

developed into a Three-Phase Theology of Communication Paradigm—models for basing the "what" in line with the "how" of biblical communication through the moving-image media. This set of paradigmatic models, collectively called the Prophetic Imagination approach, considers imagination to be the active enterprise of the "how" in implementing the format as *edutainment* and *style* as *irony* to move the audience beyond their defining commitments "to entertain alternative definitions of self, world, other and God. This is indeed the dangerous work of all serious artistic effort, that is, to lead the participant beyond what is self-evident, available and 'real' only in artistic articulation."[32]

Irony

The book of Jonah has been an exemplary piece of biblical literature that artistically communicates through the convergence of Yahweh and what Brueggemann calls "open language" to create "rhetorical/imaginative/theological space" for exilic and post-exilic communities. In this space "exiles can live their lives freely, so that the empire cannot rob them of identity, that is, cannot crush or overwhelm their baptismal identity."[33] Through the *style* of *irony* the storytelling can achieve a reconstruction of reality by revealing the dissonance between two levels of meaning that the "text" communicates (See Chapter 11). However, this is often accomplished through the process of characterization in storytelling. Here we will speak of the concretization of *irony* as *style* in narrative to surprise, reveal, and entertain through humor/*comedy* or satire/*tragedy*. "Irony then begins in conflict, in conflict marked by the perception of the distance between pretense and reality."[34] Conflict between two characters usually marks the *irony*. One character is called the *alazon*, the impostor, who is the pompous fool and pretender who pretends to be more than he actually is. The other is the *eiron*, the ironical man whom Good describes as sly and shrewd, a dissimulator who poses as less than he actually is. In the story of Jonah, it is precisely these characteristics that describe the *irony*. Jonah is the *alazon* who, as prophet, initially demands the audience's respect and awe as a man called by God, and God as the *eiron* seems unreasonable to expect such an extraordinary task of a nationalistic prophet. However, it is

32. Ibid., 59.
33. Ibid., 43.
34. Good, *Irony*, 14.

precisely in the conflict played out in the final scene that God's conversation with Jonah pricks the bubble of the imposter (Jonah), revealing the true character of Jonah's heart, while God, as long-suffering, merciful, and forgiving in his love for his creation, triumphs as the *eiron*. In this tension, the narrative uses hyperbole to exaggerate and intensify the elements that play out the conflict—for example, the great fish, the sudden storm, the large evil city of Nineveh that manifests a complete and immediate repentance. Deliberate ambiguity exists in the characterization, as the author uses misdirection techniques to result in a surprise conclusion when the true nature of the characters is revealed: Jonah as vengeful and God as sparing and merciful. The book also incorporates satire, which is not *irony* but can contain or consist completely of *irony*. Good (1965) writes, "Indeed the fact that the figure of Jonah represents all that the author of the book means to reject suggests . . . (the book) is a satire. It portrays the prophet in order to ridicule him."[35]

The Sound of Music film uses *irony* to criticize the dominant consciousness in a similar way by using Captain von Trapp as the *alazon* and Maria the *eiron*. It is Maria who, in the conflict that results between her and the Captain regarding the proper way to raise the children, bursts von Trapp's bubble when, through music, she softens his hardened heart to see the real need of the children and ultimately himself. He again is able to come to feel and love, first his children and then Maria, the source of the alternative consciousness that floods the household as agent of God to enact a Prophetic Imagination in an oppressive, hurtful milieu. The power of the story is that it is a *testimony* of actual events orchestrated by a mighty God to redeem what seemed a hopeless situation. The hope established through artistic expression, rhetoric and music, brought freedom within a family, provided an escape politically from the Nazi invasion of Austria, and even witnessed to nations as the story and music have spanned time and continents, portraying an alternative consciousness of hope and triumph relevant to both young and old.

Yahweh-Focused (Straight Up)

The test for stories with an evangelical imagination is whether they are preoccupied with Yahweh as a *character* who is credible, real, and indispensable. That means to omit Yahweh from the tale would make it col-

35. Ibid., 40.

lapse into nonsense. For exiles Yahweh must be a real and key player in their existence (see Chapter 5).

Redescriptive Speech

Redescriptive speech is not contaminated or intruded upon by the hegemonic power of the empire (royal consciousness). In the ancient exile and displacement of Jews, the treasured language was redescriptive, not determined and directed by those in charge of the empire. "It was rather derived from older speech practice of the covenanted community and sanctioned by the evangelical chutzpah of poets who dared to credit such defiant utterances as complaints, lamentations, assurances, hymns and promises. These are indeed forms of speech from Israel's 'mother tongue.'"[36] It is in the postmodern culture of rationalism that today the mother speech of Christians has been largely given up for what is imagined to be speech that is more credible and reasonable. It is time for the moving-image media—through creative scripts, master images, and musical scores—again to communicate the reality of an alternative consciousness. "Filmmakers say that over half of what we experience when we view a movie is the musical score."[37] An example of alternative consciousness made available through the effectiveness of script and music is the musical *The Sound of Music*. This film uses not only the power of testimony to evoke a powerful Prophetic Imagination with the viewer, but also a musical score and lyrics to transport the dulled empire's consciousness of a family oppressed by death and war to an alternative through the redescriptive speech of song. This is a mode of using the prophetic in lyrics and musical score that communicates powerfully and is easily accepted and assimilated into the experience of the message by the audience. This is primarily because the viewer, while being entertained, is also being educated, being played (Gadamerian idea), caught up by the paradigm of an alternative consciousness wrought through music and lyrics. The audience is invited to a response that recognizes both paradigms—that of the dominant consciousness and that of the consciousness beckoning to a freedom through faith in a favorable alternative that results in the *fairy tale* of the *Lifestyle of a Believer*. This is the whole of two worldviews discovered by the audience through creative portrayal and redescriptive speech of the

36. Brueggemann, *Cadences*, 23.
37. Schultze, *Communicating*, 40.

kind Brueggemann describes. "To speak of moral 'transformation' (with Dykstra), or arrival at a 'sacramental' stage of imaginative learning (with Harris) involves a shift, not just in some aspect of imaginal organization, but a shift in the paradigmatic imagination itself,"[38] as Kuhn's scientific research has substantiated.

A NEW RHETORIC AND COMMUNITY

"The move to (socio)rhetorical criticism as an access point into the alternative world of the text takes texts seriously in all of their particularity, without grand historical or grand dogmatic claims. Focus on particular texts insists that what is said in large measure depends on how it is said."[39] Thus, this study will turn now to the words of Marshall McLuhan, "the medium is the message," which will be discussed in terms of form and *content* in the next chapter to define the genre to communicate a Prophetic Imagination. And most of all, to establish the disciplines of readiness by which "empathetic communicators," as Quentin Schultze writes, in this case producers and directors of moving-image media messages, are "not merely brokers but are themselves deeply committed to the narratives they craft. In other words, we need authentic communicators who personally commune with others through the integrity of their stories."[40] This can be put in terms of communication as charismatic stewardship, a type of servanthood in the moving-image media that allows the communicator to provide his neighbor through the use of symbolic power an alternative worldview of reality. "A Christian focus on shalom turns our notions of symbolic power upside down. It emphasizes selfless servanthood rather than selfish masterhood."[41]

CONCLUSION

This chapter addresses popular cultural forms and their ability to redeem culture by communicating transcendental meaning, which requires more than merely superimposing Christian content on storytelling. Once content has been appropriated in terms of the audience's socio-cultural context, as Communication Model Two develops (see Appendix B), the

38. Eslinger, *Narrative*, 100.

39. Brueggemann, *Cadences*, 61.

40. Schultze, *Communicating*, 138.

41. Ibid., 99.

content must be funneled into a medium that complements the message. This becomes the goal of Model Three, as outlined in this chapter. It is a study of narrative in biblical texts composed for ancient oral communication that helps us to understand the meaning and effects of *form* and *style* on *content* and to integrate narrative and imagination theory. This is echoed by Professor Boomershine, a pioneer in the work of NOBS (National Organization for Biblical Storytellers), who says:

> Storytelling is a relatively recent methodology for the study and interpretation of Biblical narrative. . . . The importance of storytelling as a research methodology for the study of Biblical narrative is grounded in 20th century study of communication technology and its interaction with cultural formation. . . . If the medium determines the meaning, the story must be experienced in its original medium in order to experience its meaning. Changing the medium will change the message.[42]

It is studies like these that are emerging to provide valuable insights into the biblical message and its storytelling form to effectively translate, communicating an alternative biblical *Lifestyle of the Believer*. It is stories, identified and defined in this chapter as *sacred*, that have the power "to create the sense of meaning of self and world"[43] and thus to establish an alternative consciousness of Prophetic Imagination. For these stories to become agents of sanctification, this study postulates that, in accord with the Narrative Paradigm, a pre-Socratic, non-positivist view of communication as narration is considered, in which both *logos* and *mythos* form a part of the biblically based truth communicated. The three-phase interdisciplinary models include imagination and narrative theory, as examined in this chapter, with its wealth of insight into medium for the implementation of the Prophetic Imagination approach. This develops the totality of a Theology of Communication that will integrate medium and message for the active enterprise of communicating an alternative *Lifestyle of the Believer* through a new genre for the moving-image media.

42. Palakeel, *Bible*, 87–88.
43. Eslinger, *Narrative*, 6.

CHAPTER 11

Jonahre: A New Genre

INTRODUCTION

A NEW GENRE (FORMAT, *style*, *content*, and *intent*) for Christian media communication is proposed, namely, *Jonahre*. *Jonahre* is defined as the sum of identifying elements of a new genre, based on the *form* and *style* of the missiologically prophetic book of Jonah. This approach becomes infinitely more when submitted to the leading of the Holy Spirit to accomplish "newness" as God's gift. The readiness of the producer of biblical film and television narratives requires the use of "intentional disciplines"[1] to experience empowerment by the Holy Spirit to create Spirit-filled, transcendental biblical messages that will impact culture. The intent of this rhetoric in mass media narratives is to fulfill the cultural mandate of the Great Commission. The producer whose purpose it is to be an instrument of Prophetic Imagination in our culture will bring truth to the center stage of our world through Spirit-filled moving-image narratives in a medium that complements the message. This in turn will challenge the secular relativism and naturalism of the dominant culture with an alternative life system, the *Lifestyle of the Believer*. Greater than the individual parts extrapolated from (based on) the book of Jonah, *Jonahre* as a narrative genre demonstrates that appropriate *style* and *form* are critical for the message to communicate Spirit-filled truth as a powerful witness.

As stipulated thus far in the book, the biblical worldview is no longer responsible for the hegemony of the dominant consciousness; it is also no longer included in the cultural hegemony. Christianity has become a de-centered community in exile, and it is in this circumstance that an al-

---

1. Brueggemann, *Cadences*, 134.

ternative rhetoric must emerge. On the one hand, this rhetoric must have a prophetic theological purpose, "to propose a countertruth that subverts but also *a different style or mode of articulation*."[2]

As pop culture has become the mode of articulating the secular naturalism of the dominant consciousness, the question in this chapter is what *form* and *style*, *content* and *intent* are appropriate for this alternative, biblically based rhetoric to create a genuinely biblical culture by means of the moving-image media. "For the form and style always send a message of their own."[3] The medium is the message. Once pop culture has been examined, it is the producer's challenge to "take care not simply to insert Christian content into whatever style is currently on the market. Instead we should create something distinctly Christian in both content and form . . . and craft something alternative that is soundly biblical."[4] As Christian producers become creative through the power of the Holy Spirit in funneling the biblical message into an appropriate *form* and *style*, the "medium" for the message emerges as a new genre for moving-image communication that can fulfill the cultural mandate to create an authentic *Lifestyle of the Believer* based on biblical truth.

JONAH AS TYPIFIED EXAMPLE OF *FORM* AND *STYLE*

The book of Jonah has been brought center stage to serve as example to bridge the gap between theology and the narrative arts. Its ability to relate in one succinct narrative such variety, simplicity, and yet depth baffles almost every scholar seeking to categorize its genre. This biblical narrative exemplifies a genre that can best be understood by applying postmodern methodologies available to the modern reader with nothing less than an interdisciplinary methodology, such as socio-rhetorical criticism provides. The suggested approach for understanding the form and style of the book of Jonah is to accept it as communicating meaning through the inspiration of the Holy Spirit via an artistically crafted mode of storytelling. It is indeed an example of the medium suiting, and thus contributing to, the meaning of the message in order to communicate effectively. Meaning can be extrapolated from the book of Jonah by considering allegorical, prophetic, parabolic, and satirical trends, amongst others. To be inclu-

2. Ibid., 57.

3. Colson and Pearcey, *How Now Shall We Live?*, 471.

4. Ibid.

sive, the method of interpretation must therefore accept and consider the levels of meaning communicated through *form*, *style*, and *content*, all directed and moderated by the prophetic theological purpose that has been developed to show the authorial *intent* of Jonah. This book suggests the purpose for communicating to be the prophetic authorial *intent*. This purpose supports and formulates the *content* of the message and relates it to the *form* and *style*, which form the medium. "The medium is the message," as communication scholar Marshall McLuhan so profoundly stated.[5] The prophetic theological purpose for biblical moving-image narrative communicators, as also found in the book of Jonah, is typified in the narrative form termed *edutainment,* as identified in Chapter 10 in this book. The "medium" comprises the combination of *form* and *style* in narrative construction. Thus, the *form* integrated with a *style* in which Spirit-filled communication can become effective becomes the medium appropriate for the message. Prevalent in the book of Jonah is the style of *irony;* thus, as the final step in defining a new medium for moving-image narrative, this book explores *irony* as it functions in relation to the prophetic theological purpose as outlined herein.

IRONY

Irony has two levels, a literal surface meaning and a deeper meaning. Between these two levels, there must be "dissonance or tension," as asserted by Booth, Muecke, and others,[6] and it is the task of the audience to discern these competing levels of meaning. Schultze writes that once the incongruity in the ironic meaning is recognized by the audience, its task is the dynamic reconstruction, or, as some have termed it, "resolution,"[7] of an alternative worldview and, consequently, *Lifestyle of the Believer.* This can only occur as the personal and communal disassociation with the dominant meaning of a culture happens and identification with a new meaning becomes the audience's response to the ironic levels of meaning. Irony is closely related to humor, and both abound in the book of Jonah, with the distinction seemingly lying in this reconstruction or resolution of the incongruity. As Van Heerden points out, "I believe that the resolution of an incongruity sometimes is humorous, but it should not be viewed

5. McLuhan, *Understanding Media*, quoted in Williams, *New Communication*, 13.
6. Eslinger, *Narrative*, 121.
7. Quoted in Van Heerden, "Humour," 390.

as a *precondition* for amusement. . . . The ironist deals with humanness in a general sense, highlighting incongruities. The humorist focuses on humanness in a more sympathetic way."[8]

The Prophetic Theology Model helps the producer construct the authorial *intent* and purpose of the message, identifying the deeper level of meaning in the rhetorical situation. These create dramatic irony, which employs the incongruities inherent in the forms of irony, humor, puns, and witticisms to both amuse and educate by fulfilling a revelatory function through incongruity that entertains the audience. The themes of truth revealed in the biblical accounts of creation, the fall, redemption, and restoration, as outlined in Chapter 5, typically comprise the core of this deeper level of irony, juxtaposed with a more recognizable surface meaning that is readily identified by the audience in a particular culture. The surface, literal level of irony is most often subtle and covert and signaled as false, in need of repudiation. In the narrative-based *style* of dramatic irony, the interplay between reader, story plot, and characters that functions in a particular social and cultural context is described by Robert Fowler as follows:

> Because dramatic irony involves the audience in perceiving incongruity that the characters in the story do not perceive, it always has a two layered structure to it, a built in dialectical relationship between what is not understood within the story and what is understood in the audience's encounter with the story. . . . After the audience comprehends the distance opened up between the undiscerning characters, the irony continues to reverberate in the gap between the story and the audience. Dramatic irony is inherently revelatory.[9]

In the book of Jonah, dramatic irony functions repeatedly when information is shared with the audience that is not available to or received by the characters relating to each other and God in the plot (see Chapter 3). Thus, irony in this sense is somehow resident within the reaction of the audience, as the surface meaning of the narrative is presented. The narrator creates the invitation for the audience to respond to an "ironic vision" in the biblical narratives, functioning similarly as Prophetic Imagination does to create meaning in the community. Ironic vision is defined, in Eslinger's words, as:

8. Van Heerden, "Humour," 390–91.

9. Eslinger, *Narrative*, 122.

an acquired virtue of the community of believers and based on several convictions some of which are the following:

1. Christians live in numerous worlds, all shaped by storied traditions and their attended skein of imagery.

2. These worlds inevitably shape us, may equip us with certain virtues and just as surely may limit our vision to their own construals of the real and the true.

3. These worlds often are in tension with each other and with themselves, hence the occasion for irony emerges.

4. These worlds are inherently in tension with the biblical world (view) and with the character of God and Christ revealed through its narratives and images. Ironic vision (Prophetic Imagination as applied to the moving-image media ministry)[10] is "trained" as the community learns to perceive the dissonance and contradictions between story and discourse within biblical narrative.

5. Some world or other will function to shape the paradigmatic imagination such that rival interpretations are either rejected or re-visioned.

6. Discerning the ironies within the biblical narrative invites decision as to truth and performance as disciples.[11]

These convictions are applicable to the producer or critic of moving-image narratives whose purpose it is to use the prophetic theological paradigm to create or analyze the *style* of dramatic irony as an invitation to the audience for a Prophetic Imagination response. *Prophetic Imagination* and *Ironic Vision* can be understood as related in certain instances—e.g., when the terms *imagination* and *vision* and the terms *prophetic* and *irony* are explored as referring to similar concepts, respectively.

FINDING IMAGINATION IN VISION

Master images orient people to the self and world. These master images are integrated by a constant interplay of the senses. Imagination thus becomes the bond of the senses in its business of forming images to invoke vision. Vision is shaped "by the ways we imagine-that and imagine-how and by the metaphors and ironies of our stories."[12] Images contained

10. Insertion my own.

11. Ibid., 126–27.

12. Ibid., 89.

in stories become icons, and, as George Lindbeck writes, "The story is logically prior."[13] Paul Ricoeur's shift in twentieth-century imagination theory, which viewed imagination as linguistic and not merely perceptive in nature, allows the imagination to function to create new meaning through language and story. These narratives form the self and community by endowing them with character and virtues essential to their life and work. The icons formed in and through *imagineering* the biblically based stories become *metanoic*. That is, they function hermeneutically to illumine the imagination of the believer to interpret self, church, and world, thereby "transfiguring" the worshiper's imaginative vision. Anthony Ugolnik writes, "The icon's *intent* is not static but kinetic, moving and prodding the Christian imagination to shape and interpret the world anew. . . . (It) exerts its dominance over the Christian imagination, moving it to engage the culture of which it is part and transfigure it."[14] This is the establishing of an imagination via *imagineering* that is the image-shaped vision of an alternative consciousness within the dominant culture. This defines the imagination aspect of establishing the Prophetic Imagination purpose as *imagineering* that determines the biblical worldview, forming a common discipleship that seeks to co-create culture.

FINDING *IRONY* PROPHETIC

It is the task of the Prophetic Imagination narrative to speak imaginatively into a culture's dominant consciousness of meaning and to propose a biblically based alternative. This same task is achieved through *irony* in narrative. *Irony* as *style* in narrative proposes a covert intended meaning, which is often hidden by an obvious literal and easily recognizable surface meaning. The surface meaning is challenged by the beliefs and life experience of the dominant consciousness of the audience's cultural location. Precisely because they are familiar with and perhaps immersed in their worldview, the readers or hearers are relied upon to exercise the competency to reject the surface meaning. "Then the readers (or audience) must be imaginatively engaged in the tasks of proposing alternate meanings. . . . Booth both analyzes this complex irony dynamic and proposes the metaphor of 'reconstruction' to speak of this intricate reader

---

13. Lindbeck, *Doctrine*, quoted in Eslinger, *Narrative*, 85.
14. Ugolnik, *Icon*, 62, quoted in Eslinger, *Narrative*, 81.

response"[15] (insertion mine). The *irony* is revelatory to the audience in the same manner in which the prophetic theological *intent* must achieve an alternative consciousness, a new place of meaning, and invite a personal response from the individual. For the individual "to decide to build the new house of meaning in favor of remaining in the old habitation (dominant consciousness) of the surface meaning is to decide as well as to live in that new place perhaps with its new people, beliefs and customs. . . . 'Reconstruction,' then completes a more astonishing communal achievement than most accounts have recognized"[16] (insertion mine).

Prophetic Imagination narratives are the means of messaging—the medium and the message—to create, via tools of image-shaped vision and *irony, imagineering*, meaning that establishes biblical icons. These icons "transfigure" the audience through the ironic reconstruction to an alternative consciousness while the audience remains resident in the dominant cultural consciousness. The formation of a moving-image message that has a Prophetic Imagination meaning thus encapsulates the biblically based vision that our stories must foster in compiling constellations of master images. Using the three-phase Prophetic Imagination paradigm, the message becomes the medium; the result is *Jonahre*, which establishes an alternative consciousness through moving-image pictures and, consequently, the *Lifestyle of the Believer*.

This provides the book with insight into the use of Prophetic Imagination as a paradigm inclusive of theological *intent* that must guide the narrative moving-image media consisting of *form* and *style*. *Irony* is employed as the typified *style* to integrate through *imagineering* with the *form, edutainment* (discussed in Chapter 10), which results in the medium becoming the message. This ultimate product is a narrative genre with a Prophetic Imagination, designated *Jonahre*. "Jonah" means "dove," and in the New Testament the dove becomes a symbol of the Spirit of God. Messages based on *Jonahre* communicate a hope of accomplishing "transfiguration" in the audience via the power of the Spirit of God, which carries the messages forward. It is with this aim in mind that this book has attempted to identify elements of theological purpose and form that together must be at the creative core of any attempt to carry meaning

---

15. Eslinger, *Narrative*, 119.
16. Hardwerk quoted in Eslinger, *Narrative*, 120.

from the word of God to a diverse secular audience so that culture is transformed biblically.

JONAHRE AS MEDIUM

The producer of moving-image narratives must seek to receive God's newness for the message through the empowering of the Holy Spirit in order to convert the dominant culture into the alternative biblical consciousness. As demonstrated in this book, the book of Jonah has repeatedly, with Spirit-filled intensity, related its message as ironic vision through a particular didactic narrative form *(edutainment)* to create a medium that is the message, such that a Prophetic Imagination results *(Jonahre)*. It is in submission to God's sovereignty that the producer of biblical moving-image narratives awaits God-given newness that allows the message and medium to communicate through *imagineering* a Prophetic Imagination. It is this point of convergence of form, *style*, *content*, and *intent* in narrative that has a Prophetic Imagination result that this book terms *Jonahre*. "We need *disciplines of readiness*, acts to be undertaken with intentionality and discipline, to leave us ready if God should make new moves among us."[17]

DISCIPLINES OF READINESS

Producers are the instruments that must allow the *disciplines of readiness* to direct them in terms of their walk with God and their job as expressing a message of truth artistically, with Spirit-filled effectiveness. As they become available for the Holy Spirit to work newness and inspire creativity through these disciplines, the biblical moving-image narratives become vehicles for transporting exiles to a homecoming, as seen in the Prophetic Imagination in the book of Jonah. *Jonahre*, as an example of a narrative genre with a Prophetic Imagination (ironic vision) result, is achieved when the medium and message complement each other, with the *intent* to establish meaning that will transform the culture. This *intent* becomes directed and created as the producer attunes himself to the Holy Spirit's leading. The *disciplines of readiness* are exegetically explained in terms of Jonah and can be used as guidelines for the producer who engages in the task of co-creating culture through the use of *Jonahre* for the moving-image media. They are "*dangerous memories; dangerous criticism;*

17. Brueggemann, *Cadences*, 118.

dangerous promises; dangerous new songs; dangerous bread; dangerous departures."[18]

In what follows, Walter Brueggemann's thoughts on these disciplines of readiness are mainly directly implemented.

Dangerous Memories

God works newness against all counter-evidence in the face of deathly circumstances. In the *tragedy* of human deficiency, God is able to restore and save. In the process of running away from God (Jonah 1:12), Jonah is thrown into the ocean's raging storm, presumably to meet death, but is soon delivered by the sea creature that God avails. Even in the belly of the sea creature, during the most embarrassing moment for the prophet who runs from God though he should know that doing so is futile and foolish, God is there. God cannot be escaped and even in the darkest valley of death is available to deliver. That is the *comedy*. Like Jonah, we are all given chance upon chance by a long-suffering God to repent, and that truth introduces the *fairy tale* of God's promises that await. The fish spews Jonah out onto dry land alive, and Nineveh repents in response to God's warning spoken through his prophet. Brueggemann writes that *dangerous memories* seek God in the oldest and most embarrassing cir-cumstances.[19] As the parody of a prophet in the book of Jonah reveals, so Isaiah, in Deutero-Isaiah, recounts the stories of Sarah and Abraham (Isa 51:1–2). These accounts serve as dangerous memories of God's dealings with humankind, though they are often lacking in their conceptualization of an almighty God. These men and women in their humanness experi-ence God, and his otherness shapes their reality. An alternative reality that would not succumb to the imperial rationality and reality of their dominant consciousness is revealed by the miraculous interventions of God. Jonah is delivered from his most embarrassing moment as a prophet, caught up in the belly of a fish, having thought he could outrun God. Having been co-opted as a believer by the dominant culture, his heartless religiosity is a reminder to the reader that even in the darkest place of religious "exile," God is still attentive, universal, omnipresent, and able to bring home those who acknowledge his sovereignty. The initiative is God's. "By faith" is the invitation in narrative form to "reperceive the

18. Brueggemann, *Cadences*, 118–34.
19. Ibid., 119.

world as a place where the power of God works when we can neither explain nor initiate."[20] The book of Jonah encourages the reader to recognize Jonah as the anti-hero and to see with eyes of faith beyond a religion that is inclined to want to place God in a box. Jonah does not perceive God to be present with him in the belly of the fish but in the temple where Jonah's (and Israel's) faith regards God as localized. God's miraculous intervention to deliver Jonah from the fish and to send a shrub to protect him from the sun demonstrates his faithfulness to Jonah and his desire to move him out of the skewed theology that was representative of the dominant consciousness of his time.

The miraculous as technique in the book of Jonah also includes "generic signals," as termed by Alexander, of a specific genre.[21] He writes, "With regard to Jonah it is extremely important to identify these generic signals for by them the author communicates to his reader how he wishes his work to be interpreted."[22] This leads to an alternative consciousness that the author of Jonah, through the struggle between God and the character of Jonah as the antagonist, wants to render as a Prophetic Imagination. These miracles in Jonah "fit no ideology but they create communities of faith that the empire has been trying to prevent."[23] This book suggests that the alternative consciousness that is the Prophetic Imagination purpose of the author is communicated to the reader through numerous miracles, which is what Jesus in Matt 12:39–41 refers to as "the miracle of the prophet Jonah." It was the sovereignty of God's grace in refraining from justice and his lavishing of mercy in love that were signs to encourage the Jewish community of his time to embrace an alternative theology. Through the lens of ironic satire and miracles, the author allows readers to look at Jonah and to search themselves in order to understand God in a new way available to all—and thus to recognize the coming of the Messiah as part of God's sovereign plan for making available the Spirit of God to all who call on his name. It is not only in the Bible's ancient texts that these memories are contained but also within the church today, as the discipline of remembering God's accomplishments of the impossible offers concrete testimony of the Spirit of God among us. These *dangerous memories* establish, energize, and empower the contemporary metaphoric

20. Ibid., 120.

21. Quoted in Venter, "Wondervertellings," 320.

22. Ibid.

23. Brueggemann, *Cadences*, 121.

exiles of the faith to live, by faith and by the Spirit, the *Lifestyle of the Believer*. So, as memories are shared and remembered by the producer and audience respectively, "People in active touch with their memories become restless and filled with energy, prepared in a variety of ways to live beyond imperial definitions and boundaries."[24]

Dangerous Criticism

In order for the producer of moving-image media to ascertain God's newness, it is important to stay abreast of life in the context of the host empire. Dangerous criticism, as Brueggemann writes, must "keep visible the destructive seduction of the empire. . . . That criticism must assert both that the empire is incongruous with Yahweh's governance (religious critique—the *Bible* component) and that the empire cannot keep its promise of life (political critique—the *Life* component)"[25] (insertions mine).

Religious Critique

The gods of the culture must be exposed. This is the sacred texture. For this the producer must be ready, like the prophets of old, to critique the gods of the dominant culture as powerless. Similar to the author of Jonah, the poet of Second Isaiah exposes the gods made of silver and gold that "cannot move from its place. If one cries to it, it does not answer or save him from his trouble" (Isa 46:6–7). In the book of Jonah, Yahweh as the Creator God who stills the storm when Jonah is thrown into the sea is juxtaposed with the powerless gods of the sailors, who, when in danger, immediately start offering sacrifices to Jonah's God. In the contemporary culture in which the faith of Christians has been exiled, the power of the sovereign God is questioned and challenged. It is the narrative of Jonah, like the poetry of Second Isaiah, that invites Jonah's contemporaries, namely Israel (represented by Jonah), to dismiss their self-centered understanding of the sovereign God. They have become disillusioned and so succumb to the gods legitimated by the empire, though they cannot provide new and alternative realities. The Jonah narrative employing the miraculous juxtaposes the repentant actions of the pagan Ninevites to act as a foil to show up the stereotypical, complacent, hard-hearted believer, Jonah. Through its open-ended conclusion, the narrative invites

24. Ibid.
25. Ibid.

the reader to accept an alternative reality in which the intervention of a merciful God is powerfully available on a personal level. This foreshadows the redemptive work of the Messiah, who leaves the Helper amongst and for his people. This, like the poetry of Isaiah, demonstrates in whom the exiles place their hope and fosters in the community a religious criticism and, in turn, a Prophetic Imagination. The illegitimacy of the secular empire is also demonstrated by the repentance of the Ninevites. The *religious critique* of the secular empire's false gods is poignantly communicated in the narrative of Jonah through the pagans' repentance to Yahweh. This gives the message of Jonah two distinct audiences: the primary being the believer who is dominated by an incorrect theological empire, and the other being the Gentile non-believer who is co-opted by the secular dominant consciousness. Using an intricate pattern of *irony*, Israel's dominant religious consciousness is critiqued and an alternative *Lifestyle of the Believer* is legitimized repeatedly in terms of the actions of the God of creation, who can be trusted to *redeem* and *restore* human *fallenness* (as exemplified in the narrative of Jonah by God's mighty deeds of redemption of Nineveh) in response to individual repentance and sacrifice (see Chapter 5, "Prophetic Theology").

Political Critique

Political critique, as Brueggemann defines it, "addresses Israel's (the exile's) imagination. It wants Israel's sensitivity weaned from imperial realities"[26] (insertion mine). Such criticism is a prophetic act of readiness for homecoming, as it speaks of a reality beyond imperial realities to point the believer to a different home. Jonah is very sensitive to the fact that Nineveh is *the* enemy of Israel. The *political critique* of the author of the book is aimed at Israel's sensitivity toward this kind of imperial reality in the time of, and shortly after, the Babylonian exile. *Political critique* and *religious critique* are very closely knit together here. By taking Israel's enemy as an example to show Israel that God is also the God of other nations, the author places Israel's political and religious perceptions in jeopardy. Israel should no longer fear the Ninevites or the Babylonians or any other power, but should instead go and preach the Word amongst these nations, because Yahweh is the God of all nations.

---

26. Brueggemann, *Cadences*, 124.

It is thus the task of a producer of prophetic theology to speak of God's promises that have yet to be realized and to offer testimony of God's faithfulness. In so doing, the producer communicates God as a relational God who is not interested merely in administering justice but also in displaying mercy and love to each believer in terms of his or her personal walk. It is the communication of a lifestyle through the transforming power of the word of God that will effectively establish a culture of Christianity—which is the Prophetic Imagination message of *Jonahre*—through which the practice of *dangerous promises* becomes imperative. The producer seeks the disciplines of readiness to make himself or herself available for moving-image narratives, which by God's sovereignty may deliver God's gift of newness among the exiles to effect an alternative *Lifestyle of the Believer.*

Dangerous Promises

Dangerous Promises inspire hope for the exiles whose addiction to comfort and security, supplied by the host empire, has co-opted their imagination to believe that the present reality is the end in itself. The producer of a Prophetic Imagination moving-image narrative can bring, through the medium of *Jonahre*, these promises "centered around the sovereign faithfulness and the faithful sovereignty of Yahweh."[27] Jonah's message, which communicates God's faithfulness through his sovereignty, offers a newness that is a gift. It comes as a surprise to the audience when Nineveh repents, Jonah is unexpectedly delivered from the sea, and heathen sailors become God-fearing. Through God's dialogue with Jonah in the close of the book, the author desires to convey hope. God questions Jonah's anger over the plant in 4:9 as a means of prompting him to consider his overarching concern for his own well-being, which stands in contrast to his disdain for God's concern for lost people. Yahweh's deliverance of the Ninevites indicates that there is hope even for Israel. Jonah (and Israel) has to accept that God's redemption is part of his sovereign plan for the Ninevites and that he wants Jonah (and Israel) to step into a new reality. However dangerous it seems to share Yahweh with your greatest enemy, therein lies the hope. That remains, for Jonah (Israel) and today's Christians, the biggest challenge of hope. The basis for hope is not derived from a formula or powerful preaching but lies in a fresh future—in new

27. Ibid.

beginnings that result only from God's grace and gifts that are not found in the rationality of the empire. This should inspire the moving-image producers of a Prophetic Imagination *intent* to acknowledge that God's demonstration to Jonah that the fundamental factor motivating him to act is his steadfast love: "According to Nehemiah 13:22, God is asked to pity (spare) 'according to the greatness of his steadfast love' (see Jonah 4:2). God in his love desires life for his creatures, not death. For God so loved the Ninevites that . . ."[28] (insertions mine). This could not have happened within the definitions of the empire—empirical evidence cannot provide or control these realities. It is then that the author of the book of Jonah asks, as is his Prophetic Imagination *intent*, the question of Jonah and ultimately of the audience: "What gifts are yet to be given that lie outside the control and competence of the empire?"[29] The book is an ultimate foretaste, a Prophetic Imagination message, of the sovereign faithfulness, mercy, and grace of God in sending the gift of his Son, who will do what he promised, to introduce the world to his faithful sovereignty in love. In readiness, the producer of moving-image narratives must present the promise that subverts and inverts through ironic vision a new life for the spiritually exiled that will penetrate everywhere in everything with Spirit-filled richness to create the fervor of a *dangerous new song*.

Dangerous New Songs

It is in the circumstance of exile, having practiced *dangerous memories* and dangerous hopes and promises, in which the writer of Isaiah proclaims,

> Sing to the Lord a new song,
> His praise from the end of the earth!
> Let the sea roar and all that fills it,
> The coastlands and their inhabitants. (Isa 42:10)

It is in circumstances of utter despair and rampant assimilation into the dominant consciousness that the subversive act of singing is a dangerous energizing of a reality not yet received. Jonah actually sings two songs, viz. his prayer in Chapter 2 and his prayer in Chapter 4 (4:2–3). In both of these "dangerous songs," he praises the Lord. But the basis on which both these prayers are built is Jonah's selfishness and egois-

---

28. Fretheim, *Message*, 129.
29. Brueggemann, *Cadences*, 124.

tic outlook on life. Contrary to the "dangerous songs" from Isaiah that Brueggemann mentions, Jonah's "dangerous song" is not altogether a positive one, as he is still an exile belonging to the dominant culture. Only when "believers" have truly made the switch to recognize God as the God of deliverance may the church share the word of God with the world (including the moving-image media). And God is struggling with Jonah to get him to that point. Yahweh is trying to change Jonah's "confessions" into real "dangerous songs."

The expectancy of Yahweh's presence in the midst of those gathered in worship is where the "mother tongue" of the baptized is shared in community. Naming the name of Yahweh as affirmation that it is he that reigns, he that powerfully and mightily controls all things, becomes polemic. For the producer of moving-image narratives, as in the narrative of Jonah, it is the God of creation who is being named and called upon. The sailors stop worshipping their gods (Jonah 1:3) and offer sacrifices to the God of Jonah, calling upon the Lord. The Ninevites also turn to Jonah's God in repentance, as they turn to the sovereign God of creation to deliver them. The turning to the name of Yahweh as described by Jonah 1:9 is polemical, pointing to the sovereignty of the only true God recognized in the narrative as being more powerful than any other God. Through sacrifice and fasting, the characters recognize the sovereign Lord as mighty and fear him. In contrast, it is Jonah's lack of fear that leads him further and further in descent from God—first running from God onto the ship (1:3), then down to the inner part of the ship to sleep (1:5), and next into the belly of the fish (1:17). This is Jonah's "exile." In his prayer, he longs for the temple (mentioned twice: 2:4,7) in the same way that Israel had longed for the temple while in the Babylonian exile. The final picture we have of Jonah is in Chapter 4, where he is still questioning God's sovereignty and challenging the fear of God.

It is only by fearing the Lord and recognizing his all-powerful sovereignty that, in the discipline of readiness, the producer of a Prophetic Imagination can sing (worship) in the face of deathly despair. Jonah is given a second chance in the belly of the fish in a circumstance of utter hopelessness. He seeks the Lord in the form of a thanksgiving that contains elements of lament, recalling the temple as the place of communal liturgy where the "mother tongue" is spoken in worship and Yahweh is present. It is there that these dangerous new songs were commonplace for Jonah, who finds himself in the midst of an exile of arrogance and selfishness. His singing only results in old words and commonplace phrases of intertextual texts that support the displacement he experiences. Many of the words and phrases in the psalm of Jonah are reminders of other biblical psalms and texts of God's presence that are used in a new context to recover new possibilities for God to deliver people to newness: "The author used already existing psalm material to compose the Song."[30] The allegorical trends in Jonah are disputed as not very probable. West considers the fish to be the source of the prophet's deliverance, rather than his judgment (i.e., exile).[31] This book proposes that the fish be interpreted as the means of deliverance God provides for Jonah in his specific circumstances, while still giving Jonah free choice to accept or reject the Lord as the sovereign Creator God who can deliver him. Jonah and the Israelites do recognize their God, as evidenced in Jonah's confession to the sailors of God as the sovereign Creator of heaven and earth. However, the figurative and prophetic sign of Jonah in the fish also foreshadows the ultimate prophet Jesus, one of Israel's own, who is sovereignly delivered from death after spending three days and three nights in the depths of the earth, thereby ushering in the ultimate deliverance of humankind, Jew and Gentile. Jonah is the first prophet who is called out of Israel to go in person to speak God's words. "While prophets had commonly been called upon to speak against the nations (see Jeremiah 46–51, Ezekiel 25–32), no other prophet had been called upon to put in a personal appearance. To speak was one thing, to actually go there and deliver it was another."[32] The messianic framework is indeed foreshadowed, as Jesus would be the epitome of an Israelite prophet who would deliver God's word in person. God delivers Jonah based not on his heart, worship, or repentance, but because of God's sovereignty, just as he responds to the Ninevites later in the narrative. "It might be noted that the symbolic value of Jonah's activities (is) parallel to the symbolic actions of other prophets (see Isaiah 20, Ezekiel 4:1-15). What the prophet does rather than what he says becomes the vehicle for the Word of God."[33] The prophet represents Israel, the great fish represents the means by which God will deliver his people from spiritual exile, and the return of Jonah to dry land, after three days and three nights, to proclaim repentance to Nineveh represents the message

30. Fretheim, *Message*, 59.

31. West, *Hermeneutics*, 431.

32. Fretheim, *Message*, 76.

33. Ibid., 69.

of deliverance for the Gentiles as well as for Israel. Jonah's questioning of God in Chapter 4 represents in prophetic terms the wrong theology of the Jews, which endures to this day, that has prevented them from accepting the Messiah as the message and God's means of deliverance.

All of these elements point to the purpose of the message as one of a Prophetic Imagination to act as a sign—a master image of the sovereign God mercifully and sovereignly communicating his redemption for all humankind, beginning with Israel. The character of God is communicated as the sovereign, merciful deliverer of all those who repent and, in the metaphor of exile, choose to live the *Lifestyle of the Believer* that is constantly threatened and assimilated into the dominant consciousness. God is patient and forgiving to all those believers, Jew or Gentile, who in their despair and sinfulness call to him in an attitude of worship and repentance, recognizing God's act of deliverance as sovereign. This is the message of a Holy God who, through numerous examples of miraculous interventions in the *Lifestyle of the Believer* (here represented by the life of the prophet Jonah), deals graciously with those he has created. The new song thus becomes worship of a God of the miraculous, who, in response, initiates the extraordinary in and through the life of the ordinary believer (producer and audience), to affect the dominant culture in an extraordinary way.

Dangerous Bread

Included in the disciplines of readiness, which Brueggemann lists, is the concept of *dangerous bread,* taken from Isaiah 55:1–3 and relating to the daily experience of God's abundant provision in living the *Lifestyle of the Believer* and choosing God's faithfulness over consumerism and imperial security.

> Ho, every one who thirsts, come to the waters;
> And he who has no money, come, buy and eat!
> Come buy wine and milk without money and without price.
> Why do you spend your money for that which does not satisfy?
> Hearken diligently to me and eat what is good,
> And delight yourselves in fatness.
> Incline your ear, and come to me;
> Hear, that your soul may live. (Isa 55:1–3)

In this image, the poet paints a master image of the materiality of our faith. Brueggemann indicates that it begins in the "creation and culminates in the incarnation, a materiality that knows all along that our bodies count decisively."[34] With the body, food is taken in and transformed to labor, allegiance, and ultimately dependence. Thus, the biblical master image in the Isaiah narrative, as Brueggemann points out, refers us back to the narrative testimony of the Israelites, who received alternative bread (namely manna) so that they would not have to resubmit to Pharaoh for sustenance. The warning sounded in this discipline is to beware who feeds you. The provision that is God-given is a gift, not to coerce, but to exemplify God's steadfast loyalty that satisfies, as an alternative to the empire, whose bread enslaves and satiates us into silence. This image dominates the last chapter of Jonah, in which God challenges Jonah's loyalty with dangerous bread by bringing to him a discomfort that leads to a thirst that is not satisfied. This is juxtaposed with Nineveh's repentance and call for no man or beast to taste or drink, but, in repentance to the living God, to seek his faithfulness in providing mercy and, subsequently, providing for their physical needs. The materiality of faith is strikingly portrayed to Jonah when God provides a plant for shade to keep him comfortable. The loyalties of Jonah's heart are soon revealed when his discomfort becomes unbearable and God cannot be coerced to meet Jonah's desire for relief. Jonah is angry with God for taking away that "for which he did not labor" and being the cause of his discomfort. Jonah is confronted with God's love for the Gentile Ninevites. The care for the Gentiles is the "dangerous bread" that God offers to Jonah—the "bread" must be shared with Jonah's enemies, but because of his imperial, nationalistic bias, his heart is loyal to the empire, and his love for others has grown cold. Jonah has, while executing his call from God, still opted for imperial bread that leads to isolation, despair, and anxiety. He has not changed his nationalistic theology and is left with the example of the Ninevites—spared, protected, and cared for by the living God.

Today the producer of moving-image media narrative who seeks to be used as a prophet of storytelling to transform culture must, like Jonah, heed this warning and be ready to abandon what Brueggemann calls:

> junk food, the junk of social ideology, the attractiveness of consumerism, the killing seductions of security and despair; we are domesticated, silenced in our satiation. . . . What freedom there would be for us exiles if we left off the dominant hopes of our society, if we refused the dominant fears all around us, if we ate

34. Brueggemann, *Cadences*, 130.

bread that hopes only evangelical possibility and that fears only the truth of God's faithfulness."[35]

DANGEROUS DEPARTURES

For the producer, worship is the place to prepare to communicate dangerous departures for the community in exile through moving-image narrative. It is in the liturgy that the community gathers together and "imaginatively anticipates its peculiar life in the world and enacts its displacement and homelessness, its deep yearning . . . and having a vision of home."[36] The producer must, as did the poet in Deutero-Isaiah and the author of Jonah, speak to the audience in exile about moving beyond their place of worship into the cultural reality of secularism and risking not being assimilated. To live and *edutain* the culture with the alternative *Lifestyle of the Believer* is a choice to depart from the ideology of the dominant culture of the empire and to embrace the biblical worldview of a Prophetic Imagination. The departure of the exiles from Babylon is the second departure of Israel from an oppressive empire (the first being from Egypt), and of this departure the poet of Isaiah writes:

> Depart, depart, go out thence!
> Touch no unclean thing;
> Go out from the midst of her, purify yourselves,
> you who bear the vessels of the Lord.
> For you shall not go out in haste,
> and you shall not go in flight,
> for the Lord will go before you,
> and the God of Israel will be your rear guard. (Isa 52:11–12)

The exiles are commanded to depart this time from exile not as from Egypt, but without fear and panic and haste, certain of God's all-encompassing protection and safety in the midst of alienation, with him acting as their bodyguard. This departure at first is a visionary disengagement but must become the joyful act of living an alternative lifestyle, a homecoming that signifies that God is powerfully at work to restore creation as *dangerous departures* are taken.

In the story of Jonah, the narrator tells of this same departure from cultural assimilation to see God redeeming his creation. In metaphoric exile, Jonah is co-opted by the nationalistic mentality of the clergy of his

35. Ibid., 131.
36. Ibid., 132.

time. He flees in haste and is thrust into the storm without God's protection. It is only as Jonah is in the belly of the fish that God enacts miraculous newness in order to get Jonah back to dry land, where he could make a dangerous departure to obey God's call to newness. However, this alternative consciousness is not birthed in Jonah, although he acts obediently. The dangerous departure God has in mind for Jonah is that he must depart from his exile of fleeing from and resisting God. His departure is not *from* the Ninevites but *to* the Ninevites, and to any other Gentile nation. Jonah must depart from the dominant culture of complacency and selfishness in order to share his God's coming with grace for all cultures for all nations—even the Gentile Nineveh. The Ninevites repent, the oppressive power of the empire is broken, and the miraculous homecoming of these Gentile sinners becomes reality through their *dangerous departure* to live the *Lifestyle of the Believer*. The producer must allow nothing to co-opt or assimilate is or her call to create messages of prophetic newness through the power of the Holy Spirit. It is only as the disciplines of readiness make the producer available for *dangerous departures* within the resident culture that Prophetic Imagination can translate into the form, *style*, and resulting *Jonahre* genre that can transform the culture with Spirit-filled effectiveness.

CONCLUSION

From a Prophetic Imagination perspective, the book of Jonah, as analyzed by means of a socio-rhetorical methodology, and the struggles of Jonah as prophet in his own exilic circumstance and the disciplines of readiness as Brueggemann describes them, translates a message to producers today as they stand ready to be used to create film and television stories for transforming culture with Spirit-filled effectiveness. This book proposes the term *Jonahre* to describe the medium, in terms of format and *style*, to allow for Spirit-filled *content*. As the producer of moving-image narratives harnesses this medium to capture the message and seeks to present and analyze elements of truth in a culture co-opted by the dominant ideologies and false theologies of our time, it is nothing short of God's newness that can entrust stories to subvert, invert, and transform the culture. Disciplines of readiness are the acts in which the human spirit allows and waits on the Spirit of God to communicate the grace of God as possibilities not yet envisioned to establish a Prophetic Imagination through producers of film (and television) to the post-Christian culture.

CHAPTER 12

Final Applications of *Jonahre*

INTRODUCTION

*J*ONAHRE HAS BEEN DESCRIBED in this book as a genre by which the moving-image media can establish an alternative holy consciousness. (Refer to appendices A, B, and C for charts illustrating the terms discussed in this chapter.) This form of communication seeks to redeem culture by reflecting God's glory in every aspect of the *Lifestyle of the Believer* in the midst of the post-Christian, popular media "psychobabble," which regards human beings as the center of themselves. This can only be accomplished by considering the Word of God as preeminent and by pondering the glory of God as present in all of *Life*, including the dominant culture. This includes conditions and experiences such as sickness and health, prosperity and need, through which God in his sovereignty has assigned purpose to each individual's life that we might bring him glory.

Jonahre's uniqueness is that it can serve as a theological model for fictional, biblically based moving-image storytelling to transform culture, telling *Lifestyle of the Believer* **stories** that challenge the popular culture and present an alternative way to live, even, and often, implicitly. *Edutainment* and *irony* in the moving-image media is a counterintuitive form of presenting the *Lifestyle of the Believer* with the message of an alternative—communicating not the self as center, but the existence of the self for God's glory. In the moving-image narrative, it is by displaying the absence of God in the *Life* of the dominant culture that the *tragedy* of human existence is understood. Through the interaction of the holy Other in and through these conditions, the revelatory *comedy* of the *Lifestyle of the Believer* is enacted in the narrative—a counter-drama. Finally, the translation of the character of God (*Bible*) in the *Lifestyle of the Believer* in terms that are familiar to the dominant, closed definitions of reality allows for communication of the message of hope with the quality of a *fairy tale*.

Consider the parallel between the biblical narrative in 1 Samuel 16, in which Samuel goes to Jesse, the father of David, to have God show him the future king of Israel, and the *fairy tale* Cinderella, in which the prince looks for his chosen bride with slipper in hand. This analogy essentially points to the way biblical truth is communicated. Truth and holiness are on the surface level, hidden when looking with secular humanist glasses at a situation; they are often not recognized and, when revealed, surprise the reader. It is Bruno Bettelheim who suggests that our fairy tales shape the imagination of children to create alternative possibilities.[1] Play and imagination theory has been purported in this book to suggest that *irony* as a *style* in narrative makes available the reconstruction of an alternative set of definitions of self, world, other, and God.

After considering the sons presented to him, Samuel declared that none were fit to be king of Israel (1 Samuel 16:10) and inquired if there were any other. Only David, a young shepherd boy not considered worthy of this position, was absent. Similarly, Cinderella was initially not presented to the prince since she was only a servant girl in the house of her stepsisters. It was, however, her foot that would fit the slipper and make her the appointed bride of the prince. As *irony* functions in aspects of the *fairy tale*, so God in the biblical narratives has, time and again, ironically taken steps to reveal himself in the tragedies of life and amongst people where he seems absent. This turns the secular naturalism worldview of the dominant consciousness upside down, bringing about newness as an alternative—almost entertainingly so. The astonishment and amazement brought forth in these narratives is elicited by the form and *content* of the *fairy tale* element. This energizing to an alternative reality is what the proposed form, *edutainment*, encompassing truth as *comedy*, *tragedy*, and *fairy tale*, achieves and, in the context of *Jonahre* as genre, results in adoration and worship of the One who gives the newness in the first place. The goal of *Jonahre* is to employ the character of God's love and holiness displayed in biblical narrative imagination to bring the audience to re-imagine life as God has communicated it to be. Examination of

1. Bettelheim, *Enchantment,* quoted in Brueggemann, *Power,* 46.

the narrative literature of the book of Jonah and analysis of the author's aim to persuade Jonah and Israel to "re-imagine life" reveal a biblically based model to exemplify how *Jonahre* functions to effectively create and nurture an alternative *Lifestyle of the Believer* by communicating the transcendental.

The *Lifestyle of the Believer* is exemplified *par excellence* in the life of Jesus. The ultimate Prophetic Imagination message is Jesus in person, who becomes the medium to first criticize and dismantle the dominant consciousness and then to energize by establishing an alternative reality to emerge out of the dominant culture. This functions as testimony to the sovereignty and glory of God as holy, inspiring transformation and cultural renewal, which in turn leads to worship. This pattern of communication for biblical moving-image media—including the format of *edutainment*, the *style* of *irony*, and *content* and *intent* resulting in a Prophetic Imagination with the audience—is called *Jonahre*. *Jonahre*, as the narrative medium that synchronizes with the message to criticize the dominant consciousness, embodies compassion for the marginalized, while energizing in terms of biblical truth. This was evidenced in the book of Jonah, as it was analyzed in this book, applying the socio-rhetorical method to the text. Stories that do not have Yahweh at the center of truth echo Brueggemann's analysis of the use of Greek myth material to inform classical Freudian psychology: "Most of these stories are flattened into psychological transactions without robust social reality or dangerous theological force."[2] The Narrative Paradigm must become more than the sum of the parts, as *Jonahre* renders a playful reconstruction to retell our stories with Yahweh at the center, engaging and balancing *power* (*Life*), *personality* (the *Lifestyle of the Believer*), and *providence* (*Bible*—the claim that Yahweh is an indispensable character in the narrative.[3]

DISCUSSION OF SUCCESSFUL BIBLICALLY BASED PRODUCTIONS

The Passion of the Christ

It is, for many, the testimony of the biblically based production of *The Passion of the Christ* (March 2004), produced by Mel Gibson, that such a balance between *Bible*, *Life*, and *Lifestyle of the Believer*, both on and off

2. Brueggemann, *Power*, 44.

3. See Brueggemann, *Power*, 45–46.

screen, successfully captured the imaginations of the dominant, postmod-ern, post-Christian consciousness. By April 15, 2004, as the dissertation on which this book is based was being completed, the film had already taken in $350 million, making it at least the eighth biggest earner of all time.[4] As the biblical account of the last twelve hours of Jesus' passion was portrayed in Aramaic and Latin, a version of the reality of the biblical testimony was seen and experienced by audiences. In order to understand the artistic and theological integration of the subject of the film, the three-phase interdisciplinary models are applied below.

The film is predominantly an attempt to represent the biblical account of events surrounding the crucifixion, providing a real portrayal delivered more through context than proposition, with minimal teachings from Christ. Therefore, the *Bible-Content* component of the Prophetic Imagination message of Model Two is the starting point for this film. This component is informed by the consideration of the *Bible, Life,* and *Lifestyle of the Believer* components in the Prophetic Theology Model One to communicate effectively the relevance of Jesus's suffering as the God-man in the context and culture of his time. Gibson develops conceptual imagery and symbolism in order to present visually the forces of evil and the *tragedy* of the absence of God that resulted in the horrific crucifixion of Christ.[5] In the agony and grief that these images evoke, the producer criticizes the contemporary dominant consciousness of the audience through the form of *edutainment* to shock the numbed consciousness. The audience is educated in terms of the brutal reality of what the Savior suffered, and this lends historical validity to the biblical message that, through film in the present context, entertains as it communicates biblical truths, thereby impacting the dominant consciousness.

The symbolism is also employed to present every man (*Life-Audience*) in relation to God/Christ (*Bible-Content*). For example, in the symbolism of Judas and Jesus in the bridge scene.[6] Judas represents the unbeliever who cannot escape from truth, while the scene depicting Simon the Cyrene represents every man who is presented with the cross and subsequently develops a deeper relationship with Jesus. These artis-tic, poetic renderings of the biblical account illustrate the result of using

4. See Appendix A.
5. Ibid.
6. Ibid., point 9.

the first and second models to bring theological balance between the *Life–Audience* (*power*) component and the *Bible–Content* (*providence*) component to *edutain* the audience, the result of Model Three. The film creatively shows *power* as evil in the context of the life of Jesus, in relation to *providence,* God's will for Jesus, which communicated Christ's passion effectively. However, this book proposes that the subversive *personality* aspect that the audience could relate to was external to the film narrative, as this aspect was the off-screen testimony of Gibson's own personal spiritual journey in making and releasing the film. Yet this component served to balance the elements of *power* and *providence* on screen. As a follower of Christ who is also identified with mainstream personalities, Gibson and his testimony and passion for Christ became the medium for the message in this film that issued an invitation to the audience to adopt the alternative *Lifestyle of the Believer.*

This requires socio-rhetorical criticism to discover the inner texture, intertexture, social and cultural texture, ideological, and sacred texture of the text to explore what the text means. This process becomes part of models one and two, to be applied to the biblical text to extract meaning that can engage the contemporary audience's enculturation with the biblical context, evoking a Prophetic Imagination. It also influences how the message is received. Gibson's conviction and passion to see this project realized required him to fund it himself and to endure much persecution. This paralleled the message that was communicated on screen.

Model Three allows the moving-image media genre to function in *form* to entertain the postmodern culture, while educating in terms of subversive biblical truth. The term in this study for such a form of biblical moving-image media is *edutainment.* The strong images and minimal dialogue used in *The Passion of the Christ* speak to the postmodern culture, which is largely image-oriented as an aural/oral culture caught in the relativism of truth dictated by feelings. In an online review, Brian Godawa attributed the effectiveness of the biblical communication in this film to its having a form suitable to the audience's cultural postmodern milieu. In terms of this study, then, Godawa's analysis describes the elements of *edutainment's* critical function and purpose that comprise part of *Jonahre,* the medium that becomes the message, genre.

> In the Middle Ages, Passion Plays originated to dramatize the Gospel for the illiterate masses without access to holy writ. In a

similar way, many people today are largely *un*literate and image-oriented, with entertainment and media functionally operating as their canonical texts. We live in a world in the grip of post-modernism with its negation of reason, language, and discourse. People are bored with sermonizing and preachiness, especially in the arts. They just won't listen to reason. They want to *experience* your metanarrative, not mentally process it with the question-able faculties of "logocentric" rationality. Make no mistake, this postmodern prejudice is imbalanced, fallacious and spiritually destructive. But like Paul identifying to a certain extent with pa-gan philosophers on Mars Hill, so *The Passion* meets the post-modern challenge with a spiritually moving experience of Christ, that will no doubt create similar reactions from the masses. Some will sneer and others will want to know more (Acts 17:32). The story is presented through strong images and minimal dialogue that will transcend culture and denomination alike. That's the positive power of image. . . . Traditional Protestant thinking has often emphasized a word oriented theology to the near-exclusion of image, and sometimes to the *total* exclusion of image, thus suf-fering under an imbalance opposite that of the postmodern. The truth is "the Word became flesh and dwelt among us" (John 1:14), a perfect unity of word and image.[7]

It is this book's conclusion that *Jonahre* describes the medium that is the message that can result in a Prophetic Imagination, co-creating and transforming the dominant postmodern culture in terms of biblical truth. Engaging the culture through *form*, *style* and *content*, and medium and message, with the theologically appropriate prophetic paradigm, is the goal of biblical moving-image media. *The Passion* achieved the unique form, using artistically rendered images to communicate the *tragedy* of the fallenness of humankind that led to the scenes of Christ's death, which provides sinners a way of redemption. It neglected, though, to incorpo-rate a *Lifestyle of the Believer* component, except in terms of the secondary identification of the audience with the suffering of Christ. The secular movie-going audience's identification with the *Lifestyle of the Believer* that lent to the power and testimony of the biblical message of the movie was transmitted through Mel Gibson's own life. The persecution Gibson suf-fered as producer for his portrayal of his Savior was widely known and provided a framework in which the audience would receive the message. This movie successfully communicated the biblical text and interpreted

7. Godawa, 2003, 4.

it into a moving-image media message; however, without a pre-existing knowledge of the context of the biblical message, the audience would have been left without the full implications of the *Lifestyle of the Believer* in terms of the biblical narrative.

Chronicles of Narnia

It is following *The Passion* that the next big landmark for faith films in Hollywood, bringing in $744.8 million world-wide, seems to be the result of another man with a theological imagination—not only that of writer C. S. Lewis but a wealthy billionaire, Philip Anschutz, who believes it is time to project onto Hollywood screens what will capture the imagination for good. Douglas Gresham, C. S. Lewis's stepson, who manages most of Lewis's estate, says: "The main reason I went with Walden . . . is because of their mandate to produce good, entertaining movies that also educate, not merely in factual matters, but in matters of ethics and values and morality."[8] After acquiring Walden Media and Bristol Bay productions, Anschutz has also become the largest shareholder of Regal Entertainment Group, the largest theater group in America. Anschutz has thus secured the distribution of the films with a biblical underpinning that he chooses to fund. *Prince Caspian*, the second Narnia film, has teamed up with Walt Disney and is successfully capturing the audience's attention with a strong, biblically based exilic message. The prophetic prince in the story, Prince Caspian, has brought the Prophetic Imagination message powerfully to the screen by leading the oppressed Narnians to freedom through the power of the christological figure, the lion Aslan, in the mythic world of C. S. Lewis's theological, creative imagination. Theologians and academics are inspired by seeing post-Christian audiences lap up the messages of redemption, salvation, and exile closely linked to biblical texts and wondering how this is possible. Scholar Michael Ward has done a thorough analysis in his recent book *Planet Narnia,* describing the theological underpinnings of Lewis's imagination as linked to the seven planets. Although plausible in terms of how Lewis arrived at these Narnia stories in his imagination, this does not accommodate these theologically imaginative processes to the screen. Many theologians and experts such as Christopher Mitchell, director of the Wade Centre, are acknowledging that the process of taking these literary masterpieces with all their implicit meaning and transferring

8. Moring, "Hellfighter," 50.

them into a different medium has its restrictions. How does the screen accommodate such a rich text so that it will remain stories that retain the integrity of the author's intention and pave the way for others to write and produce new, Spirit-filled, theologically inspired stories for the moving-image medium? It is my conclusion in examining the films of the *Chronicles of Narnia* thus far produced, that a great deal was intended by C. S. Lewis, the author's implicit communication within these narratives, as examined by Ward. It is in this implicit communication that *Jonahre* as genre is the model to develop films not only with a biblical *intent* but as part of the structure of a new genre, a Prophetic Imagination genre that would be able to guide the moving-image media through the *imagineering* of biblically based storytelling for the screen into a new Spirit-filled medium.

Michael Ward identifies the idea of a "kappa element" in C. S. Lewis and says that "'Kappa' he (Lewis) took from the initial letter of the Greek word . . . that means 'hidden' or 'cryptic.'"[9] The quest for this secret source of the Chronicles has preoccupied many theologians and storytellers, for good reason. The kappa element, also termed "atmosphere" by Lewis, is the ingredient that provides the essence of a theologically based story, similar to that of the Prophetic Imagination purpose. As Lewis would say it, "The atmosphere should be entered into so that it comprises our whole imaginative vision."[10] Lewis understood this essence of storied communication to an alternative consciousness through the complete creative work as "difficult to put into words, for really in any given work of art, it is that whole work and its total effect, not any desiccated critical account of it, . . . so one cannot jump out of this 'state of being,' this mode of Enjoyment consciousness."[11] This alternative imaginative vision of an alternative consciousness has implicit purpose and form in Lewis's work in the Narnia Chronicles that correlates extremely well with the suggested Prophetic Imagination purpose and form—that stories with theological *content* must reflect in moving-image narratives. *Jonahre* renders this biblical purpose to take form in the complete story construction—medium, *content*, and *style* that is the message. An analysis of C. S. Lewis's construction of the world of Narnia in his explanation to Dorothy Sayers, echoes the form of *Jonahre*. Lewis said he is "concerned with the 'atmosphere' of the adventures in Narnia, and we will do better in our attempt to understand

9. Ward, *Planet Narnia*, 15.

10. Ibid., 17.

11. Ibid., 18.

the Chronicles if we approach them holistically, . . . their total effect on our imaginative palate, their kappa element, than in trying to find Biblical parallels or moral 'points.' We must remember that each Narnia story is 'something made' (poiema) [*medium*] as well as 'something said' (logos) [*message*]"[12] (italics mine). Ward's work identifies that Lewis recognized the kappa element and applied it in his stories from a very early stage in 1920, and Ward gives a new term to describe its existence in stories, namely "donegality."[13] In terms of the moving-image genre, the counterpart describing this dual purpose with *content* and *intent* that is biblically derived is *imagineering* in *Jonahre*. Both "donegality" and *imagineering Jonahre* film narratives describe the conscious effort to purpose an implicit theological *intent* in the storytelling, as in *The Chronicles of Narnia*, to have the images, in Ward's words,

> "worked into the world of the characters" . . . that the "poetic whole" that they are intended to evince consists of something that already existed in the author's mind and that he intended also to express . . . a spirit that the author consciously sought to conjure but which was designed to remain implicit in the matter of the text despite being also concentrated and consummated in a Christological representative character, the more influentially to inform the work and so affect the reader.[14]

Thus, a storyteller with a theological imagination draws from a wide variety of symbolic sources tied to the biblical text, like that of the symbolic source for Lewis in the *Chronicles of Narnia* that was predominantly the seven pre-Copernicus planets as displaying the glory of God. Ward writes that Lewis, ingeniously applying the imagery of Psalm 19, which he considered the greatest poem in the Psalter and one of the finest lyrics in the world, portrayed the divine nature as at once utterly proximate and utterly remote.

> The heavens declare the glory of God:
> and the firmament sheweth his handywork . . .
> There is neither speech nor language:
> but their voices are heard among them.
> Their sound is gone out into all lands

12. Ward, *Planet Narnia*, 22.

13. Ibid., 75.

14. Ibid., 74–75.

And their words into the ends of the world.
(Ps 19:1, 3–4 Coverdale)[15]

The planets, for Lewis as the symbolist, do more than provide an allegorical representation of the gospel; Lewis *imagineers* something concrete into a world that purposes to communicate the more than natural—the supernatural or divine—that is the hidden element of this vision. Lewis's Prophetic Imagination vision employs the planets as a new structure to encapsulate the meaning and message using symbol and allegory for this story septet.

Further, Lewis' rejection of the breakdown of the kappa element into the conscious and the unconscious, as a two-fold division of knowledge, relates to the support of screen storytelling that *Jonahre* describes as built on three interrelated variables, as a genre that accommodates the dimensions of Spirit-filled knowledge in storytelling. Lewis states, "We need a three-fold division: the Unconscious, the Enjoyed, and the Contemplated."[16] In terms of the moving-image portrayal of *Jonahre*, the three terms are *Life*, as it pertains to the "Enjoyment" of the audience as their experience framework relates to the story, *Bible*, the "Contemplated" knowledge and imagery that is derived from the Scriptures, and these two, interrelated to *edutain* the audience in the screened story, give rise to the "Unconscious," or, in terms of the Prophetic Imagination, the *alternative consciousness* of the *Lifestyle of the Believer* portrayed in the screened story as a complete whole.

This three-fold division that Lewis applied to many departments of life and literary criticism he based on philosopher Samuel Alexander's *Space, Time and Deity*, and he wrote an essay on it, "Meditation in a Toolshed," allowing us into the theological imagination of this division. The three-component model that is the theological model for the transcendental presence in *Jonahre* films brings into clear view the workings of the theological thinking and practical process associated with the *Life*, *Bible*, and the *Lifestyle of the Believer* that is translated through the *edutainment* form. In Lewis's writing he incorporates these three divisions in terms of his goal to communicate the enjoyment consciousness of the *novitas* (regenerate life by the Spirit). The Spirit-filled goal of the *Jonahre* films communicates this *novitas* as an alternative consciousness,

15. Quoted in Ward, *Planet Narnia*, 238.
16. Ward, *Planet Narnia*, 17.

the *Lifestyle of the Believer,* which, through the symbolic world of the moving-image narrative, allows the consciousness of the audience to be penetrated by the Spirit. Lewis states that this regenerate man filled with the Holy Spirit and the *novitas* he brings are exceptionally difficult to symbolize. Yet he had an equally strong belief, from examining his own regenerate life, that this presence of the Spirit is "in the presence of the Spirit flooding and transvalueing every part of a Christian life . . . hence the quiet fullness of ordinary nature."[17] It is this "quiet fullness" that is the Spirit-filled presence in the imagery of the Chronicles of Narnia, "And the imagery is 'full' in the sense that it determines the overall shape and feel of each story, governing the architectronics of each narrative, the incidental ornamentation and also, most significantly the portrayal of the Christ-like character of Aslan and the Spirit that he imparts."[18]

In *Jonahre* as screened stories this grace that is sufficient for the Spirit to impart our culturally laden stories to audiences can be understood as a way of symbolizing the Spirit that does not draw attention to itself but, by the same quiet means that Lewis understood, "getting his readers to inhabit, but not Contemplate, a Reason-saturated world."[19] This is the work of the culmination of *Jonahre,* a *Lifestyle of the Believer* that is brought through *edutainment* to the audience who is implicitly invited to inhabit this Spirit-filled world. Established through a theologically imaginative process, implementing the three interdisciplinary phases guides the producers of moving-image media through the development of the images, symbols, and *irony* in terms of *content, intent, style,* and *form,* according to the biblical paradigm of Prophetic Imagination.

Music also plays a central part. This role of music was not lost on C. S. Lewis; even in his literary work's effect, he liked to compare literary images to musical themes and the richness they can evoke through the mood they establish. Ward writes at the conclusion of his book, "The Narniad, I now started to see, was a literary equivalent of Holst's *Planets Suite*; each one of the seven heavens gave the key to a different Chronicle."[20] Music as composed for the screened stories plays an irreplaceable role in the aspect of moving-image storytelling, precisely for its ability to reflect in

17. Ibid., 39.
18. Ibid.
19. Ibid.
20. Ward, *Planet Narnia,* 251.

structure what it wants to say in meaning and message. The similarities between story and music can be compared, as Lewis often highlighted, to the similarities between the composition of a story (*fairy tale*) and the effect of a symphony on mood. This genre of the *fairy tale* is what Lewis chose to compose in, in literary form; as *Jonahre* includes the aspects of *tragedy, comedy,* and *fairy tale,* it is the *fairy tale* element that communicates the alternative consciousness that is established, but not until the other two elements have also been present and real to the characters and audience of the moving-image narrative. This often-missed quality of unconscious or alternative consciousness in the *fairy-tale* element of moving-image stories can be captured by a quote from Plato that states: "Stories that are readable by children have a good claim to being the most imaginative kind of literature that there is—and that is assuming they are read only by children. But of Course they are not only read by children, nor are they (usually) intended to be."[21]

It is then a biblically based Prophetic Imagination that can, in terms of the moving-image medium and message, provide guideposts for *imagineering* stories for a Spirit-filled *Jonahre* film. The usefulness and substantive text of the Bible as source for these imaginations for Lewis's exceptional works is proof of what the movie-makers and script-writers are capable of, if given tools that allow their creativity to be led by the images and techniques as described from a Prophetic Imagination paradigm. Lewis claimed that it was George MacDonald who "baptized his imagination," and in this comparison of literary theological genius that inspired fictional Spirit-filled literary narratives, I hope we can have our imaginations baptized to *imagineer* stories for the silver screen through a Prophetic Imagination and a medium that is sensitive to and capable of encapsulating this quiet fullness of the Holy Spirit, in submission to God's sovereignty. May these stories, like those of the prophets like C. S. Lewis and the biblical writer of Jonah, become instruments for translating the ministry of *Jonahre*: a genre for Spirit-filled moving-image storytelling of the *Lifestyle of the Believer* that communicates God's coming with grace, sufficient for all peoples everywhere in all cultures. *Jonahre is* film and television to *BLESS* (the acronym for *Bible, Lifestyle, Edutainment* for *Screened Stories*) our cultures as it transforms lives by grace.

21. Ibid., 216.

APPLYING *JONAHRE* TO *THE LAMB*

Jonahre films encompasses the aspects of *form*, *style*, *content*, and *intent* for effectively communicating a biblically based Prophetic Imagination message that is presented here in terms of *The Lamb*. *The Lamb*, scheduled for probable theatrical release in November 2009 (see Jonahre.com),[22] will be the first official *Jonahre* movie and will be developed according to the model in this book. The full implementation of *Jonahre* in the making of the movie will appear in a follow-up book released within the timeframe of the release of the movie, DV.

The quest of this author was to find a theology of communication that will be practically viable and effective for developing a new form to encapsulate fictional or non-fictional stories with an implicit or explicit Christian purpose. Currently, Christian film and television do not effectively spur society toward faith in God because they do not have a defined theological purpose that establishes an alternative consciousness with the audiences or a form and genre that meets the demands of all the aspects of the message to be captured in the medium with Spirit-filled effectiveness. The objective of this book was to define clearly a theologically based, media-oriented purpose for Christian moving-image media as found in the prophetic, narrative literature of the Old Testament. Establishing, Charis Productions, the Board of Directors, consisting of professionals in marketing, distribution, finance, and production, have written a business plan with a clearly defined goal based on an agreed upon vision and mission to make films that will communicate the truth of God to the secular audience. The director, Regardt van den Bergh, states that, "The Lamb will speak to the secular movie going audiences because it deals with real people, real tragedies and circumstances that happen to all of us at some stage in our lives."[23] In personal conversations with Regardt van den Bergh in the past several years of collaboration on the upcoming films, he has reiterated his intention to write and direct movies on a continual basis that will establish an alternative lifestyle based on God's Word—an aspect which is vital to the production of a film within the context of the *Jonahre* genre. The director's purpose for the film is thus to fulfill a call to communicate an alternative, biblically based lifestyle to the secular

---

22. Permission has been granted for this study to incorporate all aspects of the movie *The Lamb* business plan and storyline, for applying the theory and academic pursuits of this book in developing a biblically based genre for the moving-image media.

23. See Appendix F.

audience—a purpose that Regardt echoes in the business plan. Regardt states, "I truly believe that God inspired this film for a specific purpose in the history of the world; it will have a tremendous impact on mankind. I believe that I am acting on a call from the Lord to do this film. . . . Our mission is to make *The Lamb* and make it well, to develop a lasting relationship with our investors and to establish a mold for the development, financing, production and distribution of films with similar *content* and vision."[24] This book proposes that *The Lamb* and the subsequent movies in the trilogy have an authorial *intent*, vision, and mission that is in line with the defined theology of communication in this book.

Having developed the three interdisciplinary paradigmatic models, an overview of each will be applied here as a multifaceted means to explore the overall purpose, composition, and meaning of *The Lamb* for accomplishing an alternative consciousness as cultural mandate.

As the story of *The Lamb* captures the imagination of the audience by presenting an ordinary first-century family (*Life* of Model One) to a twenty-first century audience (*Life-Audience* of Model Two), one is struck by how easy it is to identify with the emotions and characters in the scenes. It is in the very real portrayal of circumstances and easily recognizable surface characterization that Model One (Prophetic Theology, see Appendix A) and Model Two (Communication Theory, see Appendix B) seem to work interdependently but in close proximity to communicate the identity of the Jewish culture at the time of Jesus.

Model One crystallizes the theological aspects involved to bring *Bible, Life,* and *Lifestyle of the Believer* to the audience in terms of biblical truth. An example is the most obvious biblical theme in the movie, the sacrificing of the Passover lamb. This biblical concept is analyzed in terms of Old Testament practices still relevant at the time of Jesus that were part of the dominant consciousness of that time. However, since the Jewish religion is also a part of today's dominant culture, contemporary viewers can also identify with this first-century Jewish tradition, although animal sacrifice is no longer enacted amongst Jews. An alternative consciousness is, ironically, didactically, and yet entertainingly, portrayed by putting the *Bible-Content* (the religious ritual of animal sacrifice) in terms of a real-life family (*Life-Audience*) to communicate meaningfully the life of Christ as a Prophetic Imagination reality. As a result, the *Lifestyle of the*

24. Ibid., 9.

Believer is created in the context of the film, inviting such a response from the audience.

Model Two integrates these themes to form the compositional and dramatic characteristics of the film, based on the understanding of the enculturation of the audience to whom the message will be communicated.

> The Lamb is not a film for the Christian community. The target audience is the cynical, secular moviegoer who frowns at anything that bears a "Christian" label. To enthrall that kind of audience, the film must be thoroughly entertaining and engage viewers in the story and characters to such an extent that they will not only want to see the film a second time, but will also recommend it to their friends. Capturing an audience without compromising the message is the real challenge for The Lamb.[25]

The movie will reflect generalized *Life–Audience* themes (see Model Two), such as: a close-knit religious family torn apart by the grief of the loss of a son; the characters' different responses to sorrow; a father who questions God's purposes and blames him for his loss; a *religious* lifestyle that does not stand up to the hard tests of life, resulting in withdrawal from both family and God (Mattias); a son who loses a brother and also his father, causing him to look for emotional comfort and solace (Joel).

In Model Two, *Bible-Content* and *Life-Audience* are brought together, ironically, to educate and entertain *(edutain)* the audience. After Joel finds a lamb that he saves from near death, the animal becomes his comfort and joy, but this relationship becomes, ironically, a parallel to his budding friendship with Jesus, who is revealed through the narrative plot to be the Lamb of God, the true Comforter and Redeemer. The *style* of *irony* is well developed via imagery involving the blood of the lamb that occurs throughout the movie, culminating in a powerful montage at the crucifixion scene. The viewer is educated about the deeper meaning of the movie in the final scene, when Mattias, the father, and Joel, his son, realize that Jesus is the sacrificial innocent Lamb who was crucified and sacrificed, his blood shed for the sin of all humankind. This revelation converts Mattias from being a religious man to a man who now has eyes to see and understand the truth as revealed in Christ. As Christ's blood is shed to redeem the sins of humankind, it runs and puddles at the foot of the cross, while images of the temple sacrifices of the Passover lambs are juxtaposed symbolically to show what is being fulfilled biblically. *Irony*

25. Ibid., 5; see also 12–13, 45.

functions clearly here to construct a reality that reveals the dissonance between two levels of meaning that the text communicates with regard to the lamb.

Conclusion

The call to a prophetic moving-image media ministry will be answered as the producer practices the disciplines of readiness to create messages that *edutain* the audience through didactic, ironic vision as part of *Jonahre,* a narrative genre aimed at accomplishing a Prophetic Imagination result. Since *The Lamb* has not yet been produced, it is beyond the scope of this book to analyze the function of all of the elements that will contribute to the movie's portrayal of *irony,* its use of the form *edutainment,* and its communication of *content* with a theologically defined *intent* to become the "medium (that) is the message" with a Prophetic Imagination result. *The Lamb,* however, is uniquely positioned to become a *Jonahre* movie according to the above analysis, indicating the combination of those elements outlined that will serve to transform culture to an alternative, biblically based consciousness in a postmodern, post-Christian context.

FINAL CONCLUSIONS

The problem was that no suitable narrative format to serve as a model for communicating an alternative consciousness as cultural mandate and Prophetic Imagination purpose exists. In this book the storytelling technique and Prophetic Imagination employed by the writer/prophet of the biblical book of Jonah is proposed as a storytelling model for communicating a Prophetic Imagination purpose in the context of the oral dominant culture of exilic/post-exilic Israel, mimicking a similar exilic/ post-Christian culture today. Employing the socio-rhetorical method, the texture of the biblical text of Jonah has been analyzed to show how the form of the book synchronizes with its *content* and *intent* to communicate with didactic deliberateness a re-imagination of life, in terms of a holy God, to establish communities of *Shalom* in exilic circumstance. Using Brueggemann's (1997) analysis of a Christian culture in exile, *Jonahre* is proposed as a genre for *imagineering* narratives for the screen by integrating theology and communication in three interdisciplinary models, to become a practical, viable form to *edutain* the numbed consciousness of the dominant culture and transform culture in terms of a Kingdom reality.

Appendix A

PROPHETIC IMAGINATION

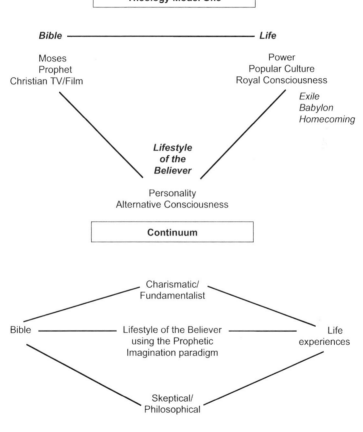

| Theology Model One |

Bible ———————————————— **Life**

Moses
Prophet
Christian TV/Film

Power
Popular Culture
Royal Consciousness

Exile
Babylon
Homecoming

Lifestyle
of the
Believer

Personality
Alternative Consciousness

| Continuum |

Charismatic/
Fundamentalist

Bible ——————— Lifestyle of the Believer ——————— Life
using the Prophetic   experiences
Imagination paradigm

Skeptical/
Philosophical

Basics

Lifestyle is living in **faith** in **hope** because we serve a God of **love.**

Aim of visual communication: to illustrate an intimate relationship with a living God, concerned passionately for his creation/people.

Method: portraying a lifestyle, instead of Bible stories, in popular culture terminology.

187

Appendix B

Communication Model Two

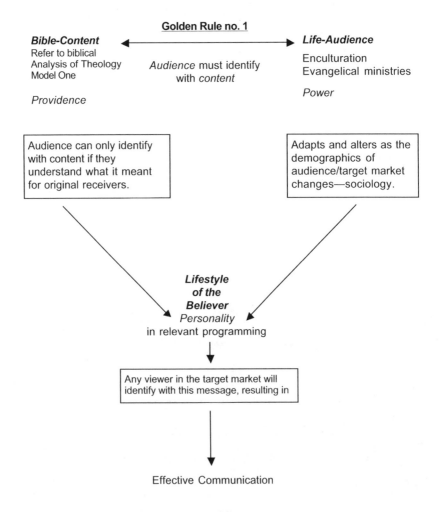

Golden Rule no. 1

Bible-Content
Refer to biblical
Analysis of Theology
Model One

Providence

Audience must identify
with *content*

Life-Audience
Enculturation
Evangelical ministries

Power

Audience can only identify
with content if they
understand what it meant
for original receivers.

Adapts and alters as the
demographics of
audience/target market
changes—sociology.

**Lifestyle
of the
Believer**
Personality
in relevant programming

Any viewer in the target market will
identify with this message, resulting in

Effective Communication

Appendix C

Edutainment Model Three

Golden Rule no. 2

Suitable *form* must be chosen for *content*

Bible ———————————————————————— *Life*

Biblical situations
must be explicated/
illustrated

Contemporary situations
portrayed/illustrated

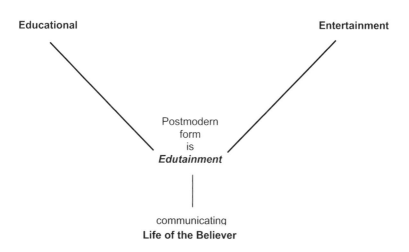

Educational   **Entertainment**

Postmodern
form
is
Edutainment

communicating
Life of the Believer

Considering theology, audience, content, intent, form, and style as genre criteria, the **Bible**, **Life,** and **Lifestyle of the Believer** approach formulates an effective Christian "medium that is the message" to communicate a Prophetic Imagination. **Genre= Format and Style + Content and Intent**
i.e. *Jonahre,* **the** *medium* **that is the** *message*

Appendix D

Socio-Rhetorical Model of Textual Communication and Inner Texture

REDRAWING THE BOUNDARIES

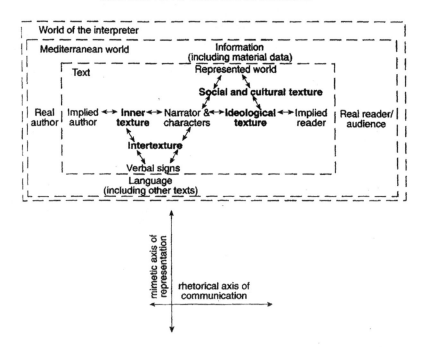

Figure 2.1 Socio-rhetorical model of textual communication

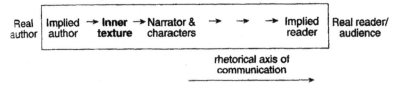

Figure 2.2 Inner texture

Appendix E

Receiver and Channel Research by Christine Gunn-Danforth 1993
See www.Jonahre.com

Appendix F

THE LAMB Business Plan used by permission of Charis Productions
See www.Jonahre.com

Appendix G

Duck/Rabbit diagram of Jastrow
See www.Jonahre.com
or http://socrates.berkeley.edu/~kihlstrm/JastrowDuck.htm

Appendix H

Notes on the *The Passion of the Christ* Symbolism
See www.Jonahre.com
or http://www.freerepublic.com/focus/f-religion/1103877/posts

Bibliography

Ackroyd, P. R. *Exile and Restoration. A Study of Hebrew Thought of the Sixth Century BC.* London: SCM Press, 1968.

———. *Israel under Babylon and Persia.* London: Oxford University Press, 1970.

Allen, L. C. *The Books of Joel, Obadiah, Jonah, and Micah.* The New International Commentary on the Old Testament. Grand Rapids, MI: Eerdmans, 1976.

Alter, R. *The Art of Biblical Narrative.* New York: Basic Books, 1981.

———. *The Art of Biblical Poetry.* New York: Basic Books, 1985.

Andrew, J. D. *The Major Film Theories.* Galaxy Books. New York: Oxford University, 1976.

Armstrong, B. *The Electric Church.* Nashville: Thomas Nelson, 1979.

Arthur, C. J. "Some Reflections on Theological Education and Communication." *Religious Education* 84 (1989) 103–30.

Bar-Efrat, S. *Narrative Art in the Bible.* Sheffield, UK: Almond Press, 1989.

Bettelheim, B. *The Uses of Enchantment: The Meaning and Importance of Fairy Tales.* London: Thames & Hudson, 1976.

Bluck, J. *Beyond Neutrality. A Christian Critique of the Media.* Geneva: World Council of Churches, 1978.

Boers, H. *What is New Testament Theology? The Rise of Criticism and the Problem of a Theology of the New Testament.* Philadelphia: Fortress Press, 1979.

Bolin, T. M. *Freedom Beyond Forgiveness. The Book of Jonah Re-examined.* Journal for the Study of the Old Testament. Supplement Series. Sheffield, UK: Sheffield Academic Press, 1997.

Boorstin, D. J. *The Americans: The Democratic Experience.* New York: Vintage Books, 1973.

Botha, P. J. "The Communicative Function of Comparison in Hosea." *Old Testament Essays* 6 (1993) 57–71.

Breytenbach, A. P. B. "Die Boodskap van die Boek Jona." *Hervormde Teologiese Studies* 59 (1983) 135–40.

Brueggemann, W. *Cadences of Home. Preaching among Exiles.* Louisville: Westminster John Knox Press, 1997.

———. *Hope within History.* Atlanta: John Knox Press, 1987.

———. *Hopeful Imagination: Prophetic Voices in Exile.* Minneapolis, MN: Fortress Press, 1986.

———. *Interpretation and Obedience: From Faithful Reading to Faithful Living.* Minneapolis, MN: Fortress Press, 1991.

———. *Old Testament Theology: Essays on Structure, Theme, and Text.* Minneapolis, MN: Fortress Press, 1992.

———. *Power, Providence, and Personality: Biblical Insight into Life and Ministry.* Louisville: Westminster John Knox Press, 1990.

Bibliography

————. *The Prophetic Imagination.* Philadelphia: Fortress Press, 1978.

————. *Texts Under Negotiation. The Bible and Post-modern Imagination.* Minneapolis, MN: Fortress Press, 1993.

Buechner, F. *Telling the Truth: The Gospel as Tragedy, Comedy, and Fairy Tale.* New York: Harper & Row, 1977.

Burke, K. *Counter-statement.* 2nd ed. Berkeley: University of California Press, 1968.

————. *The Rhetoric of Religion: Studies in Logology.* Berkeley: University of California Press, 1970.

Carey, J. W. *Communication as Culture: Essays on Media and Society.* Boston: Unwin Hyman,1989.

Chatman, S. *Story and Discourse: Narrative Structure in Fiction and Film.* Ithaca, NY: Cornell University Press, 1978.

Childs, B. S. *The New Testament as Canon: An Introduction.* Philadelphia: Fortress Press, 1985.

Christensen, D. L. "The Song of Jonah: A Metrical Analysis." *JBL* 104 (1985) 217–31.

Christians, C. G. "Redemptive Media as the Evangelical's Cultural Task." In *American Evangelicals and the Mass Media,* edited by Q. J. Schultze, 331–54. Grand Rapids, MI: Baker Academic, 1990.

Coetzee, J. H. "The Fear Motif in Jonah." *Ekklesiastikos Pharos* 75.2 (1993) 2–6.

Colson, C. W. *Chuck Colson Speaks: Twelve Key Messages from Today's Leading Defender of the Christian Faith.* Uhrichsville, OH: Promise Press, 2000.

————, and N. Pearcey. *How Now Shall We Live?* Wheaton: Tyndale House Publishers, 1999.

Conradie, E. M., et al. *Op Soek Na Jona: Verskilllende Benaderings tot die Interpretasie van die Bybel.* Bellville, South Africa: Universiteit van Wes-Kaapland, 1995.

Cox, H. *The Secular City.* New York: Macmillan, 1990.

Crites, S. "The Narrative Quality of Experience," *Journal of the American Academy of Religion* 39 (September 1971).

Crossan, J. D. *The Dark Interval: Toward a Theology of Story.* Niles, IL: Argus Communications, 1975.

Day, J. "Problems in the Interpretation of the Book of Jonah." In *In Quest of the Past: Studies on Israelite Religion, Literature, and Prophetism: Papers Read at the Joint British-Dutch Old Testament Conference, Held at Elspeet,* 1988, edited by A. S. Van der Woude, 32–47. Leiden, Neth.: Brill, 1990.

Deist, F. E. *Die God van Jona.* Cape Town: Tafelberg, 1983.

Eagleton, T. *Ideology: An Introduction.* London: Verso Press, 1991.

Ellul, J. *The Presence of the Kingdom.* 2nd ed. Colorado Springs: Helmers and Howard, 1989.

Eslinger, R. L. *Narrative and Imagination: Preaching the Worlds That Shape Us.* Minneapolis, MN: Fortress Press, 1995.

Ferre, J. P., editor. *Channels of Belief: Religion and American Commercial Television.* Ames: Iowa State University, 1990.

Fisher, W. R. *Human Communication as Narration: Toward a Philosophy of Reason, Value, and Action.* Columbia: University of South Carolina Press, 1987.

Fiske, J. *Television Culture.* New York: Routledge, 1987.

Forster, R. S. *Restoration of Israel, a Study in Exile and Return.* London: Darton, Longman & Todd, 1970.

Bibliography

Frangipane, F. *The Three Battlegrounds: An In-depth View of the Three Areas of Spiritual Warfare—The Mind, the Church, and the Heavenly Places.* Cedar Rapids, IA: Arrow, 1989.

Fretheim, T. E. "Jonah and Theodicy." *ZAW* 90 (1978) 227–37.

———. *The Message of Jonah.* Minneapolis, MN: Augsburg Publishing House, 1977.

Frow, J. *Marxism and Literary History.* Cambridge, MA: Harvard University Press, 1986.

Gadamer, H. *Truth and Method.* 2nd rev. ed. New York: Crossroad, 1989. 104–8.

Geertz, C., editor. *The Interpretation of Cultures.* New York: Basic Books, 1973.

———. *Local Knowledge. Further Essays in Interpretive Anthropology.* New York: Basic Books, 1983.

———. *Myth, Symbol, and Culture.* New York: W. W. Norton, 1971.

Goethals, G. T. *The TV Ritual: Worship at the Video Altar.* Boston: Beacon, 1981.

———. *The Electronic Golden Calf: Images, Religion, and the Making of Meaning.* Cambridge, MA: Cowley, 1990.

Good, E. M. *Irony in the Old Testament.* Philadelphia: Westminster, 1965.

Gordon, M. M. "The Subsociety and the Subculture." In *Subcultures,* edited by D. Arnold, 150–63. Berkeley, CA: Glendessary Press, 1970.

Greeley, A. *God in Popular Culture.* Chicago: Thomas More, 1988.

Griffin, E. *A First Look at Communication Theory.* New York: McGraw-Hill, 1994.

Gronbeck, B. E., et al., eds. *Media, Consciousness, and Culture: Explorations of Walter Ong's Thought.* London: Sage, 1991.

Gunn, C. "An Approach to Effective Communication for Christian Television." BA Honors Thesis, University of Johannesburg, 1993.

Gunn, D. M., and D. N. Fewell. *Narrative in the Hebrew Bible.* Oxford Bible Series. New York: Oxford University, 1993.

Hanegraaff, H. *Christianity in Crisis.* Eugene, OR: Harvest House, 1993.

———. *Counterfeit Revival.* Dallas: Word Publishing, 1997.

———. "Counterfeit Revival." *Christian Research Journal* (Jul–Aug 1997) 8–18.

Hauerwas, S. *Against the Nations: War and Survival in a Liberal Society.* Minneapolis, MN: Winston, 1985.

Hauser, A. J. "Jonah: In Pursuit of the Dove." *JBL* 104 (1985) 21–37.

Holbert, J. C. "Deliverance Belongs to Yahweh!: Satire in the Book of Jonah." *JSOT* 21 (1981) 70–75.

House, C. A. "Hebrew Prophetic Oratory: A Rhetoric of Confrontation." MA dissertation, Syracuse University, 2007.

Klein, R. W. *Israel in Exile: A Theological Interpretation.* Philadelphia: Fortress Press, 1979.

Kriel, J. R. "Jonah—The Story of a Whale or a Whale of a Story?" *Theologia Evangelica* XVIII.2 (1985) 9–17.

Kristeva, J. *The Kristeva Reader.* Edited by T. Moi. New York: Columbia University Press, 1986.

Kuhn, T. S. *The Structure of Scientific Revolutions.* 2d ed. Chicago: University of Chicago Press, 1970.

Laing, R. D. *The Politics of Experience.* New York: Pantheon Books, 1967.

Landes, G. M. "The Kerygma of the Book of Jonah." *Interpretation* 21 (1967) 3–31.

The Lausanne Movement. "Global Issue: Orality." No pages. Online: www.lausanne.org/issue-orality/overview.html.

Bibliography

Lipson, S. C. "Ancient Egyptian Rhetoric: It All Comes Down to *maat.*" In *Rhetoric before and after the Greeks,* edited by S. C. Lipson & R. Binkley, 74–98. Albany: State University of New York Press, 2004.

L'Engle, Madeleine. *Walking on Water: Reflections on Faith and Art.* Wheaton, IL: Harold Shaw, 1972.

Licht, J. *Storytelling in the Bible.* Jerusalem: Magnes, 1978.

Lichter, S. R., et al. *Prime Time: How TV Portrays American Culture.* Washington, DC: Regnery, 1994.

Lindbeck, G. A. *The Nature of Doctrine: Religion and Theology in a Postliberal Age.* Philadelphia: Westminster, 1984.

Lipson, S. C. "Ancient Egyptian Rhetoric: It All Comes Down to *maat.*" In *Rhetoric before and beyond the Greeks,* edited by S. C. Lipson and R. Binkley, 74–98. Albany: State University of New York Press, 2004.

Littlejohn, S. W. *Theories of Communication.* Belmont, CA: Wadsworth, 1996.

Mac Cormac, E. R. *A Cognitive Theory of Metaphor.* Cambridge, MA: MIT Press, 1985.

Mack, B. L., and V. K. Robbins. *Patterns of Persuasion in the Gospels.* Sonoma, CA: Polebridge, 1989.

Magonet, J. *Form and Meaning: Studies in Literary Technique in the Book of Jonah.* Sheffield, UK: Almond Press, 1983.

Malina, B. J. *The New Testament World. Insights from Cultural Anthropology.* Louisville: Westminster John Knox Press, 1993.

Marty, M. E. *A Nation of Behavers.* Chicago: The University of Chicago Press, 1976.

McLuhan, M. *Understanding Media: The Extensions of Man.* New York: McGraw Hill, 1964.

Mintz, A. *Hurban: Responses to Catastrophe in Hebrew Literature.* New York: Columbia University Press, 1984.

Moring, M. "Hollywood Hellfighter." *Christianity Today* (May 2008) 46–50.

Mouton, J., and H. C. Marais. *Basic Concepts in the Methodology of the Social Sciences.* Pretoria: Human Services Research Council, 1990.

Mouw, R. *Consulting the Faithful: What Christian Intellectuals Can Learn from Popular Culture.* Grand Rapids, MI: Eerdmans, 1994.

Muilenberg, J. "Form Criticism and Beyond." *JBL* 88 (1969) 1–18.

Newbigin, L. *Foolishness to the Greeks: The Gospel and Western Culture.* Grand Rapids, MI: Eerdmans, 1986.

Ong, W. *Orality and Literacy: The Technologizing of the Word.* London: Methuen, 1982.

Palakeel, J., editor. *The Bible and the Technologies of the Word.* Bangalore, India: Asian Trading Corporation, 2007.

Patrick, D., and A. Scult. *Rhetoric and Biblical Interpretation.* Bible and Literature. Sheffield, UK: Almond, 1990.

Payne, D. F. "Jonah from the Perspective of Its Audience." *JSOT* 13 (1979) 3–12.

Perelman, C. *The Realm of Rhetoric.* Translated by William Kluback. London: University of Notre Dame, 1982.

Perelman, C. and L. Olbrechts-Tyteca. *The New Rhetoric: A Treatise on Argumentation.* Translated by John Wilkinson and Purcell Weaver. London: University of Notre Dame, 1969.

Perkinson, H. J. *How Things Got Better: Speech, Writing, Printing, and Cultural Change.* Westport, CT: Bergin & Garvey, 1995.

Peterson, E. H. *Subversive Spirituality.* Grand Rapids, MI: Eerdmans, 1997.

Bibliography

Postman, N. *Amusing Ourselves to Death: Public Discourse in the Age of Show Business.* New York: Viking, 1985.

Potgieter, J. H. *'n Narratologiese Ondersoek van die Boek Jona.* Pretoria: Perskor, 1991.

Prinsloo, W. S., editor. *Tweegesprek met God. Die Literatuur van die Ou Testament Deel 3.* Cape Town: Tafelberg, 1987.

Reed, W. L. *Dialogues of the World: The Bible as Literature According to Bakhtin.* New York: Oxford University Press, 1993.

Rimmon-Kenan, S. *Narrative Fiction: Contemporary Poetics.* London: Methuen, 1983.

Roberts, K. A. "Toward a Generic Concept of Counter-Culture." *Sociological Focus* 11 (1978) 111–26.

Robbins, V. K. *Exploring the Texture of Texts. A Guide to Socio-rhetorical Interpretation.* Valley Forge, PA: Trinity Press International, 1996.

———. *The Tapestry of Early Christian Discourse. Rhetoric, Society, and Ideology.* New York: Routledge, 1996.

Roemer, M. *Telling Stories: Postmodernism and the Invalidation of Traditional Narrative.* Lanham, MD: Rowman & Littlefield, 1995.

Rogers, G. "Mel's Passion." *Christian Living Today* (April 2004) 23–25.

Rossouw, G. J. "Theology in a Postmodern Culture: Ten Challenges." *HTS* 49 (1993) 894–907.

Ruthven, J. "They Called Jesus a Counterfeit Too." *Charisma* (July 1997) 60–62.

Sasson, J. M. *Jonah.* New York: Doubleday, 1990.

Schrader, P. *Transcendental Style in Film: Ozu, Bresson, Dreyer.* Berkeley: University of California Press, 1972.

Schultze, Q. J. *American Evangelicals and the Mass Media.* Grand Rapids, MI: Baker Academic, 1990.

———. *Christianity and the Mass Media in America: Toward a Democratic Accommodation.* Rhetoric and Public Affairs. East Lansing: Michigan State University Press, 2003.

———. *Communicating for Life.* Grand Rapids, MI: Baker Academic, 2000.

———. "The 'God-Problem' in Communication Studies." *Journal of Communication and Religion* 28 (March 2005) 1–22.

———. *Redeeming Television: How TV Changes Christians—How Christians Can Change TV.* Downers Grove, IL: Intervarsity, 1992.

Scott, J. M., editor. *Exile: Old Testament, Jewish, and Christian Conceptions.* Leiden, Neth.: Brill, 1997.

Scott, R. B. Y. *The Relevance of the Prophets.* New York: Macmillan Company, 1968.

Shriver, D. W. "What Business Managers Should Know about the Clergy." In *Business, Religion and Ethics*, edited by D. G. Jones, 119–29. Cambridge, MA: Oelgeschlager, Gunn, and Hain Publishers, 1982.

Smith, D. L. *The Religion of the Landless: The Social Context of the Babylonian Exile.* Bloomington, IN: Meyer Stone Books, 1989.

Sternberg, M. *The Poetics of Biblical Narrative: Ideological Literature and the Drama of Reading.* Indiana Library Biblical Series. Bloomington: Indiana University, 1987.

Stuart, D. *Hosea-Jonah.* Word Biblical Commentary, 31. Waco, TX: Word Books, 1978.

TeSelle, S. M. *Speaking in Parables: A Study in Metaphor and Theology.* Philadelphia: Fortress Press, 1975.

Trible, P. *Rhetorical Criticism: Context, Method, and the Book of Jonah.* Minneapolis, MN: Fortress Press, 1994.

Ugolnik, A. *The Illuminating Icon.* Grand Rapids, MI: Eerdmans, 1989.

Van Heerden, S. W. "Imagination and the Interpretation of the Old Testament." *Old Testament Essays* 7 (1994) 343–59.

———. "Humour and the Interpretation of the Book of Jonah." *Old Testament Essays* 5 (1992) 389–401.

———. "Naïve Realism and the Historicity of the Book of Jonah." *Old Testament Essays* 3 (1990) 71–92.

Venter, P. M. "Die Funksie van die Wondervertellings in die Jonaverhaal." *HTS* 42 (1986) 312–26.

Vriezen, T. H. C. *Hoofdlijnen der Theologie van het Oude Testament.* Wageningen, Neth.: H. Veenman and Zonen N. V., 1966.

Ward, M. *Planet Narnia: The Seven Heavens in the Imagination of C. S. Lewis.* New York: Oxford University Press, 2008.

West, G. O. *Biblical Hermeneutics of Liberation: Modes of Reading the Bible in the South African Context.* Pietermaritzburg: Clusters Publications, 1991.

Westermann, C. *Isaiah 40–66.* Translated by David M. H. Stalker. The Old Testament Library. London: SCM. Press, 1969.

Williams, F. *The New Communication.* Belmont, CA: Wadsworth Publishing Company, 1984.

Wolff, H. W. *Obadiah and Jonah.* Translated by M. Kohl. Minneapolis, MN: Augsburg Publishing House, 1986.

Wolsterstorff, N. P., editor. "Communication through the Eyes of Faith." Working manuscript used at Coalition for Christian Colleges' Conference, Grand Rapids, MI, 1996.

———. *Divine Discourse.* Cambridge: Cambridge University Press, 1995.

Wuthnow, R. *The Restructuring of American Religion: Society and Faith since World War II.* Studies in Church and State. Princeton, NJ: Princeton University Press, 1988.

NON-PRINTED MEDIA

Adamson, Andrew, et al. *The Chronicles of Narnia: The Lion, the Witch and the Wardrobe,* film. Directed by Andrew Adamson. Produced by Mark Johnson and Philip Steuer, 2005.

———. *The Chronicles of Narnia: Prince Caspian,* film. Directed by Andrew Adamson. Produced by Andrew Adamson and Philip Steuer, 2008.

Barton, David. *America's Godly Heritage,* video. Directed by David Barton. Aledo, TX: Wallbuilders, 1994.

Charis Productions. "The Lamb." www.thelambmovie.com.

Gibson, Mel. *The Passion of the Christ,* film. Directed by Mel Gibson. Los Angeles: Steve McEveety, 2004.

Gunn-Danforth, Christine. "Jonahre." www.jonahre.com.

Lehman, Ernest. *The Sound of Music,* video. Directed and produced by Robert Wise, 1965.

The Mass Media Project. *Heartlines,* films. Johannesburg: Curious Pictures, 2006–07. Online: www.heartlines.co.za.

Miller, Kevin, and Ben Stein. *Expelled,* film. Directed by Nathan Frankowski. Produced by Logan Craft, et al., 2008.

Oliver, Charles. *Take,* film. Directed by Charles Oliver. Los Angeles: Chet Thomas, 2008.